Questi
&
Answers
about Islam

Dr Syed Mutawalli ad-Darsh

Ta-Ha Publishers Ltd.
1 Wynne Road
London SW9 0BB
United Kingdom

Published by:

Ta-Ha Publishers Ltd
1 Wynne Road
London SW9 0BB

Arranged, edited and typeset by Ahmad Thomson.

British Library Cataloguing in Publication Data:
A catalogue record for this book is available from the British Library

ISBN 1 897940 580

Printed by: De-luxe Printers, London NW10 7NR.

Contents

Introduction

Dr. S. M. Darsh, a graduate of Al-Azhar University, Cairo, Imam at the Regents Park Mosque and Cultural Centre, London, for many years, Chairman of the UK Shari'ah Council and, *inter alia*, a Trustee of England's first truly international Muslim aid agency – Muslim Aid, has been living in the United Kingdom for more than thirty-five years. During that time Dr. Darsh has worked tirelessly to share and apply the considerable knowledge which he possesses with as many people as possible, and in the process he has become a well-known figure in the Muslim community both in England and farther afield.

Dr. Darsh has always been concerned with demonstrating that Islam is not only a viable way of life in a twenty-first century context, but indeed provides the solutions to many of today's 'modern' ills and problems. As well as having several booklets on various subjects published in English, Dr. Darsh's book *Muslims in Europe* – which explores the experience of Muslims living as a minority community in a predominantly non-Muslim European environment – has been in print for many years.

As well as advising generally, lecturing extensively and contributing regularly to serious scholarly debate by attending many international Islamic conferences and writing articles for various Arabic journals and newspapers, Dr. Darsh's fortnightly *Questions & Answers about Islam* column in *Q-News International* – the world's first international Muslim weekly newspaper in English, has been a regular feature for the last few years, providing an easily accessible arena for straightforward questions and answers on almost any topic which affects Muslims, however minor or major they might be.

This book contains a wide selection of these questions and answers, ranging from the sublime to the ridiculous, and from the light-hearted to the profound – thereby, it is hoped, making them more readily accessible to a more general readership, for they deal in a practical manner with issues and situations which in fact affect almost everyone today, in a society in which it is not always particularly easy to follow the way of Islam in its totality – although, as the present society collapses, Islam is a way of life which is becoming increasingly viable as the old new world order changes, yielding place to new.

This book would not have been possible without the permission and efforts of Fouad Nahdi and his *Q-News International* team, and of course, the sincerity and sheer hard work of Dr. Syed Mutawalli ad-Darsh himself, to whom our thanks are especially due. *Al-hamdulillahi wa shukrulillah.*

Allah

Q : *I have heard that when a child is in its mother's womb, his personality and character – his entire life – are determined by Allah through an angel who is sent down to visit the child. My question is: If this does take place, then why does Allah choose for some individuals to follow a path of evil deeds and a rare few to follow a path of righteousness? Does this mean that as the individual's fate is predetermined, there is little he can do to change Allah's final verdict?*

A : Knowledge, Power and Free Will are among God's attributes. Nothing escapes His knowledge. All has been willed by Him, and is executed by His power. At the same time the *Qur'an* and the *Sunnah* have established that man too has knowledge, will and power, but that these are given to him by Allah.

The responsibility given by Allah to man is the result of these human attributes. Allah, Who created us, orders us to do certain things and forbids us to do others. He makes our life, in general, to follow the causes and effects which He has put in the universe around us, including the solutions to our problems. Together with the attributes mentioned, He is also attributed with Wisdom, Justice and Mercy. He does not do any injustice to any of His creation and does not impose upon a soul more than it can afford or bear. Man is asked to do what Allah has ordered him to do. Destiny will not stop us doing what is good, nor will it force us to do what is bad. So man has to do good and keep away from what is bad. He should not busy himself with discussing Allah's attributes as to whether they interfere with his actions or not. Believing in destiny helps the Muslims to carry the message of Islam. Only weak, lazy people use destiny to excuse their failures and sanction their negativity. Islam is very clear on what we are ordered to do and what we are forbidden to do. This is what we need to know and this is what we are responsible for. The destiny decided by Allah is a hidden book which does not interfere and does not handicap our manner and our attitude. This means we cannot blame God for what is hidden from us; but we can be blamed for what we know. In short, this is the kind of attitude a Muslim should have about destiny.

However, the question of destiny is not only a matter of Islam, it is the secret of the existence of the human race, and the secret of God's attributes. As Muslims who believe in Allah, we should not busy ourselves with questions that are beyond our conceptions, and we should obey the clear will of God as indicated in His revelation.

Q : *I am, al-hamdulillah, very steadfast and consistent with my prayers and other duties towards God. But for the past 26 years I have been very ill and despite serving God day and night I don't seem to get any better. In fact a period of intense prayer and good work often ends with me meeting some terrible calamity or disaster. Please tell me why this happens.*

A : It seems that you are not aware of the way Allah deals with us in this life. Please don't ever forget that this life is transitory; it is designed to be a life full of trials and tribulation. And don't ever forget that Allah has promised us an everlasting reward if we succeed through the test that is this life. The Prophet has told Muslims to recite: ***'Inna lillahi wa inna ilayhi raji'un'* – *'We are from Allah and to Him we do return'***, (*Surah* 2, *Al-Baqarah*, verse 156), whenever disaster strikes. It is also recommended to say: 'Oh Allah reward me for having borne this mishap and give me better.' Allah always rewards those who ask Him.

Remember what the *Qur'an* says: ***'Wa sta'eenu bi's-sabri wa's-salat'* – *'And seek help in the difficulties facing you through patience and prayer,'*** (*Surah* 2, *Al-Baqarah*, verse 45). And know that Allah is with those who are patient. Anas has reported that once the Prophet, blessings and peace be upon him, smiled while he was sitting with a group of Companions. He asked them: 'Do you know why I am smiling?' The Prophet then said: 'Allah does not decide anything for anyone except what is good. Please remember that whatever happens is always for the best.' One of the followers of the Companions said: 'Whenever Allah touches me with any calamity I always thank Him four times: firstly, for not having given me a more difficult test; secondly, for giving me the patience to endure it; thirdly, for having guided me to say: ***"Inna lillahi wa inna ilayhi raji'un"***; and fourthly, for the fact that He will ultimately reward me. I also thank Him that my misfortune did not affect the state of my Islam.'

We should not jump to conclusions when prayers and acts of charity do not achieve what we consider to be the best outcome in this world.

Instead we should be more patient and questioning about our own selves. While waiting for Allah to answer our prayers, we should indulge ourselves in a soul-searching exercise aimed at measuring the extent of our sincerity. The relationship with the Lord of the Universe is not a trading one – it is not equal: we need Him; He doesn't need us. More importantly, we need to have complete and total faith in Him.

Q : *When Allah has promised to feed each and everyone born in this world, why do hundreds and thousands of people die of starvation in Africa and other parts of the world? What has happened to their promised provisions?*

A : Allah has assured us that sustenance is in His hands. If we look to the earth in which we live, we can see that it has enormous potential in providing us with this sustenance. We can grow what we want. We can eat grain from the fields, butter and milk from cows and meat from the multitude of animals which Allah has made *halal* for us. Yet, there is famine in many parts of the world. Daily we hear of and watch people die of hunger. And people start to blame Allah for reneging on His promise. But what is that promise? The promise is to provide sustenance on this earth, enough to feed all of its inhabitants. There is no argument on this point. The problem is that while Allah has provided us with enough for our collective needs, human beings choose deliberately to hold back food from their fellow brothers and sisters. This is not the fault of Allah.

When nations deliberately prefer to engage in horrific civil wars instead of concentrating on economic and social restructuring programmes, whose fault is that? When the greedy, callous middlemen of Somalia refuse to feed shrivelled up Muslims, preferring to watch them starve to death instead, whose fault is that? We are often all too quick to remind the '*kufr*' West that it attracts the wrath of Allah. But we should remember one thing: few starve to death in these lands.

Q : *How can God let innocent children suffer in war? Particularly the war in Bosnia – where seven-year-olds have been raped and brutally killed. For adults this could be a 'test' or even 'punishment' – but for children? If minors have no concept of 'test' then why allow them to suffer such grotesque barbarism?*

A: The brother who asks this question forgets that this life is not the end. He should also remember that this life is far from perfect. It is a life of trial where good and evil are fighting one another. God has created the whole universe. He created our faculties of reasoning. He wants to try us out in this life and as a result He has given us full freedom of choice to do as we wish.

While our hands are capable of doing much good, they are equally capable of doing great harm. The choice is entirely ours. God does not force us; God does not compel us to do anything. How we choose to conduct ourselves on earth is part of the trial, part of the test. Killing children is no less worse than killing other people or raping women. Either way, God will not interfere. If He does, if He tries to stop these acts, He would then be taking away the freedom He had originally given each one of us. God has explained good and warned us about bad. But he has not negated our freedom of choice. He has explained the moral system by which we should live – as revealed to the Prophet Muhammad, upon whom be blessings and peace. The Prophet clearly showed us the choice of actions which we have and which we should choose and for which we will be responsible on the Day of Judgement. If we fail in our duty and responsibility to other human beings, then that is a sign of our weakness and inability to exercise correctly the responsibility which Allah has shouldered on us. If little children die in brutal, unspeakable ways, it is we who should be blamed, not God.

Q: *Why is Allah referred to in the Qur'an by the masculine pronoun, 'He', when Allah is neither man nor woman?*

A: Our concept of Allah is that He is beyond any conceivable picture that may be in our minds. In the words of the Prophet, blessings and peace be upon him, 'Whatever comes to your mind regarding the physical characteristics of Allah, Allah is far from that and that does not express the reality of Allah.'

Allah is beyond sense perception. But the *Qur'an* was revealed in the Arabic language and it speaks about God in the most perfect manner. Masculinity was considered by the Arabs to be one of the basic good qualities and this naturally found expression in their language. And when the *Qur'an* addresses humanity, it uses the language of perfection and completion.

The pronoun does not indicate any masculinity or femininity in the person of Allah.

Q : *Why does Allah refer to Himself in the Qur'an as 'We'? I know that in Christianity the third person is taken to express the idea that God and Jesus speak as one. But why is this used in Islam?*

A : The use of the pronoun 'We' in the *Qur'an* needs to be understood in the context of the Arabic language – and not the Biblical analogy which is misleading. When Allah refers to Himself as 'We', it is not in the numerical sense; but rather to denote the fact that He possesses an authority which cannot be matched. It is rather like the 'misuse' in English of the royal 'we', first used by Queen Victoria, to indicate majesty and royalty.

Some Muslim scholars add that the pronoun 'We' is used to distinguish the words of Allah from those of the Prophet – another affirmation that the *Qur'an* is a revelation of Allah and not of the Prophet, blessings and peace be on him.

The Prophet Muhammad

may Allah bless him and grant him peace

Q : *Is the celebration of the Prophet's birthday a reprehensible innovation or is it something to be encouraged?*

A : We do not call it a celebration but a commemoration of the birth of the Holy Prophet, blessings and peace be on him. This is a development which took place at the end of the sixth Islamic century according to *Imam* as-Suyuti, who researched the origins of the practice.

There are two points of view. On the one hand, there are those who consider the commemoration to be a good innovation, to remind us of the birth of the Prophet, blessings and peace be on him, to remind us of the great Islamic way of life we have inherited from his coming. In the seventh Islamic century, people became more involved in worldly affairs, and the living experience of the *Shari'ah* was in decline. As a result, scholars took the opportunity to remind people of this great event in the history of humanity. In this commemoration, Muslims revive the memory of the Prophet's achievements.

They quote the *Hadith* in which the Prophet was asked about the first day of the week, and he replied, 'That was the day on which I was born. That was the day on which I received my message, and that was the day on which I migrated to Al-Madina.' So these were days ingrained in the memory of the Prophet, blessings and peace be on him. Also, upon his arrival in Madina, the Prophet saw the Jewish community celebrating an event, and when he inquired about it he was told, 'This was the day on which God saved Moses and his people,' to which the Prophet, blessings and peace be on him, replied, 'We deserve more to look after the correct tradition of Moses.' The proponents of the *Mawlid* also point to the *ayah* in *Surah* 14, *Surah Ibrahim*, verse 5, when God says to Moses, peace be on him, ***'And remind them of the days of Allah,'*** meaning the days on which Allah graced them with so many favours.

On the Prophet's birthday, some parts of the life of the Prophet are related, the *Qur'an* is recited and food is offered to the needy, while avoiding the sort of behaviour that is Islamically reprehensible.

Those who say that commemorating the Prophet's birthday is a *bid'a* which is not acceptable are influenced by the bad behaviour that took place when people danced in the street, mixed freely with the opposite sex and danced around the villages. That is the part which is not acceptable.

One of the great Muslim scholars, in his book published this century, *Al-Ibda'a fi Mazaar'il-Ibtida'a – The Most Innovative Thing in Explaining the Harmful Things in Innovations* came to the conclusion that the two parties in the *Mawlid* debate are not talking about the same thing. The party which objects is talking about things which are not generally acceptable, while the party which encourages the commemoration is talking about things that are generally acceptable. The author concludes that if Islamically unacceptable practices are avoided then there is no harm in commemorating the birthday of the Prophet, blessings and peace be on him. This is the view of Ibn Hajar, *Imam* as-Suyuti and the recently departed great *Mufti* from Egypt, Sheikh Hasanayn Muhammad Makhluf.

Q : *What were the physical characteristics of the Prophet, blessings and peace be upon him?*

A : There are many descriptions of the Prophet, blessings and peace be upon him, which are preserved for us. The beautiful book known as

Ash-Shifa' by *Qadi* 'Iyad al-Yahsubi relates the characteristics of the Prophet, blessings and peace be upon him. He quotes from many of the Companions in describing the Prophet's qualities.

The book reads: 'Know, may Allah illuminate my heart and yours and increase my love and your love for this noble Prophet! – that if you were to look into all those qualities of perfection which cannot be acquired and which are part of one's constitution, you will find that the Prophet has every one of them – all of the various good qualities without there being any dispute about them among the transmitters of traditions.

'The beauty of his form and the perfect proportion of his limbs are related in numerous sound and famous traditions, from 'Ali, Anas ibn Malik, Abu Hurayrah, al-Bara', 'A'isha, Ibn Abi Hala, Abu Juhayfa, Jabir ibn Samura, Umm Ma'bad, Ibn 'Abbas, Mu'arrid ibn Mu'ayqib, Abu't-Tufayl, Al-'Ida ibn Khalid, Khuraym ibn Fatik, Hakim ibn Hizam and others.

'He had the most radiant colouring, deep black eyes which were wide-set and had a sort of red tint to them, long eyelashes, a bright complexion, an aquiline nose, and a gap between his front teeth. His face was round with a wide brow and he had a thick beard which reached his chest. His chest and abdomen were of equal size. He was broad-chested with broad shoulders. He had large bones, large arms, thick palms and soles, long fingers, fair skin and fine hair from the chest to the navel. He was neither tall nor short, but between the two. In spite of that, no tall person who walked with the Prophet seemed taller than him. His hair was neither curly nor straight. When he laughed and his teeth showed, it was like a flash of lightning or they seemed as white as hailstones. When he spoke, it was like light issuing from between his teeth. He had a well-formed neck, neither broad not fat. He had a compact body which was not fleshy.'

At the end of this section of *Qadi* 'Iyad's book there is a full description of the physical appearance of the Prophet, blessings and peace be upon him, which is mentioned as being related from his grandchildren. I would recommend that every Muslim buy a translation of *Ash-Shifa'*, which has been rendered into English by Madinah Press, [available from Portobello Books at 328 Portobello Road, London W10].

Q : *Please describe the type of clothes the Prophet used to wear. Did he wear trousers, a lungi, a shirt, a thawb (a long Arabian dress), or the shalwar kamiz as Pakistanis do? And what type and colour hat did he wear?*

A: The Prophet, upon whom be blessings and peace, was an Arab, born in Makka, and he lived there for 40 years before his mission began; he dressed in the manner of the time and the clothes of his community. He dressed modestly. It was the same after the advent of Islam: he used to dress with what was available, decently. He wore something like the Arabian long dress which in length was just above the ankles but with narrower sleeves; his sleeves extended no longer than his wrists.

The material which the Prophet, blessings and peace be upon him, used was called '*hibara*', one with red stripes. Sometimes he used to dress in green and reddish clothes. One of the Companions of the Prophet, Jabir ibn Samara, said that he saw the Prophet on a moonlit night dressed in a red garment; and that he looked more radiant than the moon itself. The Prophet liked wearing the Yemeni style of clothes, which had red and white stripes. He wore a small head cover, like we wear today, and a turban on top of that. His turban was not so big as to cause discomfort, but not so small that it would not protect his head from the heat or cold. Sometimes he wore a white headgear, and sometimes a black one.

The clothes which the Prophet put on were decent and modest, and ones which were also acceptable to the community in which he was living. His clothes were such that no one could deduce the wearer's pride or arrogance. There is a *Hadith* about 'lengthy garments'. The Prophet said: 'Allah will not look favourably upon the person who wears a garment that drags along behind him as a sign of pride and arrogance,' whereupon somebody said: 'Oh *Rasulu'llah*, I love to have beautiful clothes and shoes – to such an extent that I don't like it even when someone has better shoelaces than myself.' The Prophet said to him: 'This is not arrogance. Allah is Beautiful and He loves beauty. Arrogance is to look down on other people or to negate the truth.'

In *Surah* 7 of the *Holy Qur'an*, *Surat'al-'Araf*, verse 31, Allah says: ***'Oh you children of Adam, look to your clothing at every place of worship, and eat and drink. And do not be extravagant – surely He does not love those who are extravagant.'*** The Prophet's advice is: 'Eat and drink, and dress in whatever you wish, as long as you are not extravagant and proud.'

Cultural and climatic variations occur from one country to another; therefore the basic guidance to follow is that of Islam. In matters of dress one has to be decent and modest; follow that which is acceptable by the society, but within the bounds of decency and good manners, satisfying Islamic requirements. For men the Islamic requirement is that they should be covered from the navel to the knees. For women the requirement is that they should be covered from head to foot, with only their faces and hands showing – and whatever after that is respectable and good.

Q : *During a conversation with a non-Muslim friend of mine, I was asked about the miracles of the Prophet Muhammad, blessings and peace be upon him. He believes that a Prophet should have living miracles like those of Jesus and Moses. I could not give him a convincing explanation and became disheartened. Can you please suggest how I could have replied convincingly?*

A : The Prophet, blessings and peace be upon him, was challenged by the disbelievers, as is related in *Surah* 29, *The Spider*, verses 50-51, which state: ***'And they say, "Why aren't signs sent down to him from his Lord?" Say: "The signs are indeed with Allah – and I am indeed a clear warner." Is it not enough for them that We have sent down to you a Book which is recited to them? Truly in that is a mercy and a reminder to people who believe.'***

That is the logical answer to your detractors, explaining the mission of the Prophet, blessings and peace be upon him. He is the final Prophet: his signs or miracles have to be rational ones which appeal to the reasoning of the individual at any given time and without the need of the Prophet being present. This rational miracle of Allah is the *Qur'an* – and it will always be a challenge to anyone who opens its pages.

Again, referring to *Surah* 17, *Al-'Isra*, verses 90-93, the disbelievers tried to hound the Prophet to bring them physical miracles. Allah did not oblige. He said: ***'And they say: "We shall not believe in you until you cause a spring to gush forth for us from the earth; or until you have a garden of date-trees and grapes and cause rivers to gush forth in their midst abundantly; or until you cause the heavens to fall in pieces on us, as you say will happen; or until you bring Allah and the angels before us face to face ..."'***

The answer which Allah commanded the Prophet to say was very simple: ***'Say: "Glory to my Lord. Am I anything but a man, a messenger?"'*** He does not work miracles by himself, these are only from Allah. But having said that, there are abundant miracles from the life of the Prophet, blessings and peace be upon him, which have been authentically recorded. I will relate just two:

In the early days of his mission, whenever he went around outside Makka, he heard the words *'As-salaamu alaykum ya Rasulu'llah'* from many natural objects.

At the time at Al-Madina, he entered a garden where a lame camel was behaving in a restless manner. No sooner did the camel see the Prophet than it calmed down. The Prophet then said: 'This camel is complaining to me about the way it is being ill-treated by its owners. It is complaining of being over-loaded and under-fed.' After identifying the camel's owner the Prophet told him: 'Look after your camel, for it was complaining to me.'

The scholar Ibn Taiymiyyah is reported to have written that the Prophet, blessings and peace be upon him, performed over one thousand physical miracles.

Q : *How should Muslims observe the night Mi'raj? What is the significance of the 'Isra and Mi'raj?*

A : The *'Isra* and *Mi'raj* were great occasions in the life of the Holy Prophet, upon whom be blessings and peace. Firstly, it came at a time when all avenues seemed to be closed to the call of Islam in Makka. The Prophet had lost his caring affectionate wife, Khadijah, and his protector Abu Talib, and he was left to the mercy of the unbelievers. Allah wanted to show the Prophet, blessings and peace be upon him, the greatness of His kingdom and His ability to turn every thing towards His Will – and His Mercy, which is attained by all those Muslims who strive to attain the pleasure of Allah through every possible means by obeying each and every command. Secondly, we see the *Mi'raj* as a great spiritual gift. Daily prayers were not enjoined upon the Muslims on earth – but in the heavens, in the presence of the great angels. Such knowledge should affect us when praying, prompting us to experience a great spiritual elation and elevation.

There are many traditions describing the journey of the Prophet, upon whom be blessings and peace, on this night. During it, the Prophet passed by some people eating rotten, dirty, foul-smelling flesh while also leaving alone fresh, clean, pure flesh. He asked Jibril: 'Who are these people?' The reply was that they were the adulterers who had pure wives, but who abandoned them to go to prostitutes. This is symbolic of the moral degradation of man when he goes against the laws of Allah. Another *Hadith* describes the Prophet, blessings and peace be upon him, seeing people with large bellies, unable to stand up, lying on the road. A herd of people were treading on them from the beginning to the end of the day. When the Prophet, upon whom be blessings and peace, asked about the identity of these people, he was told that these were the people who consumed interest, the people of Pharaoh, who are unable to stand because of the immoral earnings in their bellies. This is another moral lesson.

There are many such lessons to be drawn from that great occasion. It is a confirmation of our faith in Allah that Islam is the final revelation of Allah, that it is a religion of justice, equality and peace. It is something to give us a great lift when we are offering our prayers, and when we remember it in daily life.

Q : *Do Muslims ascribe any significance to the start of the New Year? If so, why?*

A : Yes, Muslims do ascribe a great significance to the start of the New Year, *ra'su's-sanah.* It is a reminder of the start of the Migration of the Prophet, blessings and peace be upon him, from Makka to Madina, in search of a decent and secure place to propagate the new faith. In fact the beginning of the New Year does not exactly correspond to the time the Prophet migrated from Makka to Madina. He migrated 67 or 68 days after the beginning of the year. The year began in Muharram; the Prophet migrated in Rabi'ul-Awwal. Now the question of when to start the *Hijri* dating arose during the time of 'Umar. Before that, they used to date events according to the number of months they happened to be away from the migration of the Prophet. 'Umar was presented with a series of suggestions by the Companions, may God be pleased with them, as to when they should begin the Islamic calendar. Was it to begin with the birth of the Prophet? Was it to begin from the date that he died? Was it to start from the time when he was called by Allah?

'Ali, may God ennoble his countenance, intervened and said that it should begin from the Migration, and this was the position adopted. The Migration was a decisive turning point in the life of Islam, and it was only fitting that it should serve as the starting point. The importance of the

Hijrah was not lost on the minds of the Companions, and as such, when we consider the beginning of the *Hijri* year we remember the great sacrifice involved when the Prophet was forced to leave his home town for the safety of Madina where he could preach freely. The next question to arise was whether the calendar should start in the month of Ramadan, or Dhu'l-Hijjah, or when? The Companions agreed it should start in the month of Muharram.

Q : *Why is the crescent and star a sign/symbol of Islam?*

A : This is because Islamic dates and rituals are connected with these natural signs. We read in the *Qur'an, Surah* 2, *Al-Baqarah*, verse 189, **'They ask you concerning the new moons. Say, "These are appointed times for the people and the pilgrimage."'** From this verse we understand that the moon, the stars and the sun are natural signs which are connected with Islamic activities. That is why the moon came to symbolise the Islamic way of life generally.

Q : *Why did the Prophet, upon whom be blessings and peace, say things three times to emphasise his point? And why do we repeat phrases three times in, for example, Ruku and Sajdah? Does the number three have any great significance in Islam? I ask because I am still struggling to come away from Christianity wherein the number three has, of course, great importance, (in the trinity).*

A : At the time when there was no writing or recorders to record what the Prophet, upon whom be blessings and peace, said, it was his practice to store things in the head and pass them on by word of mouth. As such, out of his compassion and care, particularly in the area of Islamic rules and good advice, he would repeat the statements three times so that it would stick in the minds of those around him. With regards to repeating *tasbih* in *Ruku* and *Sujud*, this is a way of ensuring that we are not rushing our prayer. We are *tuma'nina*, differentiating every part of the prayer from any other. Three times' repetition is the minimum; we can say things 3, 5, 7, 9, 11 times, and so on, but always an odd number. This is because the odd number always comes back to one – and Allah is One. It has no other significance and far from strengthening the illusion of trinity, it re-affirms the reality of the Unity of Allah.

Qur'an and *Hadith*

Q : *I once heard a Bangladeshi Sheikh saying that listening to the Qur'an on video and audio cassette is haram. Is this right or wrong? Please quote references.*

A : Audio or video cassettes were not available at the time of the Prophet, upon whom be blessings and peace. But we know on the authority of many of the Companions that the Prophet used to enjoy listening to others recite the *Qur'an*.

On one occasion he asked Abu Musa al-'Ashari, one of his Yemeni Companions to read the *Qur'an* to him. Abu Musa asked: 'Should I read it to you – to whom it was revealed?' The Prophet answered: 'But I love to hear it from another person.'

One day Abdullah ibn Mas'ud, may Allah be pleased with him, was reading the *Qur'an*, when he came to the verse in which Allah says to the Prophet: ***'How will it be when We bring from each community a witness, and We bring you as a witness against these people?'***, (*Surah* 4, *Surat'an-Nisa*, verse 41). Abdullah ibn Mas'ud looked towards the Prophet and saw tears flowing from his eyes – the Prophet was overwhelmed by a feeling of thankfulness to Allah for having been chosen as a witness, on the day of *Al-Qiyama*, the Day of Judgement, to all the nations, in the Presence of Allah Almighty – so he stopped reading.

From these incidents we can deduce that Muslims have the right to listen to the *Qur'an* through any medium, as long as the reading is good and expressive. What is not acceptable in Islam is recitation of the *Qur'an* with music.

Q : *A non-Muslim friend of mine says she wants to read the Qur'an, but my Sheikh has forbidden me to give her a copy saying that the Qur'an should not be touched by the unclean hands of a kafir. What am I supposed to do?*

A : There is a *Hadith* of the Prophet, blessings and peace be on him, which is mentioned in the chapter on *Al-Jihad* in which he is reported to have prohibited Muslims from travelling with the *Qur'an* to the land of disbelievers for fear of the Book of Allah being mishandled and not being respected.

Of course that is not to say that non-believers do not have access to the *Qur'an* – they do, through the numerous copies of foreign language translations that have been written. There is nothing wrong with giving your friend an English-only translation of the *Qur'an*. But if your friend is honest and sincere and harbours a genuine wish to know about Islam, why don't you sit down with her, with an Arabic-English *Qur'an*, and go through the *ayahs* with her?

Q : *In a response to a question on giving the Qur'an to non-Muslims you said that they now have access to numerous foreign language translations of the Holy Book. What if the non-Muslim is an Arab who only speaks Arabic? Would it be wrong to give him the Arabic Qur'an?*

A : Considering the question of an Arab who is not a Muslim, yet who wishes to understand Islam, I would refer you to the *Qur'an, Surah* 9, *At-Tawbah*, verse 6, which, paraphrased, says that if any one of the disbelievers wishes to listen to the words of the *Qur'an*, Muslims should facilitate this for him or her to come and listen to the *Qur'an*. While a visitor, the security and well-being of the non-Muslim is incumbent upon the community. But while non-Muslims may listen to the *Qur'an* being recited, and discuss it with knowledgeable people, they are forbidden to touch or to read from it. It is also not allowed to give them a copy of the *Qur'an* itself. Arabic tapes of the Book, however, can be given to non-Muslims.

A *Hadith* in *Sahih Muslim*, Vol. 3, p. 1040, clearly forbids giving a copy of the *Holy Qur'an* to a non-Muslim, for fear of desecration. According to the *Hadith*: 'It is prohibited to take the *Qur'an* to the land of *kafirun* when it is feared that it might fall in their hands.' 'Umar said that the Messenger of Allah, upon whom be blessings and peace, forbade anyone travelling to the land of the enemy to take the *Qur'an* with him. But, as in the answer given to the original question, there is no harm if non-Muslims are given a translation of the *Qur'an*. A translation is not in itself the *Qur'an*. The basic definition of the *Qur'an* is that it is the Arabic word revealed to Muhammad, upon whom be blessings and peace. If it is in any other word – that is, language, it no longer qualifies as the *Qur'an*. Muslim scholars have, in addition, concluded that non-Muslims can be taught *Qur'an* by Muslims. The Hanafi school allows *Qur'an* to be taught to non-Muslims without restriction. The Shafi'i school allows tuition in limited circumstances.

Q : *Is writing 786 or 110 for Bismillah and Alhamdulillah a bid'a?*

A : Yes, this is a *bid'a*. When Muslim scholars were discussing the beginnings of some of the *Qur'anic Surahs*, like ***'Alif, Lam, Mim,'*** and the like, they said that some of the Jews came to the Prophet Muhammad, upon whom be blessings and peace, and asked him to read some of the *Surahs* for them. When he read, ***'Alif, Lam, Mim,'*** they immediately translated these letters into numbers, according to their own way of calculation. So it was they who were using this system of attributing numerical values to letters: *A* = 1; *B* = 2, and so on. This is not Islamic. The best way is to write '*Bismillah*', etc., in full; this is clear and understandable and in Arabic as it is read.

Q : *What is the origin of the numerical representation of ayahs of the Qur'an, for example, the use of the number 786 to denote Bismillah-ir-Rahmanir-Raheem?*

A : Muslims adapted the science of Arithmology, the representation by numbers of letters, from the People of the Book, who in turn had inherited it from Babylonian Cosmologists. The numbers, incidentally, do not represent *ayahs* but letters. Each letter of the Arabic alphabet has an associated number. The first letter, *Alif*, is represented by the number '1', the second letter by the number '2' and the third by the number '404', and so on.

The earliest recorded use of Arithmology in an Islamic textbook was found in al-Qurtubi's *tafseer* of the *Qur'an*. According to an incident narrated by Ibn 'Abbas, a group comprised of the People of the Book approached the Prophet, upon whom be blessings and peace, when they heard him reciting the letters ***'Alif, Lam, Mim,'*** from the beginning of the second *Surah* of the *Qur'an*. 'Are these words from God?' the group is reported to have asked the Prophet, upon whom be blessings and peace. When he said, 'Yes,' members of the group told him that the letters which he had recited added up to 71, (*Alif* = 1, *Lam* = 30, *Mim* = 40). 'How can we accept a faith as true when it is just 71 years old?' they said. The Prophet, upon whom be blessings and peace, replied that if the letters *Alif* = 1, *Lam* = 30, and *Ra* = 200 from another *Surah* were added together, the total would increase to 231.

The uses of Arithmology are not that many. The figure 786 is usually substituted for ***'Bismillahir-Rahmanir-Raheem'*** on paper, in books and other publications, to avert possible desecration. Beyond this, Arithmology has no other significance in Islam whatsoever. Magic squares and other arithmetical permutations have no place in a rational, clear, well-explained and common-sense faith like Islam. Some years ago, an attempt to prove that the number 19 had special mystical significance in Islam was declared totally false by practically every single scholar of Islam.

Q : *Can you please advise the Islamic position regarding disposal of Qur'anic verses, texts of Hadith, Name of Allah, etc., which are in newspapers and other literature? Please quote full references or, at least indicate the source of references.*

A : The revolution in printing and publishing, which has given rise to the sheer volume of *Qur'anic* literature produced every day, makes this question one of the most important issues that needs addressing today. For an answer, I have chosen to go back to early teachings, to the days of the four rightly-guided *Khalifahs.* During the *khilafah* of Abu Bakr, the *Qur'an* was recorded by the *huffadh*, a select group of people who committed the whole Book to memory. But when increasing numbers of them were killed on the battlefield, 'Umar, Abu Bakr's eventual successor, suggested to the *Khalifah* that one copy of the *Qur'an* should be written down and kept in safekeeping – just in case none of the *huffadh* survived, or if spurious versions began to appear.

Indeed, this is exactly what happened. Years later, when conflicting versions of *Surah*s began appearing, the *Khalifah*, 'Uthman, ordered the collection and burning of all parchments which did not tally word for word with the standard volume recorded during the time of Abu Bakr. The event of the burning is authentically recorded in Islamic history by many different commentators. Mus'ad ibn Sa'ad ibn Abi Waqqas writes in Vol. 9, pp. 13-17 of *Sahih al-Bukhari*, of the day when – led by 'Uthman – lots of people gathered to burn parchments of the *Qur'an* which differed from the original. The event of the incineration is also recorded by Anas in *Sahih al-Bukhari.* Therefore, I would say that burning is an acceptable way of disposing of used, loose or frayed copies of *Qur'anic* portions. Alternatively, disposing of them in the ground by burying them is an equally acceptable way of disposal.

Q : *What is the Islamic way to get rid of religious written material? I have heard that you can burn paper or throw it into the river. Is this correct?*

A : The standard way of getting rid of such material is to burn it. This will erase any trace of writing. We follow here what happened during the *khilafah* of 'Uthman when, together with Hafsa, a Mother of the Faithful and the daughter of 'Umar, he made a number of standard copies of the *Qur'an* and had all the remaining material burnt – with the acceptance of the consensus of the Companions. This is the best way of disposing of religious material.

Some people say that you can also wash away the writing from the paper. This was acceptable in the past, when the ink was not absorbed by the paper. Whilst this may remain the case in rural areas, where children can wipe away writing from slates, etc., in our society most of the matter is printed and cannot be washed off. Even if it is thrown into the sea, the material may end up in a place which is not honourable or decent. So we follow the example of 'Uthman, even though some of the Companions had reservations about burning holy texts. 'Ali rebuked these people, saying, 'If I had been ruler during that period, I would have done the same to dispose of written *Qur'anic* material.'

Q : *How should one dispose of sheets of the Qur'an or papers with Qur'anic verses written on them? Is the rule different when dealing with Qur'anic verses that are transliterated into, for example, Turkish or Urdu?*

A : Dealing with the second part of the question first, it is important to remember that although Arabic is the language of the *Qur'an*, and thus accords more respect, parchment from translations written in other languages, should be treated with equal consideration. This is because, although not exactly the *Qur'an*, a translation nevertheless represents the writer's utmost effort to convey its meaning.

Parchments of the Book which need to be disposed of should be burnt. Muslim countries tend to organise the process by having '*Qur'an* receptacles' dotted around various parts of cities and villages in prominent places. Unlike traditional refuse bins, the contents of these receptacles are not tipped into refuse trucks, together with rotting food and waste – they are taken away for burning.

In the absence of such a meticulous system of disposal, you're probably asking what should one do? I personally keep an old envelope used to collect parchments so that they should not, at any point in the process, come into contact with other waste. The paper should be burnt, or buried, or washed with water only, until the ink of the words is no longer visible.

Q : *I recently came across a group of people who told me that Muslims need only refer to the Qur'an and not the Hadith for guidance on how to live their lives. The Hadith literature, they argued, was more like the gospels in that it was unreliable, sometimes contradictory and written many years after the death of the Prophet, upon whom be blessings and peace, and should be avoided. This group, therefore, says that the massive numbers of Muslims who follow Hadith are not Muslims but 'Muhammadans' – just as 'Christian' is a reference to today's followers of Christ. As such, I was told, many of today's 'Islamic' traditions were not at all Islamic and in some cases amounted to shirk. If an Islamic rule – like praying five-times-daily, or wearing Hijab for women – was so important, this group claimed, it would have been included in the Qur'an and would not have been left to a questionable medium like the Hadith. Please comment.*

A : This question is very serious indeed. I myself have also been bombarded with similar 'Islamic' literature dismissing as irrelevant the use of the *Hadith* of the Prophet, upon whom be blessings and peace, in Islamic affairs. Again, let me make it absolutely clear, make no mistake, that anyone - man, or woman or organisation - who rejects the *Sunnah* of the Prophet, upon whom be blessings and peace, in its entirety can no longer be considered a Muslim – they are regarded as an apostate. This is not my personal opinion, it is the unanimous verdict of all the major, recognised schools of Islamic thought. Let me refer you to one of the leading texts on Islamic *fiqh* which, fortunately, has been translated into English and is published by the Islamic Texts Society. The leading Muslim scholar, *Imam* Ash-Shafi'i's *Risalah*, or *Treatise on The Foundations of Islamic Jurisprudence*, available at all good bookstores and a must for the bookshelf of all conscientious Muslims, sums up this issue and confirms that all those who reject the *Hadith* must be considered to be outside the fold of Islam. I will reproduce a portion of the summary below:

'In whatever form it may take, God has made it clear that He has imposed the duty of obedience to His Apostle and has given none of mankind any excuse to reject any order which he knows to be the order of the Apostle of God. God has rather made men have need of him in all matters of religion and He has given the proof for it by providing the *Sunnah* of the Apostle which makes clear the meaning of the duties laid down in His Book. Thus, it should be known that the *Sunnah*, whether in the form of specifying the meaning of God's commands as provided in the texts of the Book, or in the form of legislation in the absence of such text in either form, represents God's commands and is in full agreement with that of His Apostle. Both are equally binding in all circumstances. This has been confirmed by the Apostle by the tradition of Abi Rafi' which has been cited.'

If you cannot get hold of the treatise, I suggest you try and buy an excellent booklet entitled *The Place of Hadith in Islam*. This booklet, published by the Muslim Students' Association of the USA and Canada, is a compilation of papers presented to a seminar on the subject, '*The Relevance of the Hadith of the Prophet, upon whom be blessings and peace, to Religious and Social Life in Modern Times*.' Maulana Syed Abu'l-Hasan 'Ali an-Nadwi presented the keynote paper, with major contributions from top *Hadith* scholars, including Professor M. M. Azami's '*Rules for Accepting and Transmitting Hadith*'. This seminar was held specifically to help clarify the position of the *Sunnah* in the Islamic way of life.

Q : *Apart from the Qur'an and the collections of Hadith, which book on Islam would you recommend to a newly-converted English-speaking Muslim?*

A : There are many, many books which serve as good introductions to Islam. The best in my view is *Islam in Focus* by Dr Hamoudah Abdalati. This covers good ground. If anyone needs more detail, they should consult *Islam*, a five-volume work by Sheikh Muhammad Nu'mani, which is very well written.

Muhammad, by Martin Lings, is a very readable account of the life of the Prophet, blessings and peace be on him, published by the Islamic Texts Society of 22A Brooklands Avenue, Cambridge, CB2 2DQ.

In the Beginning

Q : *Is it true that Hawwa, Eve, was created from Adam's rib, since this is not an idea that is mentioned in the Qur'an?*

A : This is not mentioned in the *Qur'an*, but we take our point of view from the numerous *Ahadith* speaking about the creation of Hawwa from a rib. When Ibn Hazm, the great explicator of *Imam* al-Bukhari, was working out how to interpret this, he said that there are two possible interpretations, apart from the literal one. The first is that perhaps Hawwa was created from a simple element that may be represented by the weight of a rib. Or it could be that the *Hadith* gives us a simile. The *Hadith* might be saying that women (and even men) are by their nature 'bent', and it should not be attempted to straighten such a rib because it will break. Once you marry a woman, you will not be able, as it were, to 'straighten', that is change, her. This means that we have to tolerate each other and compromise.

Purity and Cleanliness

Q : *Water is pure in itself and it purifies other substances and so for cleaning we use water and cloths. Are there any other substances with the properties of water? And if we use dry, clean cloths, to prepare for Salat, is it valid in front of Allah the Almighty?*

A : In Shaikh Rashid Ridha's introduction to the book of *Al-Mughni* by Ibn Qudama he set out a lengthy discussion about purifying and purification. He said that the Shafi'i and Hanbali schools of thought are the two strict schools as far as this question is concerned. Only pure and purifying water is acceptable in the act of ritual purification. The Hanbali school also considered the intent of the *Shari'ah.* What is required, in its point of view, is that a Muslim should be in the best state of purity when he is offering his prayers. Any liquid fulfilling this requirement is acceptable. Gasoline, according to this view, is purifying; coca-cola is purifying, etc. Once the actual dirt, *najasa,* itself is removed, the place where it was – whether on cloth, body or earth – becomes clean.

As far as dry-cleaning is concerned, this is becoming the question of our time. There are many manufactured materials which we use and which say 'dry-clean only'. In Muslim countries this may be an easy matter, because Muslims generally avoid soiling their clothes with impurities. But in a non-Muslim country we give our clothes to the dry-cleaner who also receives clothes from people who may have a concept of hygiene but not purity. In the cleaning system, the evaporated water goes into all these clothes. So what is the fate of such clothing belonging to Muslims?

The answer is given in the Hanafi textbook of Hashyat ibn Abideen in the section on *Impurities*, Vol. I, p. 325. In the body of the section, under the heading of '*Impurities which do not Affect Acts of 'Ibada*', it says: 'and the vapour of impure material'. In the margin Ibn Abideen explains that such vapour does not cause things to become impure unless the smell of the impurity can be smelt from such articles.

Q : *I have terrible arguments with my husband over matters of hygiene and cleanliness. His hair is greasy, he does not cut his nails and he smells of cigarette smoke. If I suggest he take a bath, more often than not he threatens to divorce me. However, he does have high morals, is intelligent and Islamically aware, though he does not pray very regularly and says that women have no right to interfere in these matters with their husbands. Is he correct?*

A : I really find it surprising how a person who you say is smelly, dirty and who does not pray regularly can be described as having Islamic awareness . If he is truly 'aware', then his conduct would be far from what you have described. The Prophet, blessings and peace be upon him, was very firm and explicit on the question of personal hygiene. Men are allowed up to a maximum of 40 days before they have to clip nails, and remove hair from other parts of their body. And as for having a bath, it is a strong *sunnah* to take one every Friday, followed by decent, clean clothes before going out to pray. These are not just good manners – these are religious duties, and the sister should realise that it is her Islamic duty to remind her husband of them.

The sister should also remind her husband that smoking is strongly discouraged in Islam. I hesitate to use the term '*haram*' in this respect as the Hanafi opinion, in particular, discourages the wanton use of this classification. But nonetheless, smoking can be safely considered as being *makruh*, 'permitted, but severely reprehensible'.

Q : *I understand that Islam requires its followers to wash and clean themselves several times a day, e.g., before prayers and after going to the toilet. Is this a compulsory requirement? It seems to me that this amounts to an over-excessive use of what is a very scarce resource. I know that Islam is an equitable religion that shuns waste and extravagance. So, why wash so many times each day? What are Muslims supposed to do when there is a water shortage?*

A : *'Splashing. Splashing.'* Veterans remember how that apostate from 'The Satanic Verses' affair, Salman Rushdie, used these words to ridicule Islam's concern for cleanliness and hygiene by suggesting that, by washing regularly, Muslims are somehow guilty of wasting water. I may be wrong here, but having read the question, I detect a similar line of argument. I feel that the questioner is not entirely sincere. I just hope she didn't get the idea for the question from reading 'The Satanic Verses'.

In one way, this question denies logic. You know, it is odd, even ironic, that on the one hand people complain how standards of hygiene and purification will fall if the government goes ahead with its plans to install water meters in every household – yet Muslims, one of the most hygiene-conscious groups of people in the world, are now being asked to explain why we keep clean. This is absurd.

Anyway, to answer the question, I will begin by stating, in no uncertain terms, that Islam is a pro-hygiene religion. We make no apology for this fact. If people want to ridicule us for the fact that we are particular about washing our bodies, cleaning our nails and teeth, wearing clean clothes – let them. Perhaps it is just a reflection, a sign of the degree to which this society has plunged; or an indicator of how much importance the so-called civilised west actually places on keeping clean and tidy.

Secondly, we need no lectures from anyone about the necessity for conservation and the importance of avoiding waste and extravagance. Muslims have been 'green' from the beginning of time. We did not need scares about deforestation or global warming, or the hole in the ozone layer, to remind us not to waste scarce resources. The Prophet, upon whom be blessings and peace, instructed Muslims never to waste or use excessive amounts of water during *wudu*. He even went as far as saying that this rule has no exception. Even if Muslims perform *wudu* from rivers, it does not give them licence to use more water than is strictly needed, the Prophet is understood to have said.

So, while, technically, Muslims need to wash 'five times daily' – although in most cases it is less – the amount of water we use is far less than the gallons and gallons that gush out of the average house equipped with the latest style of mixer-taps and power-showers. And this is my final point. If you want to talk about wasting water, perhaps it is worth questioning the logic of installing running water households without issuing guidelines about the need to be conscious about conservation. While Muslims are required to conserve water, the same cannot be said for the population at large. There is no similar secular commandment urging Britons not to leave the water running while they brush their teeth each morning. I'm quite confident that if people stopped doing this, there would be enough water for another two million Muslims to do their *wudu* – properly.

Q : *Is a person allowed to pray immediately after using body deodorants? Or does the application of such an accessory mean that the person has to change his clothes and have another wash?*

A : There is no prohibition on a person praying after using various bodily cleansing and refreshing agents like deodorants. These things are clean and pure and thus do not invalidate a person's *wudu* in any way. There is no need to change clothes nor to go and have a wash.

Q : *Does wudu have to cover the finger nails? I know of many women who paint their nails three or four times each day – every time they need to perform wudu. If anything, it seems like an awful waste of nail varnish. Is this right?*

A : The women you speak of might be wasting nail varnish, but in removing it before doing *wudu*, they are doing the right thing. Generally speaking, if there is any hard, impermeable material covering any part of the body which has to be washed during *wudu*, then that material must be removed – nail varnish included. As Allah has clearly prohibited waste and extravagance, it might be an idea for you to suggest the use of an alternative to nail paint: henna. As henna does not prevent water from reaching the nails, it does not need to be removed before doing *wudu*, and thus does not prevent the ladies from performing prayers either. Plus it is equally attractive and, very important in our times it seems, friendly to the environment.

Q : *I wear foundation make-up during the day. Does this affect my wudu, the way nail varnish does (by not allowing the water to penetrate through the varnish and wash the nails)? What I mean is, will my wudu be adequate if I am wearing this make-up?*

A : If the make-up forms a solid barrier which prevents the water from washing the skin which has to be wet during *wudu*, then it constitutes a barrier which is not acceptable for a *wudu* to be valid. If the powder or whatever is like henna, which colours the skin but does not form a barrier and allows the water to touch the skin, then it is permissible.

Q : *I have been told not to dye my hair using chemical colourings because they stop water from reaching the hair, and therefore do not allow me to perform a valid wudu. Should I take this advice?*

A : I do not think this is good advice. Women are entirely free to colour or shape their hair in any manner liked by themselves for their husbands. This colouring does not prevent the water from reaching the hair or the skull. What is obviously not acceptable is a dye that prevents water from reaching the limbs that are supposed to be wetted during *wudu* or *ghusl*. Apart from that, it is recommended that we should colour our hair when it becomes grey or white. The acceptable colour for men is any which does not seek to deceive others into believing the wearer is younger than he actually is. There was an incident during the time of 'Umar when a man presented himself to a family as young, having dyed his hair black. However, after the marriage the colour started to wear off – and 'Umar started lashing at him, 'You have deceived people!'

Q : *Is someone allowed to recite the Name of Allah when in a state of impurity – given that both men and women cannot touch the Qur'an when they are unclean?*

A : Yes, both men and women are allowed to recite the Name of Allah when in a state of impurity. There is an authoritative *Hadith* in which 'A'isha, the wife of the Prophet, upon whom be blessings and peace, is reported to have said that the Prophet remembered Allah at all times, even when he needed to take a bath to clean himself. The need for a Muslim not to lose touch with Allah and with His Book, the *Qur'an*, is so important that some scholars insist that men and women should not be banned from reciting passages just because they are in a state of impurity.

These scholars doubt the authenticity of the *Hadith* which states that reading from the *Qur'an* is forbidden to menstruating women and to men who need to clean themselves with a bath, a *ghusl*. If followed to the letter, the *Hadith* effectively cuts off women from the *Qur'an* for up to a whole week every month. While a quick bath is all a man needs to clean himself, the menstrual cycle for women can last anything up to six days. Six days, according to the scholars, is far too long a period for any person to go without reading from the *Qur'an*. Passages recently memorised might be forgotten. If a woman needs to consult the Book for something important, she should not have to put her life on hold until the end of her periods.

As such, these scholars have agreed that while menstruating women should not touch copies of the *Qur'an*, there should be no prohibition on reciting those parts of the *Qur'an* which they know off by heart.

Q : *After menstruation is it necessary to remove pubic hair and hair from under the armpits, as well as cutting the nails of the feet and hands and changing the bed sheets? Also, in the case of ghusl after marital relations, is it necessary to do the above again? Or is it okay to just have a straight-forward shower?*

A : No, there is no need for that. What you mention is not a condition for making *ghusl*. This is considered in the *Hadith* of the Prophet, blessings and peace be on him, as a matter of natural decent good manners. The Prophet is reported by Abu Hurayrah as saying that there are five things which constitute natural decent good manners. These include being circumcised in the case of men, trimming the moustache, plucking pubic hair and the hair from under the armpits, and cutting nails. Another *Hadith* reported by Anas says that pubic hair and hair from under the armpits should not be left to grow for more than 40 days.

It is unfortunate to watch so many young people nowadays who follow the culture here – where hair from different parts of the body and nails are left to grow unchecked. Often their bushy armpits are embarrassingly visible while praying. This is against the *Sunnah*. As far as *ghusl is* concerned, the main difference between the *ghusl* after menstruation and that after marital relations is as follows: *ghusl* after marital relations tends to occur quite often and as such women do not need to untie their hair when they wash. After menstruation, women have to make sure that all their hair and the skin underneath get washed while making *ghusl.*

Q : *Why are Muslim men required to remove their pubic hair? I was once told that removal of this and hair from other private parts, etc., applies only to those Muslim males living in hot climates like Saudi Arabia, and not to people living in cooler countries like Britain. Is this so?*

A : Hair is removed to maintain hygiene and cleanliness. There are many *Ahadith* in which the Prophet, upon whom be blessings and peace, emphasises the need to stay clean and thus wholesome. As people who live in cold climates are not exempt from the need to stay clean and healthy, the requirement to cut nails, get circumcised, etc., applies as much to them as it does to hot-country dwellers.

Q : *Is it compulsory for an adult male to be circumcised?*

A : Yes, it is. There are many *Ahadith* of the Prophet, upon whom be blessings and peace, which speak of the importance of cleanliness and hygiene. Top of any list – for men – is the need to be circumcised. In another authentic *Hadith* on cleanliness – this time recorded from the time of the Prophet Ibrahim, upon whom be peace – circumcision comes top of five acts of cleanliness which men are asked to perform: cleaning the armpit and pubic regions, cutting the finger and toe nails, trimming the moustache, and growing a beard are the other four.

Circumcision has at least one other recorded use. It is sometimes the only way a dead man can be identified as a Muslim if he dies in a strange land. One last point: Muslim *fuqaha* have questioned the acceptability of offering prayers behind an *Imam* who has not been circumcised.

Q : *Is it Islamically permissible to read books, newspapers and magazines while sitting on the toilet-seat? I live in a one-bedroom flat. When the place gets busy with guests and visitors, my toilet – which is very clean – is often the only place where I can get some time to be myself, think and read.*

A : There is nothing in Islam preventing you from reading newspapers, magazines, etc., while sitting on the toilet-seat – just so long as your choice of reading matter does not contain words from the *Qur'an*, that is, either in Arabic or in translation, or any references to the name of the Prophet, upon whom blessings and peace. The Prophet himself always removed his ring, which was inscribed with the Name of Allah, before going to the toilet.

But while there is little harm in indulging in a bit of occasional light toilet reading, the toilet-seat is no place for long, intense, concentrated study. The toilet is, essentially, a place where people go to relieve themselves. It is not a library, nor a reading room. If you want time and space to read, think and reflect, then there are many other places you can go – like the public library.

Besides, occupying the toilet for excessively long periods holds up others who may want to use it. Also – medical sources would confirm this – it is not very healthy, however 'clean' the toilet is. What might be necessary to point out is that toilets, no matter how 'clean' they are, are nevertheless, in the final analysis, nothing more than repositories for excrement.

Q : *What are the circumstances in which a follower of one of the four Sunni schools of law can wipe his feet, masah, in lieu of washing them?*

A : The Hanbali school, as interpreted by the scholar Ibn Taiymiyyah, permits the wiping of socks as a substitute for washing the feet for a period of up to 24 hours for residents – and up to 3 days for travellers – after a complete *wudu,* ablution, has been performed. The only other proviso for such an act is that the socks, which need to be opaque – i.e. made from material which hides the colour of the skin – must be worn above the ankles.

Ibn Taiymiyyah backed his opinion with evidence from at least 18 Companions of the Prophet who are reported to have wiped their socks instead of washing their feet when they performed *wudu.*

Other schools, however, are much firmer and have laid down many more conditions before the wiping of socks is permitted. One of these conditions is for the socks to be made from thick animal hide, known as *khufs*, which should be waterproof.

Shahada

Q : *At present I am a Catholic in religion, but some of my friends are converting to Islam. I would also like to do so, but I do not think I am yet prepared. I know only how to do the Salat, from 'Allahu Akbar, Bismillahir-Rahmanir-Rahim' to 'Qul HuwAllahu Ahad'. If it is not a big burden on you I would like to ask for a copy of your book, the Holy Qur'an, in English.*

A : Once Allah has opened your heart to the right path, do not hesitate in declaring, formally, your Islam. I am saying 'formally' because once your heart is opened and you learn some Islamic terms and say the declaration, '*Ash-hadu an la ilaha ill'Allah, wa ash-hadu anna Muhammadar-Rasulu'llah*', you are already a Muslim. Your Islam does not depend upon you knowing a great deal about your new faith. This is a long process of learning which should come gradually. Go straight to any official department in the town or the city where you are, register yourself as a Muslim, and you will be given the translation of the meaning of the *Qur'an*. There are many centres of teaching, at a time suitable to you. I am sure you will be welcomed and supported spiritually as well as emotionally in this new phase in your life. But do not wait. No-one knows when he or she will be leaving this life. May Allah guide you.

Q : *Although I was bought up in a Muslim home, as a teenager I studied the faith of the Jehovah's witnesses and became convinced of the 'truth' of their message. I was not baptised, however. Later, I realised the error of my ways and came back to Islam. Do I have to make Shahadah in front of witnesses like a 'new' Muslim?*

A : Even new Muslims do not have to say *Shahadah* in front of witnesses. Once they have said that they believe in no other deity except Allah, and that Muhammad is the Messenger of Allah, they are Muslims.

Part of being a member of the Muslim community and of behaving in an Islamic way is the *Shahadah*. That is why we differentiate between the acts of faith and what is in the heart. No one has access to that except Allah. The outward expressions of our faith are in our daily prayers, fasting , etc., and these are the real indications of our Islam. If we say the *Shahadah* in front of witnesses but distance ourselves from the practice of Islam, it does not indicate a good Islamic attitude.

Q : *Why is it considered 'OK' for non-Muslims to convert willingly to Islam but not vice versa? A lecturer has posed this question to me, relating it in the context of Rushdie, Taslima Nasreen, and so on, so your help would be useful.*

A : Conversion in Islam is not a personal attitude alone; it affects the whole fabric of the family. No one searches the head of a person, but once a person declares a rejection of Islam, it means that he is rejecting his family, his children, his wife; he cannot inherit from them, nor they from him. It is a rejection of the whole system under which he is living. If this system is a just, compassionate and decent system and he rejects it, he is considered to be committing treason. Allah will question such people about their faith – but we must consider the harm done to personal relationships, family relationships and the state which is governed by Islamic Law. It is not simply an individual issue – there is a state issue involved in the act of conversion out of Islam. Hence, it is treated very seriously indeed.

Q : *I believe in One God and am a follower of Jesus. There is a command in the Holy Book that we must visit those who are sick. I have observed that the Muslims visit those people who have a physical sickness. But what about those people who do not have a strong faith? Why does it seem to be more important for the Muslims to visit a sick person in the hospital than to visit those who are not active in their faith?*

A : The heart is the seat of faith. Acts of goodness, prominent among these being the prayer, are the outward expression of that faith. To respect the integrity of the faithful, we do not question his or her sincerity. This is beyond the scope of the human being. We do not spy on people, nor intimidate them, nor bombard them with literature which indicate unfaithfulness.

We encourage Muslims to discuss, in a rational manner, any questions that may arise concerning basic religious concepts. There is nothing hidden, irrational or secretive about such concepts. They do not defy reason or understanding – both for the ordinary as well as for the highly intelligent educated person. Please bear that in mind.

We are not ritualistic or mechanical in the observance of our rituals, as some outsiders may try to imply when they are dismayed to see the meticulous observance by Muslims of their external acts of worship, while seeing their own followers dropping out and their places of worship closing.

As far as visiting sick people is concerned, there is an act of grace involved. It is not a matter of walking a few steps or riding to the hospital. We are assured that during the few minutes we spend there, we are really seated in the Mercy of Allah. This is a point to be remembered by those who consider that they are doing the sick person a favour – in fact it is the other way round.

I do not wish, once again, to question the integrity of the ordinary praying Christian. He has been brought up in that tradition and may not have been exposed to other traditions. He may have even been brought up to be prejudiced against it. The truth is, *Al-Islam* is the final, authentic revelation which has abrogated the other earlier religions. Allah Most High said: ***'And whoever seeks a religion other than Al-Islam, never shall it be accepted of him, and in the Hereafter he shall be one of the losers.'*** (*Surah* 3, *Surah Ali 'Imran*, verse 85**).** This is not a personal or a human opinion, for in the matter of faith we do not opinionate – it is the clear text of the revelation. I hope that this short answer will satisfy you.

Q : *When giving Da'wah, can it ever be said that the end justifies the means, thus condoning going into pubs, discos, etc., with the intention of trying to lure any Muslims inside away from haram acts?*

A : This is a very strange question. In Islam, the end does not justify the means: if the end is to be good, the means must also be good. There is great danger in going to such places to give *da'wah* as they are not places where *da'wah* can be given easily. People there may not only resent it but also may do harm to the *da'ee*. We are not allowed to visit places wherein *munkar*, wrong-doing, is the main activity. When I was in Sweden, in Lund, a young Muslim was in the dance hall. There was a fight and he was arrested. The chairman of the Islamic Society was invited to stand bail for him and he asked the young man what he was doing there in the first place. When he replied that he was making *da'wah*, everyone laughed at him. That is not the place to make *da'wah*. There are many places with a healthy, pure atmosphere where people will be far more inclined to listen to you.

Q : *I want to learn more about Islam from a teacher, but don't really know how to select one or, indeed, where to look. How does one go about finding the right person? And what qualities should I look out for in a person who is to teach me to understand and live my faith?*

A : You have not made clear in your question whether you are looking for a teacher in the conventional sense, or whether you want a spiritual guide. If it is a spiritual guide you are in search of, then, I'm afraid, I cannot help you. But if you want a step-by-step structured guide to the Islamic faith, I recommend you attend the classes organised by the Islamic Circle Organisation that take place at Regent's Park Mosque, 146 Park Road, London NW8 – nearest Tube Baker Street or St John's Wood – every Saturday at 3.00 p.m. If you are looking for in-depth knowledge of Islam, you ought to contact the *Dar'ul-Uloom al-Arabiyyah al-Islamiyyah* in Holcombe, Bury.

Prayer

Q : *Where should the hands be placed while giving the adhan?*

A : If we try to understand the function of the *adhan*, it will become clear where the hands should be placed. The function of the *adhan* is to let people know that the time for prayer has arrived, and hence the practice of delivering it from the highest place in the mosque. In the early days, there were no minarets or ladders, and in the Prophet's Mosque, the ceiling was not strong enough to support the weight of a *muadhdhan*. For this reason, a house belonging to one of the female Companions, which was near to the mosque and the highest-situated house in the area, was used by Bilal as a place from which to call the *adhan*. So, the idea is to make the *adhan* audible as widely as possible. This is why there exists the practice of placing the thumbs in the ears while delivering the *adhan*: this allows the *adhan* to be louder and thus carry further.

Q: *What are the reasons for an Imam reciting aloud parts of the Fajr, Maghrib and 'Isha prayers and reading in silence the same parts of Dhuhr and 'Asr prayers?*

A: We pray today in the same way that the Prophet, upon whom be blessings and peace, performed his *Salat*. He said: 'Pray as you see me offering my prayers.' Some Muslim scholars contend that the silent recitation of the daytime *Dhuhr* and *'Asr* prayers dates back to the early days of Islam in Makka, when believers would pray in total silence out of fear of being ambushed or intimidated by hostile non-Muslims.

Q: *Is no prayer – i.e. not praying at all – better than praying mechanically, without concentration? I am an isolated, thoroughly depressed young mother who finds it hard to concentrate on prayers with small children to bring up. I have been told that praying with more concentration will help me overcome my depression. But I feel my prayers are bouncing off the ceiling. They're certainly not achieving the things they are supposed to. Please help.*

A: You seem to have decided already, on Allah's behalf, that your prayers are redundant. That is not fair. Your job is to pray. Pray as hard as you can. Pray regularly. Pray on time. Pray that your prayers be accepted. Leave the rest to Allah. I have further news for you. The fact that you continue to pray despite your difficult circumstances will benefit you. Keep at it. Sometimes you will feel spiritual. On other occasions, you will feel mechanical, devoid of soul. The important thing is never to stop praying.

I have just one other point to make. You say you are depressed. My guess is that this is due, in part, to your lonely existence and isolation from a community life. Couples and families, when deciding where to set up home, need to give high priority to the need of having a community around them. This is a necessity and not doing it is very wrong. Unfortunately many people don't understand this, but being part of a community is integral to the Islamic way of life. You cannot live an isolated existence. Apart from the innumerable practical benefits of being part of a vibrant, dynamic community, there are also many, many other benefits, spiritual and temporal, that are essential for one's wholesome existence. You seem to lack this – and here lies a large part of your problem. This may sound like asking too much, but life would become infinitely more pleasurable if you took the plunge and made a conscious decision to move closer to a place with some kind of Muslim community life.

In the meantime, talking to people will help. Go out and talk. Talk about anything. About the weather. About health. About life. Just talk and share your problems with others. You've heard of the proverb, 'A problem shared is a problem halved.' Believe you me, it works.

And finally, please, never, under any circumstances, abandon your prayers. Prayer is your one regular channel to God. It is the opportunity you have to strengthen and communicate directly with your Creator and Sustainer. Don't let it go and don't lose it.

Q : *I feel as if I am losing my grip on spirituality after more than a decade in Islam. I long to grow spiritually, but just don't know what to do or where to look. I was briefly attracted to Sufism, but began to get worried when I encountered idolatrous practices among some Sufis. Nonetheless, this branch of Islam remains the only one concerned with the soul. All the rest seem to be obsessed with mechanistic, legalistic issues or high-level intellectual matters. I admire the Salafi/Wahabi approach to purity in religion, but find them incredibly dry spiritually. What should I read and who should I contact in my continuing spiritual quest?*

A : Spiritual experience cannot be judged by decades, centuries or even millennia. Spiritual enrichment is unquantifiable. It is not rational either. You cannot project, predict or calculate spirituality. The experience of one day may be such that it surpasses the quest and journeying of decades. Only Allah knows – but how to acquire spirituality? Again, I will return to a theme which I have introduced during an answer to another question: community.

To repeat myself, Islam is not an isolated religious experience. Any person who wants to flower spiritually must be part of a community. Present yourself to your community. Get involved in community affairs. Offer your services in areas where you think you can better the life of your community members. You will find this to be an incredibly enriching and rewarding experience. But this is not just a question of feeling good about yourself. In serving others, you are serving Allah. Remember, Islam is more than praying, which is important in its own right. Islam is more than going to the mosque everyday. Islam is a practical, everyday religion. It always has been throughout its history, right down to the present day. And strange as it may sound, spiritual enlightenment has a good chance of flowering by doing seemingly ordinary, practical work in your community.

You probably know this already: Muslims are not homogeneous, we are a very diverse *Ummah*. Some of our people are 'obsessed' with rational matters, others spend their time worrying about the letter of the text, while others, still, are men and women with purity of soul. This last category, I suspect, are the people you want to find. Keep looking and one day, *insha'Allah*, you will find them.

Q : *I am in the habit of offering 'Isha prayers at midnight, just before going to bed. I find it most rewarding. Is this wrong?*

A : If there is a mosque near you and a *Jama'ah,* congregational prayer, takes place regularly, that is where you should go. If there isn't, then it is right to offer your prayer late – the later the better.

Q : *In the summer, Salat'ul-'Isha starts very late, at about 11 p.m. I find it difficult to stay up so late to offer the prayer, especially since I have to wake up at 5 a.m. to pray Salat'ul-Fajr, and then get up early to go to work. Salat'ul-Maghrib is also very late. Is it possible that I pray my 'Isha a little earlier before its time has started?*

A : This question of praying *'Isha* a little earlier has been discussed in a number of Islamic conferences. In 1984, in a big conference at Regent's Park Mosque in London, attended by many jurists and astronomers, it was decided that such a course of action is allowed for women who are looking after children, for students in secondary and university education, and for people whose work is so hard that it requires them to rest. For all these categories of people, performing *'Isha* together with *Maghrib*, i.e. *jama' taqdeem*, is permissible.

This decision was confirmed at a subsequent conference in Belgium. In a *Fiqh* seminar in France in 1992, I presented a paper about offering *Maghrib* and *'Isha* together for the above mentioned categories of people, and it was accepted and agreed. There is a collection of the traditions of the Prophet by Ibn Abi Shayba in which it is related that a man came to

Sa'id ibn Al-Musayyib, who was one of the successors of the Companions and a great scholar, and said, 'Look here Sa'id, I am a camel-herd. I milk the camels. When it is time for *Maghrib* prayers I offer them and go to sleep and can't get up to perform *'Isha*.'

Sa'id ibn Al-Musayyib said to him, 'Do not go to sleep until you have offered your *'Isha* prayer. If you fear that you will not be able to get up, you may combine the two prayers.'

Q : *What is the Islamic position regarding an Imam leading simultaneous congregational prayers in geographically separate areas, or in mosques in different cities linked up by telephone or a giant video screen relayed by satellite?*

A : The concept of an *Imam* leading simultaneous prayers beamed across the world '*via* satellite', in the way you describe, is not only unacceptable according to Islam but also defeats the very object of the concept of praying together in *Jama'ah*.

There are numerous *Ahadith* of the Prophet, upon whom be blessings and peace, that reiterate the importance and necessity for Muslims to pray in groups. However, the idea behind this recommendation is not to put on a grand show of numbers: congregational prayers are part of community building. The *musallis* go to the mosque, a place of worship in their local community, to pray with members of that community behind an *Imam* from that community. However, even if someone were to argue that large prayer gatherings attracting tens of thousands of worshippers are not uncommon, such as during *Hajj* and *'Id*, these are always held in one place. The worshippers, in addition, stand in continuous, unbroken rows behind the *Imam*.

In normal *Jama'ah* prayers, the potential for disasters is pretty slim. If an *Imam* were to make a mistake in the performance or recitation, people behind him would always be there to correct him; the *Imam* could therefore correct the mistake. Similarly, if an *Imam* were to fall ill, someone would be there to take his place. In the hi-tech world of satellite television, a small technical hitch resulting in a blank screen or loss of sound would instantly ruin the prayers of thousands, potentially millions of people.

Congregational prayers are meant to be simple and effective. Technological advances in this area are unwanted and undesirable.

Q : *Scientifically speaking, the sound heard from a radio receiver is neither aks as-sada, reflection of sound, nor naql as-sada, conduction of sound. Naql means the conduction or transmission of the sound itself without any transformation. For example, heat may be transferred by conduction as well as radiation and convection. An iron rod conducts heat without transforming it. Heat is conducted from one iron crystal to the next one and thus from one end of the rod to the other. The voice of a reader is heard by conduction, that is naql as-sada, by the people within ear-shot: the vocal cords in the larynx in the throat become tense and the air blown from the lungs sets them, the two fleshy cords, into vibration when we talk. These vibrations set into vibration the air molecules surrounding them and this is conducted to other air molecules and eventually to our ears. Sound propagates in the form of a spherical pressure wave in the air. The air conducts sound, it does not travel, or carry sound, itself. Sound travels at 340 metres/second in dry air, at 1,500 metres/second in water and at 5,000 metres/second in glass and steel since solids conduct sound much faster.*

The sound waves propagating in air or water change their direction when they hit a solid smooth surface like a wall or a rocky cliff. The reflected waves give a second sound of similar qualities. This second sound is called aks as-sada or 'echo'. Although the reflected sound or echo is similar in quality to the incident sound, it is said that it is not necessary to perform sajdat at-tilawa, to prostrate, when one hears the echo of the Qur'an since this is not the Qur'an. This sound is not called the word of Allah ta'ala.

A voice on the radio is neither the naql, conduction, or aks, echo, of the voice of the qari'. It is a sound different from and only similar to the voice of the qari'. Once the sound waves from the reader reach the microphone they are converted into electrical impulses and then electro-magnetic waves. These electro-magnetic waves, when received by the antenna of the radio-receiver, are converted back into electrical impulses and then into new sound waves.

How, then, can a transmission of the Qur'an which involves transformations or conversions into another sound be called the Qur'an – while even an echo of the Qur'an is not? And what about an Imam who conducts Salat through a loud-speaker?

A : Leaving aside the jargon of science you bombard us with, let us first consider your argument in bare form. We do not prostrate when we hear one of the *Qur'anic* verses of prostration on the radio, not because what we hear is not the *Qur'an*, but because one of the conditions for prostration is not there. This is for two reasons: Firstly, the radio is not good to offer prayer behind because there is a lack of human communication. You cannot reach the *qari'* in a way which does not break your prayer. It is allowed for an *Imam* to conduct the prayer through a loudspeaker because the *musalli* can reach him without breaking his prayer. The human contact is there in the last lines of the *musallis*. Secondly, because there is no *tamyeez*, discretion, on the part of the set. It does not have the power of choice, the freedom or understanding of what it is transmitting. It can be compared to hearing it from a parrot. This is the reason why *sajdah* is not required.

As far as the scientific analysis which you give is concerned, you have to differentiate between the *Qur'an* as the eternal word of Allah, one of His Attributes, and the way in which this eternal word is conveyed to us. This is how Allah Most High has explained to us the various ways in which He, Glory be to Him, has communicated with His Messengers and Prophets: ***'And it is not for any human that Allah should speak to him, except by revelation, or from behind a veil, or by sending a Messenger to reveal whatever He pleases by His Command – surely He is the Most High, the All-Wise. And thus have We revealed to you.'*** (*Surah* 42, *Ash-Shura*, verses 51-52).

The word of Allah, in whatever language it has been revealed, has always been understood as Allah's word, whether it has been written in Hebrew, Syriac or Arabic. The important thing is that it has always been in the language of the people to whom it was being addressed in the first place. It says in the *Qur'an*: ***'And with every Messenger whom We have sent, We made him convey the Message in the language of his own people, that he might make all matters clear to them.'*** (*Surah* 14, *Ibrahim*, verse 4).

This is the basic consideration: to make matters clear. In whatever form this message is delivered and understood it will have achieved its purpose. The most distinctive thing about the *Qur'an* is that it had to be conveyed in its original language, i.e. Arabic: the same words which were given by Allah to Jibril, were given to Muhammad, were given to humanity.

The matter is much deeper than scientific analysis could indicate, and this was the reason for the great historical debate about the nature of the *Qur'an*. What interests the believers in this debate is not the nature of the means through which the message was delivered – it is the clarity and understanding of the message. This is exactly what was given in the *Qur'an*: ***'And if any one of the idol-worshippers seeks protection from you, then grant him protection so that he may hear the words of Allah,'*** (*Surah* 9, *At-Tawbah*, verse 6). Hearing the words of Allah and understanding them is enough to establish the fact that they are His words and His proofs for them – and against those who reject them.

Q : *Do the rules regarding crossing the path of people who are praying apply equally to men walking in front of women? I ask because I was praying in front of my wife and when I finished I left the room by walking in front of her. When she finished her prayer, she complained that I had done this.*

A : There appears to be a misunderstanding here, because there are a number of *Ahadith* which state that a man's prayer is invalidated by a woman walking directly in front of him. The correct interpretation of these *Ahadith* is that any person, man or woman, doing this invalidates prayer. This is why it is a *sunnah* to put a *sutrah*, or barrier, between the person praying and the area in front of him or her – on the other side of which people may walk.

Q : *According to an authentic book on prayer, 'Sifat'us-Salat'an-Nabi', during Sajdah, prostration, the heels should be together. However, someone has told me that there is a Hadith saying that if the right foot moves from its place during Salah, the Salah is lost. Which is correct?*

A : I do not know why this brother is making a lot of fuss about this issue. What is needed in *Sujud* is for the five parts of the body mentioned by the Prophet, upon whom be blessings and peace, to touch the ground; they are: the forehead, the nose, the hands, the knees and the toes. If the feet are together, that is all right; if they are spread apart, that too is all right. What is unacceptable is for the feet to be off the ground altogether during *Sujud*; the toes must be touching the ground during the *Sujud*. If the feet are moved during the prayer, as long as it does not constitute what is deemed to be unacceptably excessive movement, the prayer is valid. For example, when we stand up after *Sujud* we look at our feet to make sure we are still standing in a straight line, and move if necessary. That does not spoil our prayer.

Q : *Is there a correct number of Sunnah prayers that the Prophet, upon whom be blessings and peace, recommended Muslims to offer after completing their Fard, compulsory, prayers? My local mosque is the scene of endless argument over this subject. The time and positioning of Witr prayers after 'Isha is another hot potato. Is Witr the last prayer of the day, or should Muslims, as some brothers suggest, offer two Sunnah prayers afterward?*

A : While the number of *Sunnah* prayers recommended to offer after *Fard* prayers does, indeed, vary according to which school of thought you follow, none can be considered to be wrong or incorrect. All the numbers and performance sequences have their roots in Prophetic traditions. The Prophet, upon whom be blessings and peace, practised each at different times in his life.

The widely accepted combination is that suggested by the Companion Abdullah ibn 'Umar. According to this version, the Prophet performed 10 *Sunnah raka'ahs* at various times of the day: 2 before *Fajr* prayers, 2 before and 2 after *Dhuhr*, and a further 2 *raka'ahs* after both *Maghrib* and *'Isha* prayers.

Followers of the Hanafi school pray the most *Sunnah* and *Nafil raka'ahs*: 2 before *Fajr*, 4 before and 2 after *Dhuhr*, 2 *Sunnah* and 2 *Nafil* after *Maghrib*, and a combination of 13 *raka'ahs* before and after *'Isha* including *Witr*.

The Prophet, blessings and peace be on him, once put the question of *Witr* prayers to his Companions 'Umar and Abu Bakr. Abu Bakr replied that he would pray *Witr* just before going to bed, while 'Umar did not perform his *Witr* prayers until well into the night – just before *Fajr*. 'You are cautious,' the Prophet told Abu Bakr. While 'Umar, he said, was strong, as he was able to offer *Witr* by getting up early, before dawn.

The timing and positioning of *Witr* prayers is also the subject of much contention among Muslim scholars. Some scholars contend that *Witr* is the last prayer of the day, while others say that 2 *raka'ahs* of *Sunnah* should be offered after the 3 of *Witr*. Again, neither are wrong. The former base their opinion on a *Hadith* which states that the last prayer of the day has to be *Witr*, after which no prayer should be performed. However, it has also been widely reported that the Companions of the Prophet were often seen offering *Sunnah* and *Nafil* prayers after their *Witr*. In fact, according to Umm Salamah, one of the Prophet's wives, the Prophet himself even offered 2 *raka'ahs* after *Witr* one night – although the commentator ash-Shawqani in his book *Nayl'ul-Awtar* later clarified this by saying that this was a prayer exclusive to the Prophet only.

The consensus opinion says that *Witr* is the last prayer before sleeping. But, if someone were then to wake up before *Fajr*, he or she would be free to offer whatever number of *Sunnah* or *Nafil* prayers he or she chose.

Q: *I have often seen my relatives who are from Pakistan and India perform their Nafil prayers sitting down. Why is this so?*

A: Some time ago, while *Imam* at Regent's Park Mosque, I used to know a Sudanese postgraduate student who later met and married a Pakistani girl, also pursuing graduate studies. Some time later I came across the newly-married husband who asked me if I could explain the Hanafi approach to prayers as, 'at night-time my wife just seems to pray and pray and pray. Sometimes sitting down. Sometimes standing up. What is this?'

I don't know, but there is a *Hadith* of the Prophet, upon whom be blessings and peace, which says that Muslims who pray sitting down, when they are in good health, can expect only half the rewards of a prayer performed while upright.

Q: *As far as I know raising hands for du'a is a sunnah. However, if one person, the Imam, says a du'a and everyone else just says 'amin' this is a bid'a. If I am faced with such a situation, I could a) walk out of the room, as I do not want to participate in this bid'a, or b) I could, like all the other people raise my hands, but I would say my own du'a while the others would be saying 'amin'. Which of these two alternatives is more correct?*

A: I think the second option is the best to take. Stay in the room and make your own *du'a*. Do not withdraw as this will cause a lot of misunderstanding and animosity in the community. All of these actions include some which are acceptable and some which are 'minor' *bid'a*, and if our brother withdraws he will be doing something which is not good at all, by causing friction.

Q : *How can Muslims make up for missed prayers? If I am unable to perform Fajr, or 'Isha, etc., should I just add extra raka'ahs to my next prayer, or is there something else that needs to be done? Also, in which order should late entrants to congregational prayers complete missed raka'ahs?*

A : In the event of either *Fajr* or *'Isha* being missed, the position is very clear: whoever has missed prayers should immediately make up for them the minute he or she realises it. There is no alternative on this issue. If you were to 'forget' about a prayer you should immediately stand up and perform it the minute you 'remember'. Each prayer is a self-contained self-sufficient act of worship. Do not add extra *raka'ahs* to existing prayers: we are not allowed to add or subtract to or from the prescribed number of *raka'ahs* in a prayer. Missed prayers are to be offered in full, separately.

If you enter a mosque – let's say for *Maghrib* prayers – and say you join the congregation while it is performing the third *raka'ah*, this would count as your first *raka'ah*. Once the *Imam* finishes the prayer, saying, *'As-Salaamu Alaykum'*, you are supposed to continue and finish the remaining two *raka'ahs* to make up the three *raka'ahs* that make up *Maghrib* prayers. The point is that any time you join *Jama'ah*, congregational, prayers – while the *Imam* is still in *rukuh* at the very latest – you consider the *raka'ah* which you have joined as your first one. When the *Imam* sits for *tashahud* you sit and do it with him, just for the sake of reward for congregational prayers, and then you continue.

Q : *Sometimes I have noticed that people who arrive late for Jama'ah prayers, instead of joining in, wait to form their own congregation. Is that permissible?*

A : The Hanafi, Maliki and Shafi'i schools of thought do not encourage extra *Jama'ah*, congregational, prayers in mosques where one has already taken place. Multiple *Jama'ahs*, according to these *Imams*, could be construed as a sign of a divided community, and therefore have to be discouraged. Worshippers who have deliberately arrived late for the main prayers so that they can lead their own separate congregations, as a sign of open rebellion, are not encouraged.

The Shaikhs did not want to promote an activity which could later sow the seeds of discord. However, I understand the question does not refer to rebellion-induced *Jama'ahs* within divided communities, but talks about second *Jama'ahs* performed by mosque-goers who have genuinely missed the main congregation. Rather than join in a prayer which is due to finish, there is no harm if this group do perform their own congregation – but after the main one finishes.

This, however, does not apply to Friday congregations. I am aware that here in Britain, small mosques' limited space often dictates the need for two or sometimes even three consecutive *Jama'ahs* on Fridays. But this tradition is very difficult to justify, Islamically speaking. Once a mosque has been filled, it is better if late-arriving worshippers pray the *Dhuhr* prayers and do not perform an extra Friday congregation at the same spot. According to one *Hadith*, *Jumu'ah* is for those who offer it first. In addition, another *Hadith* says that Friday prayers are to be offered in one single great mosque, not in lots of small mosques, as is the case here in the UK.

Q : *I began to pray regularly rather late in life, at the age of 38. Having been born a Muslim, I have always wondered about the prayers which I missed. Do I have to 'catch up' on these, or is there any other way I can 'atone' for them? Is the answer the same for someone who has converted to Islam?*

A : There are two points of view concerning the question of missed prayers. The first says that non-praying born Muslims were *kafir*, unbelievers, prior to their truly discovering Islam, while the other postulates that such people are no more than sinful Muslims. The Hanbali school, the first category, asks followers who did not pray in the past to make *tawbah*, to ask Allah for forgiveness. Being considered non-Muslims before, there is no obligation on them to catch up on missed prayers. They should begin to pray regularly from the day they 'entered Islam'.

According to the second opinion, after making *tawbah*, the person – who is considered to have been a Muslim all along – should calculate the number of prayers missed. These prayers then have to be completed whenever time allows. One method involves performing a missed prayer immediately after finishing a *Fard* prayer – e.g. praying a missed *Dhuhr* at mid-day, a missed *Maghrib* prayer after the proper *Maghrib Salat* after sunset, and an extra *'Isha* prayer at night, etc., to make up for those missed. The choice of method rests with the individual, and depends entirely on personal circumstances, state of *Iman*, faith, etc.

A person who has recently come to Islam is under no obligation to fulfil anything from the past. His position is akin to that described in the Hanbali example above. Detailed Islamic obligations like prayer are incumbent only on believers, as illustrated by this *Hadith*: 'Amr ibn al 'Aas, ready to accept Islam at the hand of the Prophet, blessings and peace be upon him, withdrew at the last minute. The Prophet asked him if he had changed his mind, to which 'Amr replied that he wanted to make sure that Allah had forgiven him for the past sins which he had committed against Islam. "Amr,' said the Prophet, blessings and peace be upon him, 'didn't you know that Islam erases your previous mistakes with *tawbah*. Islam is a new, clean page in your life. Your test begins from the day you become a Muslim.'

Q : *How does Islam define the word 'travelling' when used to allow Muslims to shorten their prayers? As a salesman my work keeps me on the move five days a week. Some days I can go to a European city and come home on the same day. Does this constitute 'travelling', according to the Islamic definition, and entitle me to pray reduced raka'ahs?*

A : You are allowed to shorten and combine your prayers if your journey exceeds 60 miles, 100 kilometres. This has been agreed upon by all schools of thought. Shortening a prayer allows Muslims to perform two *raka'ahs* instead of the obligatory four, during *Dhuhr*, *'Asr* and *'Isha* prayers. *Fajr* and *Maghrib* prayers stay the same. Permission to combine a prayer allows Muslims to perform *Dhuhr* and *'Asr* – mid-day and afternoon, and *Maghrib* and *'Isha* – sunset and night-time, together, respectively.

While opinion varies regarding what length of stay constitutes a 'journey' in the Islamic sense, I will try to give a consensus viewpoint illustrated by some examples. Take the case of someone who comes to London from overseas for a medical check-up and does not know how long his stay will last. Should he pray as a traveller, and if so, for how long? According to most schools, he can shorten and combine his prayers for up to 18 days, after which he must pray as a *muqeem*, local resident.

For other travellers, for example, holiday-makers, a stay of 4 days or less – or 20 consecutive prayer times or less, is the maximum time that permits Muslims to shorten prayers. But if you arrive at your destination, go directly to the hotel and reserve a week-long booking, then excepting the days of arrival and departure, you are not allowed to shorten your prayers from the moment you put your suitcase on the bed.

Q : *Whenever I am travelling, I get confused about whether or not I should shorten my prayers and join Dhuhr/ 'Asr and Maghrib/ 'Isha together. I try to follow the Hanafi School of fiqh, and I understand that it is disliked to join the prayers; but when I am with a group of brothers following different schools, and they join two prayers together, I tend to join with them for the sake of unity. Is this right?*

A : Yes, it is allowed; there is no problem about offering the prayer with the group with whom one is travelling. *Imam* An-Nawawi, in his book *Al-Muhaththab Al-Majmu'a*, after explaining the Shafi'i point of view, says: 'Our *madhdhab* allows the joining of two prayers, at the time of the first and at the time of the second – and that is the view of the overwhelming majority of the Muslims, from the predecessors and the ancestors.'

There are many *Ahadith* in this connection which are sound and correct. Ibn 'Umar said, 'The Prophet, upon whom be blessings and peace, used to join together *Maghrib* and *'Isha* when he was hard-pressed in travel.' Anas said, 'The Prophet, upon whom be blessings and peace, used to offer his prayer of *Dhuhr* if it was time for it before travelling; if it was not time, he would delay it until the time of the *'Asr* prayer, and then he would offer the two together.' Again, Anas said, 'The Prophet, upon whom be blessings and peace, when he wished to join the two prayers together, would delay *Dhuhr* until the beginning time of *'Asr* and would join them together.' These are reported in *Sahih al-Bukhari* and *Sahih Muslim*.

One of the Shafi'i School said, 'There are many sound, correct reports of the Prophet, upon whom be blessings and peace, allowing the joining of two prayers together. There is no way of watering down or explaining these in any other way.'

Q : *When we travel, why don't we shorten our Sunnah prayers in the same way we cut the Fard, compulsory, prayers?*

A : The way we pray is derived from traditions of the Prophet, upon whom be blessings and peace. He did not perform *Sunnah* prayers while travelling, except early in the morning – when he always prayed 2 *raka'ahs* before the obligatory 2 *raka'ahs* for *Fajr* prayers, and at night – when he never failed to perform the three *Witr raka'ahs* after *'Isha* prayer. Muslims, as such, are required to do the same.

During the early days of Islam, each prayer-time consisted of just two *raka'ahs,* irrespective of whether a Muslim was travelling or at home. The present 2, 4, 4, 3, 4 format was designed to extend home prayers. Away prayers remained the same.

Q : *How important is it to offer Tarawih prayers?*

A : *Tarawih* is a strongly recommended *sunnah* dating from the times of the Prophet, blessings and peace be on him, who said that Allah will forgive the past sins of whoever offers *Tarawih* for the sake of Allah.

But *Tarawih* prayers must not be considered an obligation. The Prophet, blessings and peace be on him, offered *Tarawih* prayers on the first night of Ramadan on his own, but was later joined by a few people who grew in numbers so that by the fourth night, the Prophet, blessings and peace be on him, seeing an overflowing mosque, decided to stay at home until it was time for *Fajr* prayer. When asked why he had not come out, he replied, 'I knew you were in the mosque last night, but did not come out in case you thought that *Tarawih* has become an obligation for you. I did not want to make things difficult.' The Prophet, blessings and peace be on him, did not continue to offer *Tarawih* prayers collectively in the mosque for that reason.

However, after his death, people would offer *Tarawih* both collectively and individually in the Prophet's Mosque in Madina. On any one night, one would witness many small *Jama'ahs* taking place in different parts of the Mosque at the same time – all praying *Tarawih*. 'Umar ibn al-Khattab, may Allah be pleased with him, the *Khalifah* at the time, observed this for some time, and decided that it would be better to combine the various small *Jama'ahs* under one *Imam* – which is why the conventional *Tarawih* as we pray it today is a traditional *Sunnah* which was endorsed by the *Sahaba* and continued during the reigns of the other *Khulafah* who followed.

The *Tarawih* prayers, offered in nightly combinations of twenty *raka'ahs* are agreed upon by all the major schools of thought. And *Imam* Ahmad ibn Hanbal said, 'Prayer is a good thing. Offer as much of it as you can.' Nevertheless, someone wanting to offer less than 20 *raka'ahs* in his or her *Tarawih* should not be condemned, as according to a tradition narrated by 'A'isha, the Prophet's wife, he never offered more than 8 *raka'ahs* in one session.

Q : *It is authentically reported that Tarawih is 8 raka'at. In most Masajid 20 raka'at are prayed. Should I pray 8 raka'at at home instead of 20 raka'at at the mosque, or pray in the Masjid, making the intention of Tarawih for the first 8 raka'at and the intention of Nawafil for the other 12?*

A : I wonder where the brother has got his 'authenticity' that *Tarawih* is 8 *raka'at*. 'A'isha, may Allah be pleased with her, said that the Prophet, upon whom be blessings and peace, did not pray, either in the month of Ramadan or in any other month, more than 8 *raka'at* at night. This is a statement of 'A'isha, not a saying of the Prophet. However, there is a paper prepared by Sheikh Isma'il al-Ansari, a researcher in the highest religious authority in Saudi Arabia, Dar al-Ifta' concerning the *Hadith* related to the *Tarawih* prayer. He quotes Ibn Taiymiyyah as saying, 'It is well established that Ubay ibn Ka'ab used to lead the people in prayer for 20 *raka'at* during Ramadan and made *Witr* with 3 *raka'at*.' Many scholars consider this to be the *Sunnah*, because Ubay was leading the prayer of many of al-Muhajirin and al-Ansar and none of them dissented at his action.

Some other scholars prefer to offer 39 *raka'at* because this was the action of the people of Madina. It is also well-established in the *Sahih* that 'A'isha said that the Prophet, upon whom be blessings and peace, did not increase his *raka'at* in Ramadan or any other month more than 13 *raka'at*. What is clear is that there is no definitive number of *raka'at* to be offered during Ramadan. Those who offer the greater number use a 'short' reading of the *Qur'an*. We know that the Prophet sometimes read *Al-Baqarah*, *Ali-'Imran*, and *An-Nisa* in one *raka'ah*, so that the length of standing was more than enough to compensate for the number of *raka'ahs*. When Ubay was leading the prayer, he was leading a large number of people so he could not lengthen the standing; instead, he offered more *raka'ahs*.

The research paper was summed up by quoting Yazid ibn Hudhaifah who said that the *Tarawih* during the time of 'Umar, may Allah be pleased with him, consisted of 20 *raka'ahs*. This is sound and authentic, and there is no way to say that it is unacceptable. Also, 'A'isha did not specify *Tarawih* or any other prayer during the night; these are *Nafilah* – and people who perform these are free of any constraints on the number of *raka'ahs* to be prayed.

Q : *I am a student in London and pray at whichever mosque happens to be most convenient. In Ramadan, this poses a problem with Tarawih prayers. At some mosques only 8 raka'at are performed, at others 20. I was raised in a community which offered 20, and feel guilty when I perform only 8. My friend says I shouldn't worry. Is he right? He also insists that Tarawih is a sunnah, whereas I have always understood it as wajib. Who is correct?*

A : To take the second part of the question first, *Tarawih* are supererogatory, additional, optional, prayers: they are strongly recommended and are a *sunnah* and not *wajib*.

As regards the number of *raka'at*, those who claim that *Tarawih* is only 8 *raka'at* are new arrivals on the Islamic scene. Traditionally, Muslims everywhere have offered 20 *raka'at*. This is inherited from the times of the great *Khalifah*, 'Umar ibn al-Khattab, during whose time there was no dispute on this. The Prophet, upon whom be blessings and peace, said, 'Follow my *Sunnah* and the *sunnah* of the rightly-guided *khalifs* after me.'

And from that period there is a sound, correct *Hadith* explaining how to perform *Tarawih*. 'Umar found people in different groups offering their *Tarawih* in the Prophet's Mosque in Madina, so he gathered them together under one *Imam*, Ubay ibn Ka'ab. Since that time Muslims have been offering 20 *raka'ahs* for the *Tarawih* prayers. However, there is some variation here. Some reports say that at the mosque of the Prophet, upon whom be blessings and peace, 36 *raka'at* were offered, but we take the standard, which is 20 *raka'at*. Those who argue for 8 *raka'at* depend upon a statement of *sayyidatuna* 'A'isha, in which she was talking about the night prayer, *qiyam'ul-layl*, of the Prophet, upon whom be blessings and peace. That does not change the fact that *Tarawih* is 20 *raka'at* and this is confirmed by the focal point of Muslims world-wide, the Great Mosque in Makka, which subscribes to this *sunnah*.

Q: *I have seen some Imams recite from a copy of the Qur'an whilst leading Salat, particularly in Tarawih prayers during Ramadan. Is this right?*

A: *Imam* Abu Hanifa disliked this habit very much, and he considered the action of turning the pages of the *Qur'an* during *Salat* an action that spoilt the prayer. However, two Sheikhs from his own School, Abu Yusuf and Muhammad – and all the other Schools of thought too – accept that the practice is allowed, particularly during the *Tarawih* prayer, without spoiling the prayer of the one who is praying. So basically, it is allowed, with the proviso that *Imam* Abu Hanifa did not think it acceptable. Those who allow it consider it to be an act of worship which does not affect the prayer in a negative way.

Q: *Where I live the mosques are always packed to bursting-point for Tarawih prayers. Yet for the rest of the daily prayers, the turnout is much lower. Is Tarawih more important than the other prayers?*

A: *Tarawih* is not more important than the daily prayers. The daily prayers are obligatory, whereas *Tarawih* is recommended. But this should not obscure us to the fact that *Tarawih* is synonymous with the month of Ramadan and the recitation of *Qur'an*. *Tarawih* takes place in the evening when people are generally freer to go to the mosque.

Fasting

Q: *Ramadan is described as the month of the Qur'an. Why? And how should Muslims approach the reading of the Holy Book in this blessed month?*

A: Three points can be made here. Firstly, we read in the second *Surah* of the *Holy Qur'an*, *Al-Baqarah*, verse 185: ***'Ramadan is the month in which the Qur'an was revealed.'*** This verse establishes the link between Ramadan and the *Qur'an*. We know that the Prophet, blessings and peace be upon him, was in the habit of retreating to Mount Hira during Ramadan and it was during one of these periods of contemplation that the Archangel Jibril appeared to him with the first revelation. So Ramadan marks the beginning of the call to Islam and the prophethood of Muhammad, blessings and peace be on him.

Secondly, when fasting during Ramadan became obligatory, the Prophet used to recite the *Qur'an* with Jibril. Jibril used to descend from the heavens every night to read everything that had so far been revealed to the Prophet, blessings and peace be on him. Thirdly, when we offer our *Tarawih* prayers, it is recommended that over the course of the month the whole *Qur'an* be completed. This presents a great opportunity for those who haven't read the whole *Qur'an* to hear it read out.

Q : *Are there any additional prayers or supplications which are recommended during Ramadan?*

A : Ramadan is the month in which the *Qur'an* was revealed. It is also the month in which the Prophet, blessings and peace be upon him, and his Companions stepped up their reading of the *Qur'an*. Later on, the four schools of *fiqh* closed their books during this month, suspending all teaching and research, and devoted as much time as possible to the *Qur'an*.

The first thing all conscientious Muslims can do is to read the *Qur'an* more. During the last ten days of the month, Muslims are encouraged to go into *'Itikaf*, seclusion in the mosque, to spend Ramadan's final days 'away from it all' in reflection and reading the *Qur'an* and in anticipation of the *Laylat'ul-Qadr*, the Night of Power, in which the *Qur'an* was first revealed.

Q : *Fasting is compulsory, I know, but is it true that there are exemptions for the disabled and schoolchildren?*

A : Fasting becomes obligatory on all Muslims once they reach the age of puberty. However, parents and young people themselves should start practising much earlier. According to one *Hadith* of the Prophet, upon whom be blessings and peace, children should start training from the age of ten. Certainly no one should wait beyond the age of fifteen, unless he or she falls into one of the exempt categories. These include the sick, the elderly, menstruating women, and travellers. However, with the exception of the chronically ill, all the others mentioned have to make up the missed fasts later. Disability is no excuse for not fasting. People with medical ailments should also fast unless, of course, they need to take frequent medication.

Q : *How does fasting during the month of Ramadan differ from that on other occasions?*

A : The only difference is in intention, *niyyah*. During Ramadan, the intention to fast has to be made the night before, unlike in other months when fasting is not obligatory – in which case one can leave the final decision until *Dhuhr* time of the following day.

The significance of Ramadan is clearly mentioned in the *Qur'an*, where Allah, *subhanahu wa ta'ala*, especially chose this month to reveal the final mission to the Prophet, blessings and peace be on him. The fact that the Prophet enjoyed great intimacy reading the *Qur'an* with Jibril during Ramadan is an affirmation that Ramadan is the signpost for the beginning of the Islamic mission. It is extremely important for believers not just to read the *Qur'an*, but to pay attention to its message.

Q : *What is the meaning of the Hadith that the devil is chained up during Ramadan? In most people's experience, evil persists all year round including Ramadan. For instance, the Serbs and their friends never declared a truce for Ramadan last year.*

A : The *Hadith* may be referring specifically to the Muslim *Ummah*, that is, to the absence of sedition and evil thoughts from the minds of Muslims in this holy month. The Prophet, blessings and peace be on him, said, 'Shaytan runs through the veins like blood. So tighten your veins to stop shaytan entering into your thoughts and deeds.'

Fasting is a means of self-discipline and of recognising that shaytan exists inside and outside of us. Shaytan whispers to us and incites us constantly to commit sins. Fasting is like a lock against shaytan, closing up his access points to the inside. That is why when we look into the Muslim community during Ramadan, evil seems to be very much reduced. Muslims work to improve themselves during Ramadan. Their awareness and spirituality is so intense that the devil finds it hard to get the better of them.

But when it comes to the situation of a community other than the Muslims, shaytan is there all the time and that explains why Muslims are under oppression in so many places. Even within Muslim nations, one leader has prevented the Muslim population from fasting because shaytan was whispering to him that fasting reduces productivity. So we also have to differentiate between shaytan's influence through leaders at a national level and his influence at a personal level.

Q : *Why is there a difference in the timings of Suhur and Iftar in timetables published by different people and organisations?*

A : Let us make it clear that there should be no differences in the timings for *Iftar*, at sunset. All organisations have access to the times that are published in advance from bodies like the Meteorological Office or the Royal Greenwich Observatory, and as such there should be no discrepancies in Ramadan timetables.

As far as the end of *Suhur* is concerned, believers are asked to stop eating as soon as ***'... the darkness of the night is distinguished from the clear full light of the day,'*** as described in the *Qur'an, Surah* 2, *Al-Baqarah*, verse 187. But unfortunately for us here in Britain, excessive cloud-cover on many nights means that it is often very difficult to make the precise distinction between the end of the night and the beginning of the day, which is why the Hanafi opinion allows believers to delay the start of *Fajr* prayers for a short period of time (10 to 15 minutes), just to be one hundred per cent certain that day has begun.

Unfortunately our modern day scientists and astronomers have as yet been unable to come up with an exact method to calculate the distinction as described in the *Qur'an*. So far their results are restricted to approximating that the fast begins roughly one and half hours before sunrise.

Q : *I know that fasting is compulsory for Muslims – but what should those whose work requires 100 % alertness do when they are bound to feel tired and groggy towards the end of a fasting day? This question relates to operators of potentially hazardous complex machinery, for example at building sites, or to surgeons.*

A : A person who has no alternative to working in high-pressure/high-precision employment during Ramadan is allowed not to fast during this month but to re-do his fasts at a later date. I know that there are many employment situations, including the medical and building industries, where the safety of lives depends on hairline precision, a high degree of skill – and there's absolutely no room for human error which can be brought about by excessive tiredness. In such situations, the people concerned should, if at all possible, try and take holidays during the month of Ramadan. If they are unable to do so, they should perform their fasting later on.

Q: *Our mother lavishes the table with all manner of delightful foods to appease our hunger in Ramadan. We always close the fast with dates because it is a sunnah to do so, but are there any other foods that Muslims have been recommended during Ramadan?*

A: There are no other foods that have been recommended. But the whole business of lavishing tables with delicious foods, which are rarely cooked throughout the rest of the year, is something which negates the whole purpose of Ramadan. An incident which occurred during the life-time of the Prophet, upon whom be blessings and peace, occasioned the revelation of a verse of the *Qur'an*: One Companion had been working all day whilst fasting and when he returned home he could find no food. His wife went out to gather some food but when she came back, she found her tired husband fast asleep. A *Qur'anic* verse was revealed, permitting during the nights of the month of Ramadan those things which had been prohibited during the day. The Companions, therefore, were not living luxuriously or extravagantly, preferring instead to struggle and sacrifice in order to build a Muslim community.

Today there have developed so many 'ritual' foods specifically for Ramadan that one would be forgiven for mistaking this to be the true purpose of the month. Ramadan is about breaking our daily habit of filling our bellies. It is therefore a reminder to Muslims to be caring, compassionate and kind. Rather than indulging ourselves, we should be making an effort to save more during Ramadan and give to those who are more needy.

Q: *Is eating an egg for Suhur during the month of Ramadan 'makruh'? Please answer according to fiqh and Shari'ah.*

A: There is no such restriction on eating an egg for *Suhur*. All *halal* food is acceptable for *Suhur*. It may be that there is a social reason for people saying it is *makruh*: after *Suhur* people may sleep before digesting their food, and an egg, particularly a boiled one, may cause a foul smell! But the word '*makruh*', undesirable – permitted but disliked, is an Islamic term which should not be used to describe an action without proof from the *Shari'ah*.

Q: *A person living in Jeddah once broke his fast during Ramadan earlier than in Makka due to hearing the adhan from his local Mosque. The* *break of fast in Jeddah should be 5 minutes after Makka and this is what the residents used to do. On this occasion the muadhdhan gave the adhan by mistake and he has apologised for this. What is the status of the fast broken early because of this reason? Does it have to be repeated during Shawwal?*

A : If a person breaks his fast earlier than the time of sunset due to a mistake on his part, or on the part of another person (like the *muadhdhan*), he has to repay that day once it has been established that it was before time. Al-Bukhari reported of Asma', who said: 'During the lifetime of the Messenger of Allah, blessings and peace be on him, we once broke our fast before sunset. The cloud broke up and the sun was still there.' Hisham, who reported the incident, asked: 'Were they ordered to repay it?' He answered: 'It is a must to repay.'

The main thing here is that they did not do that intentionally, so there was no sin – unlike the one who breaks his fast intentionally. During the rest of the year, apart from the two days of *'Id*, 'A'isha, may Allah be pleased with her, said that she used to repay the missed days of Ramadan, especially during the month of Sha'ban the following year. But, of course, it is better to repay at the earliest opportunity. No one knows when his or her last hour will come and it is better to part without any delayed *'ibada*.

Q : *For breaking the fast, or failure to keep it on medical grounds, what does one have to do?*

A : If someone is taken ill while he is fasting, he should break his fast and then complete the fast when he gets better. Similarly, if someone unintentionally breaks his fast by e.g. accidentally drinking water, his fast is not destroyed and he can continue.

If someone is unable to fast, as he or she is suffering a permanent illness, then they have to pay what is called *Fidyah*, expiation. *Fidyah* involves providing a Muslim with two meals each day for the whole month. This can also be in the form of *Suhur* and *Iftar*, or in the form of an equivalent sum of money – e.g. £3 per meal per day for the month amounts to £180. *Fidyah* should be given to needy people and can be given to mosques.

Someone has committed a grave sin if he deliberately breaks his fast – it is as if he had denied his faith. Ibn 'Abbas reports the Prophet, blessings and peace be on him, as saying that a person who wilfully abandons the nuts and bolts of the faith – *Shahada*, the prayer, fasting during the month of Ramadan – is a disbeliever. This is a sound *Hadith* which is confirmed by Adh-Dhahabi. Commenting on it, Adh-Dhahabi said that whoever deliberately chooses not to fast during Ramadan, without any legitimate excuse, will suffer a fate worse than that of a fornicator or an alcoholic. His faith is suspect.

Q : *Since it is not possible to feed the poor in Britain, what can one do as a substitute?*

A : Who said we cannot feed the poor in this country? If there are no such people in your locality, then you can always seek out those people who prepare for their *Iftar* in the mosque and give them food or its cash equivalent. If you like, you can also arrange for food to be despatched to deserving people in Muslim countries.

According to the Maliki tradition, if someone is very poor or terminally ill or very old and thus unable to fast, he is relieved of any responsibility regarding *Fidyah*. In other words he does not have to fast and he does not have to give any expiation in lieu of that fast.

Q : *Are there any special rituals that are required to be performed in Muharram?*

A : There are a number of traditions of the Prophet, blessings and peace be upon him, speaking about the value of fasting during the month of Muharram. Once someone asked him, 'O Prophet of God, is there any month in which you would prefer I should fast?' He said, 'During the month of Muharram. It is the best month to fast.' There are other traditions speaking of the fast of the 10th of Muharram, which is called *Ashurah*. In *Al-Bukhari*, the Prophet is reported by 'A'isha as having observed the fast of *Ashurah* during his time in Makka. And when he went to Madina he found there the Jewish community observing the fast of *Ashurah*. When the Prophet enquired about this practice, he was told that this was the day on which God had saved Moses and his people from the oppression of Pharaoh. The Prophet replied that he was more entitled to preserve the tradition of Moses than the Jews and ordered the Muslims to observe the fast of *Ashurah*. Later on, when fasting during the month of Ramadan became obligatory, the Prophet lifted this obligation, saying that Muslims could fast if they wished to on *Ashurah*, or not.

There is another tradition in which the Prophet is reported to have said, 'If God spares me for the following year, I will fast on the 9th and 10th of Muharram.' All these reports show that fasting and the remembrance of Allah, *dhikru'llah*, are considered to be meritorious during the month of Muharram.

Zakat and *Sadaqa*

Q : *Is Zakat exempt on those people who are on social security benefits like family credit or income support?*

A : The amount of *Zakat* that someone has to pay has nothing to do with his or her social security status. Whether or not you pay *Zakat* depends on the extent of your savings. Supposing at the beginning of the year, day one of Muharram, you had £1,000, and on day 30 of Dhu'l-Hijjah you have £2,000, then you will have to pay *Zakat* regardless of your DSS category. Remember that *Zakat* amounts to two and a half per cent of your savings.

However, there is a threshold at the beginning of the year before which *Zakat* is payable – what we can call a '*zakat*-exempt sum'. This is 85 grams of gold. To pay its cash equivalent you would have to look up the conversion rates in your daily newspapers. If you have savings that are less than the equivalent of 85 grams of gold, you don't need to pay *Zakat*.

Q : *In the absence of a proper Islamic State administering social welfare, where should Muslims in Britain pay their Zakat? What is the criterion for deciding where the money is given? Should we pay money to an organisation, or cause, in this country or should we concentrate on paying Zakat to the needy in Muslim countries?*

A : This question was also raised at the time of the Prophet, upon whom be blessings and peace, when a man came to him demanding a share of *Zakat*. The right to demand *Zakat*, said the Prophet, did not even rest with Messengers. *Zakat* could only be distributed to those mentioned by God in the *Qur'an*. *Surah* 9, *At-Tawbah*, verse 60, elaborates: ***'Alms are for***

the poor and the needy and those employed to administer them (*the funds*); and for those whose hearts have been (*recently*) reconciled (*to the Truth*); and to free those in bondage and in debt; and in the way of Allah; and for the wayfarer: (Thus is it) ordained by Allah, and Allah is full of knowledge and wisdom.'

The well-known scholar of Islam, *Imam* Abu Hanifah, said that *Zakat* should be given to individuals and not to institutions, as the money is meant for persons in need and not groups or organisations. Broadly speaking, Allah has specified, in order of priority, eight categories of *Zakat* recipient. First on the list is any needy person who lives nearby or in your own locality. If no one in your immediate area falls into this category, then the rational Islamic way would be to look further until you do find someone who really is in need of help.

It is obvious that there are many thousands of people here in Britain to whom *Zakat* ought to be allocated. And if we directed our efforts to these people alone, we might never get to the priority cases of famine and natural disaster which are now a regular feature of life for so many Muslims in Muslim countries. This is why a balance needs to be struck. *Zakat* ought to be distributed both at home and abroad *via* the specialist relief agencies set up by Muslims to cater for Muslims in the developing world.

One final point. Please remember that *Zakat* is not charity. It is an obligatory act of worship to Allah. By paying your two and a half per cent, you are doing favours for no one but yourself.

Q : *Recently, I was criticised for donating a fairly substantial sum of money to a well-known non-Muslim charity based in Oxford. I was told that the money would have been better spent had it gone to a Muslim relief organisation like Muslim Aid or Islamic Relief. However, I justified my action by saying that my chosen charity was much better at providing disaster relief to Muslims all over the world, and that it was a hundred times bigger, more effective, much less bureaucratic and much more efficient than any Muslim charity I could name. What do you think? Was I right?*

A : The criticism of your action, in my opinion, was justified. It is not that we Muslims are against non-Muslim charities like Oxfam or Save the Children. But condemning our own organisations for being too small and ineffective, while in the same breath withholding a 'substantial sum of money' to benefit a non-Muslim charity does not help the cause of Muslim relief work. If you keep your money away, how do you expect Muslim charities to grow and respond to disaster emergencies with the speed and professionalism expected of modern relief work?

You must also understand, as I indicated towards the end of the last answer, that the intention behind Muslim relief work is different to that of non-Muslims. While Muslim relief organisations are reduced, for want of a better word, to using the term 'Aid' in their literature, they are not 'aiding' anyone, nor are they doing any favours.

Similarly, their work, or money handed out, must never have any strings attached, and they must never demand favours in return. Muslim relief work is all about worshipping Allah. It is about following Allah's commandments – since everything on this earth is given to man on trust, for which he is answerable, and which he must therefore spend wisely and equitably. Muslim relief work is not about making the needy feel guilty about being helped.

I suggest you go and contact Muslim relief organisations and read their statements of aims and objectives for a clearer picture. Finally, I'm afraid the facts do not support your contention that Muslim relief organisations are excessively bureaucratic and inefficient. As far as my information goes, administrative costs for both Muslim Aid and Islamic Relief are well below Oxfam's figure of 12.5 per cent of the total amount of money received from donations.

Q : *Many people postpone their charity until the month of Ramadan, when they believe their deeds will be more generously rewarded. Is there any justification for doing this – for poor people need money all the year round, don't they?*

A : This is simply a more convenient way of organising one's finances. In this country, for example, April is the month in which the fiscal year starts. Similarly in the Islamic calendar, the year starts with the first month of the year, Muharram – or with Rajab or Ramadan.

Also, many people look to the month of Ramadan as a month of increased spiritual awareness in which our duties should be fulfilled, and so they keep their *Zakat* until this month – when they will especially remember that it is due from them. Moreover, many people take time off work to take advantage of Ramadan and so for some it is the only time they can find to take stock of how much is owed.

On the other hand, people may be confusing *Zakat* with *Zakat'ul-Fitr*. *Zakat* is obligatory for all those who possess a specified amount and may be paid at any time of the year – but *Zakat'ul-Fitr*, which is the *Zakat* for the end of Ramadan, is due only during that holy month.

Q : *What is the significance of Zakat'ul-Fitr, who is obliged to pay it, when should it be paid, and how much and to whom?*

A : *Zakat'ul-Fitr* is a compulsory contribution of food or money payable to the needy at home or abroad. Persons who are heads of families, or breadwinners, are responsible for the payment of a set amount on behalf of their dependants. Grown up children living on their own do not count as dependants and have to pay their own *Zakat'ul-Fitr*. *Zakat'ul-Fitr* has to be given before the end of the month, so that the recipient receives it in time for the *'Id*. In the early days, *Zakat'ul-Fitr* amounted to 'four double-handfuls of staple food'. In other words, four double-handfuls of rice, or flour, or dried milk, or dates, or raisins, etc., making a combined weight of approximately three kilogrammes. Three kilogrammes of any one commodity were also perfectly acceptable.

Nowadays, the scholars have permitted payment of a cash equivalent. So instead of giving rice, for example, I am permitted to pay the equivalent in cash of the market value of three kilogrammes of rice for each member of my family. Clearly not all commodities cost the same, as some are more expensive than others. This is why the final monetary figure for *Zakat'ul-Fitr* set should reflect an average for many commodities. The figure which has been agreed upon for this year is £2.50. Only followers of the Hanbali school of thought still insist on 'edible contributions'.

Zakat'ul-Fitr is an indication of how the community cares for those who are less fortunate during the feast at the end of Ramadan. The payment of *Zakat'ul-Fitr* also enables Muslims to cleanse their fasts of any 'improprieties' they may have unwittingly made during the month.

Q : *Is it valid to give financial donations, Zakat, Zakat'ul-Fitr and skins of sacrificed animals to political parties or groups who are clearly involved in terrorism, killings and other heinous crimes?*

A : Absolutely not. Allah Most High says: ***'Help each other in what is good and pious, and do not help each other in what is sinful and hostile, and fear Allah – surely Allah is severe in punishment.'*** (*Surah* 5, *Al-Ma'idah*, verse 2). It is really amazing for a good Muslim to lose his Islamic common sense and, in looking at a clear-cut case of what is harmful to the Muslim community, to ask if a most noble action, the donation of *Zakat* or *Sadaqa*, can be given for the most horrifying things. This means that there are some people who are unaware of the terrible consequences of supporting or encouraging such elements in their ruinous activities.

Hajj and *'Umrah*

Q : *I have never understood the ritual of Hajj, revolving as it does around the structure of the Ka'aba. What is the significance of the Ka'aba and does it contain any heavenly objects?*

A : Al-Ka'aba stands as the symbol of the unity of the Muslim nation and of the oneness of the worship of Allah, as is mentioned in the *Qur'an* when it relates that Ibrahim, *alayhi salam*, called upon Allah, saying that he had built a structure and put his offspring next to it just to offer prayer to Allah. Al-Ka'aba is a symbol from that early history of Islam, expressing the oneness of God, the oneness of the human race and the oneness of our destiny. It is not a structure as such, but a great religious symbol, gathering the hearts of those who have accepted the faith of Ibrahim and Isma'il and of Muhammad – who brought the final phase of the revelation of Allah, blessings and peace be on them.

As far as heavenly objects go, there is nothing in particular inside al-Ka'aba itself – but in the structure there is a Black Stone set in the corner where Muslims start their circumambulating around the Ka'aba. The Prophet used to kiss and touch the Black Stone when he started performing his circumambulations. It has been related that the second *Khalifah*, 'Umar, was kissing the Black Stone one day and as he was doing so he said, 'I know that you are only a stone, and you do not have the quality of benefiting or harming anybody, but I saw the Prophet kissing you and so I am kissing you, following his example.' When 'Umar looked around he saw 'Ali who said to him, 'Oh, 'Umar! This stone is a witness of harm and benefit, because when you touch it, that represents a testimony of your acceptance of the Unity of Allah and of your obedience to His call to offer pilgrimage around it. That, on the Day of *al-Qiyamah*, will weigh greatly in the scales of your deeds.' There is another sound *Hadith* which says that the Black Stone was a jewel from heaven which Allah gave to the Ka'aba.

Q : *I have just returned from Hajj. I saw that people kissed the Black Stone set in the Holy Ka'aba and know that the Prophet, blessings and peace be upon him, did so. There is another corner, Rukh al-Yamani, which some people kiss when they do the tawaf. Could you please explain the background for their doing so and what the proper ruling concerning that is. May I also ask, what is the proper name of the semicircular space next to the Ka'aba where many people offer prayer?*

A : There are two corners of the Ka'aba which date back to the time of the Prophet Ibrahim, peace be on him, the Yamani corner and the Black Stone. Touching the Yamani corner, not kissing it, is a *sunnah* of the Prophet, blessings and peace be upon him; it is *sunnah* to kiss the Black Stone. The other two corners are not built on the foundations which date back to the time of the Prophet Ibrahim. Their history goes back to the time when the Quraysh were first re-building the Ka'aba but were not rich enough to replicate the size and foundations of the Ka'aba of the Prophet Ibrahim. As such, they had to settle for two out of the four corners being situated at their corresponding positions from the time of the Prophet Ibrahim, with the other two corners falling short of their previous positions. This is why it is not a *sunnah* to touch either of the newer corners.

The semicircular place you ask about is called Al-Hijr, which means 'the restricted area'. It is also called Hijr Isma'il, the area concerning Isma'il. The origins of this name are linked with evidence that suggests that the Prophet Isma'il and his mother are buried there, peace be on them.

Q : *Briefly, what are the main, or compulsory, rites of Hajj and what is their significance?*

A : The essential aspects of the *Hajj* differ according to the *madhdhahib.* The Hanafis consider these to be only two: standing on Mount Arafat, and circumambulating the Ka'aba.

For the Shafi'i school of thought, the donning of the *Ihram* is compulsory. The significance of this lies in the fact that the Muslim is starting a journey to Allah in which he or she is abandoning everything connected with this life and proceeding to the House of God in the most simple, humble way.

The second act is standing on Mount Arafat. This is the greatest moment, an earthly foretaste of how on the Day of Judgement everybody will be gathered before God to account for their actions.

The third is circumambulating the Ka'aba. The Ka'aba is the symbol of the oneness of the Muslim nation. Once they are in the Holy Sanctuary, no matter where they stand, pilgrims will be facing the Ka'aba, symbolising oneness of purpose and direction. The Ka'aba is their focal point – and this is also very symbolic, for it is from the Ka'aba that the expansion of al-Islam took place.

The fourth ritual is running between the two small hills of as-Safa and al-Marwa, reminiscent of what Hagar did when she was searching for the source of life for herself and her child, until the mercy of Allah appeared in the form of the well of Zamzam. To run between these two points is to remind ourselves of the dedication of that young mother in following the command of Allah.

Q : *Why did the Prophet Ibrahim leave his wife Hajirah (Hagar) and son Isma'il all alone in the desert?*

A : The answer is very simple. When the Prophet Ibrahim, upon whom be blessings and peace, left his wife Hajirah and son alone in the desert with few provisions, she cried: 'Why are you abandoning us like this?' When she got no reply she repeated her question twice more, adding the third time, 'Is this a command from Allah or are you doing this of your own accord?' He finally said that he was acting on God's orders.

Do not think that the Prophet Ibrahim was a callous or stone-hearted person. He was not. No father would wilfully leave his family alone in the desert without reason – particularly the Prophet Ibrahim, who had fathered a child so late in life. In his case, Allah had set the ultimate test of loyalty: would he obey a command of God, even if it meant leaving his loved ones alone in harsh surroundings? He was on trial: would he choose personal love or obedience to Allah?

Q : *I heard it said that one of the purposes of Hajj is to allow a believer to immerse himself in the community of Muslims, the Ummah, and to forge a closer bond of unity with fellow Muslims. Is this the primary purpose of Hajj or just an accidental effect?*

A : This is part of the benefit Muslims get from the experience of *Hajj*. Allah mentions in the *Holy Qur'an* that He summoned Ibrahim to call everyone to offer pilgrimage in order to witness benefits. These benefits are spiritual, moral and social. To have all the pilgrims congregated in that place at one time is to experience how to live and get along with one another, irrespective of colour, language or culture. The manner in which pilgrims should conduct themselves during the *Hajj* also serves the purpose of unity. The *Qur'an* says with respect to *Hajj*, **'Let there be no licentious talk, no bad action and no arguing.'** (*Surah* 2, *Al-Baqarah*, verse 197). These are three essential qualities which make for a friction-free, humble and peaceful occasion to let man experience the oneness of humanity.

Q : *I saw a speech advertised recently about the political significance of Hajj. Unfortunately, I couldn't make it to the talk, but I was reflecting that Hajj is a spiritual exercise designed to cleanse the soul and rejuvenate the spirit. Is there really any political significance to Hajj?*

A : There is a political significance in the sense that after the liberation of Makka in the eighth year of the *Hijrah*, the Prophet, blessings and peace be on him, asked Abu Bakr to publicly declare the beginning of *Surah* 9, *Al-Bara'a*, verses 1-12, proclaiming that there is no place in Paradise for non-believers, that no idol-worshipper would be allowed to come and perform *Hajj*, that no-one would be allowed to perform the *Hajj* naked, and that any treaties agreed with the idol-worshippers would be allowed to run their course – but that those among the idol-worshippers who did not have any pacts with the Muslims should be warned that the Messenger of Allah would fight them. Later on, the Prophet sent 'Ali to proclaim the same message during the time of the Pilgrimage two months later in order to give it the widest publicity. This was done to demonstrate that the Ka'aba was no longer a sanctuary for unbelievers, and that the un-Islamic practices of the pre-Islamic era were no longer acceptable.

Once the place was clean and pure and all these practices had been stopped, the Prophet, blessings and peace be on him, came in the last year of his life to perform his farewell pilgrimage. The declaration made the year before was to clear the Ka'aba from all evil and unclean practices and to stop the idol-worshippers from coming.

There is another political significance: *Hajj* in the past was an occasion when Muslim leaders from all parts of the world came together to discuss the affairs of the *Ummah* and to inform the head of the Muslim nation what was happening in all the regions under his rule

As far as shouting slogans goes, there is no precedent for this practice after the promulgation of *Al-Bara'a*. After this, the only slogan pilgrims shouted was, '*Labbayk, Allahumma Labbayk*' – '*At Your service, Oh Allah, at your service*'. As far as the ordinary Muslim is concerned this is a time to realise the great spiritual benefits of *Hajj*, to cleanse the soul, and to experience the oneness of humanity – all worshipping Allah in different languages and living together in harmony and peace.

Q : *My friend's family are going for Hajj this year and they will be travelling overland, passing through many Muslim countries, where they will have an opportunity to visit the graves of famous saints and Sahaba. I see this as a great way of touching base with one's Islamic heritage, but a colleague told me that such a way of getting to Hajj is bid'a. Is he correct?*

A : We say that in a sense he may be correct. There is a *Hadith* in which the Prophet says that Muslims are not allowed to journey except to three sacred mosques, al-Masjid al-Haram at Makka, the Prophet's Mosque in Madina and the Bait'ul-Muqaddas in Jerusalem. If the person has the intention of visiting the graves of saints and Sahaba, we say that this is not acceptable to the school of thought which considers itself 'Salafi'. They stress that a Muslim is not allowed to visit any but the three mosques mentioned.

But if a pilgrim starts out with the intention of performing *Hajj*, and he happens to pass by these places, there is no harm in him stopping to say *Salaam* to the people buried there, or to make supplications for them and to remember the great spiritual and moral achievements of such luminaries. This is the point of view of those who consider that the above *Hadith* does not place restrictions on the number of mosques to which Muslims may travel, but merely emphasises the importance and the stature of the three greatest mosques.

Q : *Is it true that one's Hajj is not accepted by God until all one's debts have been repaid? If so, what is the definition of debt here?*

A : When Allah enjoined pilgrimage upon Muslims, the *Qur'an*, according to the basic principle of not burdening a soul with more than it can bear, has taken into consideration that not everyone will have the means to do so. For example, there are people who accepted al-Islam far, far away from Makka. So the *Qur'an* makes the obligation of *Hajj* dependent on the ability to perform it. Muslim scholars say that the debt of a believer has priority over the performance of *Hajj*.

Nowadays, people may be indebted and these debts may be repaid over a number of years. If the debt is a long-standing, structured debt and the believer is not under any obligation to repay it immediately, then he is allowed to go and perform *Hajj*. If a Muslim has large debts, he should not go. Borrowing money to go for *Hajj* is generally discouraged unless you have the means to repay the loan. If one is a little short of the sum needed and is sure that the money can be repaid, it is permissible to borrow.

Q : *Is it permissible to go on Hajj with money borrowed from a relative?*

A : Yes, it is; if the person has some wealth from which he will he able to repay the amount he borrowed. *Hajj* becomes obligatory on someone when he becomes financially able to provide for his family and dependants, back home, during his absence. If he is a little short of the money needed, and provided he is employed and able to make repayments, he is allowed to take out a loan from relatives. However, relatives can prevent him from going if he has large debts.

Q : *I have been told I cannot go on Hajj without clearing outstanding debts. Does this also apply to the fasts I missed over previous months of Ramadan? Are these classified as debts as well?*

A : No, these are not classified as debts. Fasting and other incomplete religious obligations do not prohibit someone from performing *Hajj*. Scholars tend to follow the example of 'A'isha, the wife of the Prophet, upon whom be blessings and peace, who went for *Hajj* despite having missed certain days of the fast during the previous Ramadan.

Q : *Is it Islamically permissible to perform Hajj on behalf of someone who is living? I am thinking of going on Hajj for my grandmother who has never been on the pilgrimage but cannot now go on account of her age and physical state.*

A : '*Proxy-Hajj*' is allowed on two conditions, based on the following *Ahadith*: When the Prophet was performing his farewell *Hajj*, as reported in *Al-Bukhari*, a woman from the tribe of Qasa came to him and asked if she could do *Hajj* on behalf of her father who was old and who 'could not sit properly on his mount'. The Prophet, blessings and peace be upon him, told her that she could.

The second *Hadith* reports an incident where the Prophet, blessings and peace be upon him, heard a man during *Hajj* calling out, '*Labbayka* on behalf of Shubruma'. When questioned by the Prophet, the man explained that he was performing the *Hajj* for Shubruma who was a friend. When the Prophet, blessings and peace be upon him, heard that the man had not been on *Hajj* for himself, he told him to '... first perform *Hajj* for yourself – and after that you are free to offer for whomever you choose.'

From this the *fuqaha* have ruled that *Hajj*-by-proxy is conditional on a person having done it himself or herself first. Also, *proxy-Hajj* only applies in the case of the elderly, handicapped and infirm. Strong, able-bodied people must perform the pillar themselves. They cannot expect others to do it for them.

Q : *I have heard that the Hanafis say it is better for a woman not to do Hajj if a mahram does not travel with her. What is the evidence for this? Is this a majority opinion? What if it is impossible for a mahram to go with her? Does this not contradict Qur'anic verses encouraging performance of the Hajj?*

A : Opinion on the question of *Hajj* for unaccompanied women is divided between the two great scholars, *Imam* Abu Hanifah and *Imam* Ash-Shafi'i:

Al-Kafani, the author of a leading Hanafi textbook, writes in the chapter dealing with *Hajj* that women who are unable to find *mahram* men (men whom they are forbidden to marry), or their husbands, to accompany them on *Hajj* are forbidden to go on the pilgrimage. *Imam* Shafi'i, however, disagrees and says that not being able to find a suitable escort is not a valid reason to prevent a woman from performing *Hajj*. A group of trustworthy women is just as good an escort, according to *Imam* Ash-Shafi'i.

A careful analysis of the Hanafi opinion reveals one escape clause: If the journey to Makka from the woman's house takes less than three days, she does not need her husband to go with her, nor indeed a *mahram*, according to the *Imam*. A *mahram* is only needed if the journey takes more than three days.

Furthermore, *Imam* Shafi'i says, in the section on *Expiation for Hunting*, that in one of the *Hadith* it is reported that 'Umar, the Companion of the Prophet, allowed the wives of the Prophet to perform *Hajj* without the Prophet, accompanied only by the Companions 'Uthman and Abd ar-Rahman ibn Awf – and no *mahram*. The commentator Ibn Hajar wrote in *Fath al-Bari* that this tradition could be cited as evidence for women to be allowed to go on *Hajj* in all-female groups. He added that none of the other Companions had objected to 'Umar sending 'Uthman and Abd ar-Rahman ibn Awf with the female group. And he pointed out that if this practice was good enough for the wives of the Prophet, may Allah be pleased with them, it had to be good enough for other women too.

Ibn Hajar also quoted from a *Hadith* of the Prophet, blessings and peace be on him, which records a conversation with the Companion Adi ibn Hatim. The Prophet is reported to have told Adi of a time when women would be able to travel from Al-Kheera, now in Iraq, to the House of God without any *mahram* escort. While some scholars have pointed out that the Prophet's prediction did not necessarily make it permissible for women to go for *Hajj* on their own, Ibn Hajar contended that it was a sign of the times when Islam would be well established and that travel circumstances would also change.

Finally, in an answer to a question posed by his wife, 'A'isha, who had asked to accompany the Prophet on *Jihad*, the Prophet, blessings and peace be on him, replied that *Hajj* was more rewarding, and a greater *Jihad* for a woman.

Q : *In a reply to a question on Hajj last year, you said that women could make the trip without men, so long as they were in a group. Does the same hold for 'Umrah?*

A : The same holds true for *'Umrah* as well. There are a number of *Ahadith* in the collection of *Al-Bukhari* – together with incidents from the life and times of the Prophet, upon whom be blessings and peace, and his Companions – which support this position. To quote an example taken from section 26, entitled *Pilgrimage for Women*, 'Umar, a Companion who later became the second *Khalifah*, is reported to have let the wives of the Prophet perform a *Hajj* without a *mahram*, a permitted male escort, although the Companions 'Uthman ibn 'Affan and Abd'ur-Rahman ibn Awf were sent to accompany them.

However, a story from the life of the scholar Ibn Hajr shows that even all those years ago, the issue was constantly being debated. Ibn Hajr refers to a *Hadith* which is the result of a conversation between the Prophet, upon whom be blessings and peace, and Adi ibn Hatim, one of the Companions. The Messenger of God asked the Companion if he had ever been to Al-Kheer, then a non-Muslim town which is somewhere in today's Iraq. When Adi replied that he had not, the Prophet, upon whom be blessings and peace, said that a day would come when, 'Muslim women will travel, alone, from Al-Kheer to Makka for *tawaf* and *Hajj*.'

Ibn Hajr's comment caused controversy at the time, with some scholars questioning his conclusion. While acknowledging the authenticity of the *Hadith*, they nonetheless maintained that it was not sufficient to give licence for women to travel to *Hajj* alone. The *Hadith* simply points to signs of the times, according to one scholar, and therefore should not be taken out of context. However, Ibn Hajr had other ideas and pointed out that the *Hadith* indicated two things: that Islam would spread to Al-Kheer, and that the road would be safe enough for a woman to travel on her own without fear or hindrance.

Q : *A widow in her fifties wishes to offer 'Umrah but cannot manage to have any close relative, mahram, to accompany her. What should she do?*

A : The good news for her is that she can go as long as she travels with a group of trusted, good Muslim women – the total number must not be less than three. If any of her companions has a *mahram* with her, so much the better.

Q : *Is it permissible for women to take medication to stop their periods for Hajj? If so, what did the early Muslim women do? But, how can we justify tampering with nature?*

A : Yes, it is. There is a *fatwah* by Shaikh Abd'ul-Aziz bin Baz, the *Mufti* of Saudi Arabia, allowing women to take medication during the month of Ramadan so that women can fast the whole month, without the anxiety of impending periods. The *'ulama*, Muslim scholars, do not consider it to be an act of interference or tampering with nature – rather, it is considered an act of regulation so that Ramadan and *Hajj* can pass free from anxiety. There is nothing wrong with using available resources to help Muslim women in their acts of *'ibadah*, worship, during these times. This is not a permanent act of interference with human nature.

Q : *A 9-year-old boy travelled to Makka, in Ihram, with the intention of performing 'Umrah. However, his mother fell seriously ill and he had to return to Makka and remove his Ihram since his mother was admitted to hospital. The boy also did not cut his hair. In the light of Islamic law what should this boy do with respect to his intended 'Umrah?*

A : This is known as *Ihsar*, i.e. being prevented from doing *Hajj* or *'Umrah* by reasons beyond the power of the person whose intention it was. The young boy should offer a sacrifice in accordance with the *Qur'anic* ruling: ***'... if you are prevented, then make such offering as may be feasible, and do not shave your heads until the offering reaches its destination.'*** (*Surah* 2, *Al-Baqarah*, verse 196). It is better for the offering to be sent to the sacred territory. If the boy has already shaved his head in ignorance of the rule, Allah will forgive him.

Q : *At 'Id'ul-Adha should only the Hajjis perform the ritual sacrifice, or is this something that is recommended for all Muslims?*

A : The sacrifice is not solely connected with the pilgrimage. It is recommended for all Muslims. It is mentioned in the *Qur'an* in *Surat'ul-Kawthar*, where Allah says, ***'Surely we have granted you the abundance of***

al-Kawthar, so pray to your Lord and offer sacrifice.' (*Surah* 108, verses 1-2). A lot of commentators of the *Qur'an* have said that this refers to the sacrifice of *'Id'ul-Adha*. Anas reported the Prophet, blessings and peace be on him, as having sacrificed two beautiful, healthy rams, saying, '*Bismillah, Allahu Akbar*.'

By the consensus of the Muslims, sacrifice is a ritual to be performed on *Id'ul-Adha* – to the extent that the Hanafi School considers it to be an obligation. Abu Hurayrah is recorded as reporting that the Prophet, blessings and peace be upon him, said, 'Whoever is able to offer sacrifice but does not do so, let him not come to our place of prayer.' According to the majority view, sacrifice is strongly recommended for anyone who can afford it. It may be considered as a commemoration of what Allah did with Ibrahim when he asked him in a dream to sacrifice his son Isma'il. Once it was established that Ibrahim was seriously prepared to carry out the command of Allah, Allah saved Isma'il by replacing him with a ram. Then Allah called to him, ***'O Ibrahim, you have fulfilled the dream.'*** (*Surah* 37, *As-Saffat*, verses 104-105). And when the Prophet, blessings and peace be upon him, was asked about the sacrifice he replied, 'That is the way of your father, Ibrahim.'

Q : *What animals can be sacrificed and how should their meat be distributed?*

A : The animals to be sacrificed are mentioned in the *Qur'an*, *Surah* 5, *Al-Ma'idah*, verse 1, where Allah says, '***baheematu'l-an'am***'. This is understood to mean camels, cows, sheep and goats. There is a minimum age for animals to be sacrificed – at least seven months in the case of rams, one year in the case of goats, two years in the case of cows, and five years in the case of camels.

As sacrifice is a recommended act, there is a recommended way of distributing the meat. One third of the meat goes to the family, one third to relatives or friends and one third goes to the needy. It is however all right, but less preferred, to give all the meat to the poor, or for the family to keep it all, or to give it all to friends or relations.

Q : *What are the recommended religious observances to be carried out on Id'ul-Adha and what do they signify?*

A: The first recommended act is to offer *Id'ul-Adha* prayer in the morning. This, again, is a collective commemoration of the manner in which the pilgrims are offering their pilgrimage, so that people can participate emotionally and spiritually in that great event which they have not attended in body. The second is offering the sacrifice – and this is what the Prophet, blessings and peace be on him, meant when he said, 'The first thing we do today is to offer our *Id'ul-Adha* prayer. The second is to sacrifice the animal. Whoever has already done his sacrifice should do it again, for sacrifice can only take place after the prayer.' But before both of these, after the *Fajr* prayer on the 9th of Dhu'l-Hijjah, Muslims should say the *takbir: 'Allahu Akbar, Allahu Akbar, Allahu Akbar. La ilaha il'Allah. Allahu Akbar, wa lillahi'l-hamd.'* – '*God is Great, God is Great, God is Great. There is no god but Allah. God is Great, and to God is all praise.*' This is repeated after each of the five daily prayers until the third day of *tashriq*, that is, the days of stoning the devils at Mina. After *'Asr* prayer on the third day, the *takbir* stops. According to some schools of thought it is also to be performed after the *Dhuhr* prayer on the Day of Arafat.

There is a great historical event to be recalled by the *takbir*. When the Prophet, blessings and peace be upon him, re-entered Makka at the head of his army in the 8th year after he had made *Hijrah* to Madina, he recited the *takbir* as a show of humility to God – Who had fulfilled His promise that Islam would be permanently established in the Haram ash-Sharif. The Prophet used to say, 'He fulfilled His promise, granted victory to his servants and humiliated the unbelievers.'

Once more, *Id'ul-Adha* is a reminder of the great occasion of the Pilgrimage – and there are other basic things to be observed. It is a time to show care and affection for our friends and relatives and other Muslims. It is also a time for Muslims who are not on good terms to reconcile themselves. There are so many meanings to the *'Id* and each one is an affirmation of our dedication and responsibility to strive and struggle to establish Islam even if it entails making huge personal sacrifices.

Q: *'Id is a time of celebration, but is it meritorious to remember those who are less fortunate than ourselves on this day?*

A: Yes. *'Id* is not simply a matter of celebration and joy, It is also a chance to share the feelings of those around us. That is why the sacrifice is offered and shared with friends, even with non-Muslims. We are not stopped from sharing with those of our neighbours who are non-Muslim. Charity is very important and meritorious on the two *'Ids*. It is an affirmation of our responsibility to the community in which we are living.

Q : *If 'Id'ul-Adha is the most important feast of the Islamic Calendar, why are the Hajjis not expected to observe it? Why do we celebrate such an occasion anyway?*

A : We celebrate these occasions because feasts are natural, human phenomena which people remember in their lives. They are civic and religious occasions. In Islam we have only two: *'Id'ul-Fitr*, the celebration of the completion of Ramadan, and *'Id'ul-Adha*, the commemoration of the great sacrifice which God asked Ibrahim to perform with his son, Isma'il, peace be on them. That was a great spiritual test for Ibrahim – whether he would obey the commandment of Allah, or be swayed by his love for his son. Ibrahim passed the test – and so as he was about to bring down the blade on his son, God replaced the little boy with a ram. As for the pilgrims themselves, they are commemorating this in some symbolic, far removed way – but they are re-enacting the Abrahamic episode for themselves.

Q : *My relatives and friends always return from Hajj with plenty of dates and Zamzam water. They say that Zamzam should be drunk while standing and that it has special spiritual, even healing, qualities. Is this true?*

A : Those returning from the Pilgrimage bring back gifts from those places because they are considered to be places of blessing and grace. The easiest thing to do is to buy dates and carry Zamzam water with you. Zamzam water has the qualities mentioned in an authentic tradition of the Holy Prophet, blessings and peace be upon him, in which he is reported to have said, 'Zamzam is for what it is drunk for,' which means that if it is drunk for asking the forgiveness of Allah, then Allah will forgive us. If it is drunk for seeking knowledge, Allah will grant that. Whatever the wish the drinker has in his mind, then Allah has the power to grant that, so long as it is not cursing anyone, or calling the wrath of Allah on other people. Those who are drinking Zamzam water should start by saying, 'In the Name of Allah,' and then say, 'Lord, grant me good knowledge, bounteous maintenance, satisfaction and the feeling of being full and satisfied, cleanliness and purification, and cure everything in my heart.' It is recommended to drink in three sips beginning each one with 'In the Name of Allah'. There is nothing in the *Hadith* to say that it must be drunk while standing. We drink in the normal *Sunnah* way, which is while sitting.

Q : *Are there any books which a prospective Hajji might read before making the journey for Hajj?*

A : The prospective Hajji should start reading as soon as possible. The following titles might be useful: S.A. Hussain : *A Guide to Hajj* – a simple, handy pocket-sized book which is reasonably comprehensive. M.A. Ghazanfar : *Talim'ul-Hajj* – simple and informative and quite readable. S.A. Qadri : *How to Perform Hajj* – an awful publication, but one that contains all the information you'll ever need to know. A.R. Salli : *The Book of Hajj* – a complete manual which goes into considerable detail. It is a shame that it doesn't seem to be that widely available.

But as with everything else, the best way to learn about *Hajj* is to approach a learned man and to also get in touch with people who have had first-hand experience about the journey.

Mosques and Islamic Centres

Q : *Is it necessary, Islamically speaking, for a purpose-built mosque to have a dome and a minaret?*

A : It is not necessary to have a dome and a minaret. The mosque at the time of the Prophet, upon whom be blessings and peace, was very simple. Even when the time came to extend it, 'Umar told the person supervising the work to prepare a place which could shelter people from the heat of the sun, from the rain, and which was not coloured red or yellow. He clearly wanted a simple place of worship. But the development of Islamic architecture has progressed to such an extent that the dome and the minaret are both firmly part of our architectural heritage, an indication that the building which supports them is a place of worship. Domes and minarets have become architectural landmarks that indicate a place where God is being worshipped according to the Islamic way of life.

Q: *Why is it so common for Muslim establishments to be so dirty, even those which are supposedly high-profile? Anyone using the toilets in Regent's Park Mosque, the Muslim World League and so on must be appalled.*

A: I am not sure of the fussy argument about these places. It is the mosque authority which is responsible for keeping the place clean, and I trust that the two places mentioned here are in a reasonable condition. It is also the responsibility of those using these places to keep them tidy and clean. However, the numbers involved and the use of so much water in *wudu, istinja,* etc., makes it understandable why they are sometimes in a less than acceptable condition. I would expect our brothers and sisters in charge and the users to keep such places clean as this is a basic Islamic principle.

Q: *As a new, English-speaking Muslim, I find it very frustrating not to be able to understand the Khutbah in my local mosque on Friday, which is always in Urdu. I am sure that it is not Islamically correct to give the week's most important community message in a language which lots of people do not comprehend. What do the Qur'an and the Hadith have to say about this?*

A: The *Khutbah,* Friday sermon, in Islam is a very simple matter, particularly according to the Hanafi school of thought. While the Shafi'i school insists that *Khutbahs* have to contain recitals of '*al-hamdulillah*', '*ashhadu-an la ilaha illa'Allah*', verses from the *Qur'an* and advice to stay pious and to seek the forgiveness of Allah, none of these are essential in the Hanafi point of view. Any speech which advises goodness and adherence to Islamic principles is considered to be a *Khutbah* in the Hanafi point of view.

Khutbahs in Britain tend to be in Urdu as the majority of first generation Muslims do not understand English very well. Of course, for the second generation Muslims the opposite is true: they are, so to speak, more at home with English than Urdu. As their numbers continue to grow it is only natural that the situation *vis-a-vis Khutbah* language will change, reflecting the situation on the ground. Hence it is only a matter of time before a group of second generation Muslims in Britain – who are, Islamically speaking, well-versed, knowledgeable and with the right scholarly skills – take up the task of preaching, teaching and leading the community within the mosques and outside. Right now our predicament is only temporary. We are in the midst of a cultural change-over which will not last for ever. Ideally, *Khateebs,* the men who give Friday *Khutbahs*, have to be culturally aware of trends in their society and problems that affect the Muslim community. They need to gauge the implications of changes in their societies' social, moral and spiritual fabric. These people have to then reflect the Islamic attitude and correct Islamic point of view so that they can enlighten their congregation on current and topical events. Of course people who do not understand *Khutbahs* can, if they want, find alternative mosques, but the fact that they are present in a congregation, is itself an act of worship to Allah.

Q : *How can we get our local Imams to introduce relevant topics into their Khutbas? I am thinking of things like sex education, morality, the environment and so on – things which we Muslims should be leading the world in, but somehow fail. Is there an easy answer?*

A : This brother is expecting too much from our *Imams*. In one education meeting I attended there were many representatives from the church; a philosophy lecturer spoke and said to those who were graduated from universities, 'You are not knowledgeable enough to lead, answer and direct young people. They expect too much from you and you are not qualified for that.' I am sure that if he looked at the majority of our *Imams*, that lecturer would not mince his words and would dismiss the whole question! In 1988, the then Home Secretary, Douglas Hurd, was reported in *The Times* as trying to raise the standard of *Imams* coming into Britain by refusing to grant visas to non-graduates. This promise was not fulfilled and the *Imams* still come with a bare minimum education, just suited to an uneducated village community. We do not have an administration to look after the *Imams*, their qualifications, their salaries and their appointment. We import *Imams* with minimal qualifications and give them the lowest wage possible. We imprison them in the mosques – they do not go out, they do not mix, they do not read; what they then give to our children is only what they themselves have learnt in their own country. Until such time as our community is aware and selective in such appointments, looking for well-educated young Muslims, we will continue to have *Imams* who are functioning at a very basic level and transferring that to our youngsters.

Q : *I was recently elected President of my local mosque. During the campaign, I promised that I would make the mosque more young-person friendly. Sadly, I failed in my task, so I resigned. One of my promises was that I would appoint an Imam, who, although not necessarily young, would be well-educated, articulate in English, Arabic and one other language, sporty and fit and would demonstrate a fair understanding of the issues affecting today's British Muslim youth. The trouble was, I was not in a position to offer such a person the salary he deserved. The mosque committee have since appointed some poor soul all the way from India who is quite happy to work for £8,000 yearly. In my resignation letter I told the committee that our children needed the best teachers and scholars for which we would have to pay the proper rates. Third-rate pay would only guarantee us third-rate teaching and eventually third-rate children. I didn't want to act like the martyr, but I believed that someone had to take a stand on this issue for the sake of our future generations. Was I right to resign?*

A : Before answering this question, I would like to take the reader back to an incident in 1988 concerning a certain Mr Douglas Hurd, Home Secretary in Margaret Thatcher's Government. Out of the blue, Clifford Longley, then Religious Affairs Correspondent for *The Times,* wrote an article alleging that the Home Office was going to do its bit to raise the quality and standard of our mosque *Imams* by refusing to admit into Britain any *Imam* who did not possess a first degree. At the time I thought it was a very positive gesture by the Government, as it aimed at improving the education of Muslim children while ensuring that our *Imams* come up to certain standards. Unfortunately, the story was mere hot air as nothing ever came of the proposal.

Coming back to your question as to whether you ought to have resigned from the post of President, I feel a few words should be said about the nature of your campaign promises. I know you sincerely wanted to enhance the quality of education in your mosque, but, I am afraid, you were far, far too idealistic. I wonder, before you promised your local Muslim community an 'articulate, well-read, sporty and fit Imam', did you ever, at any stage, consider how you were going to pay for someone fitting that particular description? All our mosques could do with high-calibre *Imams*, but the reality is that many of our mosque-goers happen to be men and women drawing on the dole who can barely afford to send their children to weekend *Qur'an* classes. Your promises were simply not realistic, given the economic situation of Muslims in Britain today. I am afraid that until we become wealthier, better educated and more prosperous, no local Muslim community will be able to employ the sort of *Imam* we badly need – but, sadly, cannot afford.

Q : *I am worried about my nine-year-old brother. Every day that he returns from his madrassah at the mosque, he cries because the Imam regularly beats him. Apart from the damaging effect this is having on his development, I fear that the experience may put him off Islam for ever. What should I do?*

A : This scandalous tradition reflects the attitude of many, many *Imams* in this country. These are people who are ill-educated and who have no idea how to teach children at all. Almost all of them come from *madrassahs* where they themselves have been beaten throughout their childhood and youth, so when it comes to discipline, they know of no other method than extreme corporal punishment.

You must go to this *Imam* straight away and talk to him. Be firm and strong and explain to him that children's experiences in schools compared to *madrassahs* could not be more polarised. Tell the *Imam* that teaching children in this country must be done with love, kindness and consideration, especially for those with learning difficulties. As you rightly say, children with bad experiences will not come back, and moreover, will ensure that their children in turn don't go to mosques either. Children who go to mosques are greeted with damp, dark and draughty surroundings. Met by intimidating *Imams* with beards down to their navels and sticks in their hands, who can blame a child if he never wants to see a mosque again?

If the *Imam* does not change his attitude, then don't just pull you brother out. For the sake of all the children, raise the issue with your mosque committee or Islamic association, get other parents together to lobby those in authority for change. Don't rest, for this is too important an issue just to be left aside.

Q : *A mosque in Leicester has a big sign at the door saying that children under the age of seven are not allowed inside. Is it* ***a)*** *lawful, and* ***b)*** *desirable, to ban young children from our mosques?*

A : I think our brothers are a little rigid in their viewpoint. Of course, a commentary of Ibn Abideen on an authoritative Hanafi *fiqh* work, *Radd'ul-Muhtar*, Vol. 1, p. 656, states that '... it is not allowed to admit small children, or mad people, or animals, into mosques.' This is based on a *Hadith* recommending, among other things, that parents should avoid taking their children to the mosque. Now this particular *Hadith* on which they depend is unsound. In the same book, however, it is recalled in the section relating to rules of behaviour in the mosque that the Prophet, blessings and peace be on him, led the prayer carrying his grand-daughter Umayma in his arms. Moreover, when the *fiqh* books talk about prohibiting children from mosques, they are referring only to those children who have not reached the age of discretion – which is four years or a little over. The prohibition is designed to prevent against children urinating in the mosque and polluting it. If we consider that today, strong nappies are available which eliminate the possibility of leakages, so this reason is no longer valid. The other reason that is usually given for stopping children from being in the mosques is noise. But I think that children over the age of four are controllable.

Q : *My question concerns the admission to mosques for prayers, lectures and other events. Until recently, I lived in London where my wife was able to attend the Islamic Cultural Centre as well as our local mosque. I am now in a provincial town. It has a fine mosque with ample capacity for women – only they are not allowed inside. How can this be justified?*

A : There is no justification, whatsoever, for harbouring such a narrow-minded and, frankly, anti-Islamic attitude. I am saddened to acknowledge that the majority of prayer facilities in this country lack adequate provision for women; I am often left wondering whether this really is because of a shortage of money, as is often suggested, or whether it is the men's lame excuse to exclude the other half of the Muslim population. Whatever its origins, the decision by so many *Imams*, Presidents and mosque committees to shut the mosque doors on women is certainly not rooted in Islam. Even a cursory reading of the numerous *Ahadith* from the life of the Prophet and his Companions, blessings and peace be on him and them, should demolish forever this myth that mosques are meant to be 'men only' clubs.

'Do not stop the female servants of Allah from entering the houses of Allah, but ensure that they are decently dressed,' urges one *Hadith*. In another tradition, the second *Khalifah*, 'Umar, may Allah be pleased with him, was publicly challenged in the mosque by a lady to justify, in accordance with the *Qur'an*, his call for dowries to be reduced. Unable to do so, 'Umar had no choice but to back down and concede in public that he was wrong and the lady was right. Mosques were not only just places for men and women, but young children were welcome too, according to yet another *Hadith*.

The Prophet, blessings and peace be on him, is reported to have cut short a long recitation during prayers one day when he heard the shrill screams of a baby from somewhere in the midst of the congregation. 'The mother must be praying behind me,' the Prophet is said to have thought, as he promptly cut short his *Surah*. The final tradition – but by no means the last – refers to a *Sahabiyyah* who memorised the whole of *Surah Qaf* just by listening to the Prophet during the Friday *Khutbah* in the mosque.

In the light of such insurmountable evidence, how can anyone even try to prove from Islamic history that women were not allowed to attend mosques? Unfortunately, people have tried to do just that. Challenged to find evidence to support their ban on women in mosques, *Imams* and local community leaders have been known to reach out for a line taken from the teachings of *Imam* Abu Hanifa: According to certain community leaders, *Imam* Abu Hanifa is alleged to have discouraged women from attending mosques on the strength of the following saying of 'A'isha, the wife of the Prophet, blessings and peace be on him: 'If the Prophet knew what women were going to invent after him, he would not have allowed them to go to the mosque.'

Such a sloppy attitude has been responsible, to a large extent, for the absence of deep Islamic knowledge in many of our wives and mothers – who are charged with the responsibility of bringing up the young: teaching them, playing with them, acting as role model. Recently, a man from a city in West England approached me with a view to opening up for women one of the city's two magnificent mosques. Nine ladies had just converted to Islam, he told me, and were keen to pray in the mosque. But when I approached the *Imam*, he threatened to resign if a woman ever set foot inside his mosque. Faced with overwhelming evidence to the contrary, the *Imam* insisted he could do nothing until he received a *fatwah* from his *Dar'ul-Uloom* in India. We are still waiting.

I remember being asked to intervene in a mosque dispute almost 20 years ago between members of the Pakistani/Bengali community and their English *Imam* who wanted to open up the mosque to women. What an irony! The two communities, which, up until the appointment of the *Imam* had been at war with each other, actually joined forces to kick him out.

Q : *I was in Dewsbury recently with my family and was shocked to note that what appears to be arguably the biggest mosque in Britain has no facilities for women. As a traveller, this meant that although I could relieve myself, perform wudu and pray, my wife could not. Shouldn't all mosques have at least some area for women for cases like this, or is there some reason why women are excluded in this way?*

A : I remember visiting a mosque in Sheffield recently. I found many taps for the men and only a few for the women. I said to the brother there, 'Muslims are allowed to marry four wives. If men in the community have two or three wives, shouldn't the women have two or three times the number of facilities in the mosque?' This problem stems from the Hanafi school of thought and its attitude towards women. Sadly, they discourage women from going to the mosque.

In the late seventies, I visited the Oxford mosque where the two factions, the Pakistanis and the Bangladeshis, agreed that our revert brother, Ahmad Bullock, could be the *Imam*, simply because he did not belong to any group. They were happy until some women approached him to make an adjustment to allow them to attend the *Jumu'ah* prayer; at this, the groups agreed to get rid of him from the *Imamat*. Women have every right to offer prayers in the mosque.

The Prophet, upon whom be blessings and peace, said very clearly, 'Do not stop the female servants of Allah from going to offer their prayer in the houses of Allah, but let them go in a decent, modest manner.' That was the advice of the Prophet. There are examples which show that women used to offer their prayer behind the Prophet. He said, 'The best lines are the first lines for males, and the last lines for females.' One lady said that she memorised *Surah Qaf* from the lips of the Prophet, blessings and peace be on him, because he often repeated it during the *Jumu'ah*, We have the

Prophet's statement, upon whom be blessings and peace, 'On many occasions I go to the prayer with the intention of reading long *Qur'anic* passages, but when I hear a child crying I shorten the prayer for fear of disturbing the heart of his mother who is reading her prayer behind me.'

We could go on with many such examples – and so if we are to make facilities for prayer for males, we must also do so for females especially. Prayer in the mosque is a great spiritual experience and we should not deprive our women of that.

Q : *British mosques have a scandalously poor standard of facilities for women; that is, when they exist at all. Can a Muslimah offer her Tarawih prayers at home?*

A : There is no question that people may offer their *Tarawih* at home. But the more important question here is the right of a Muslim woman to attend mosques. Women have an undeniable right to enter mosques for prayer. There are ample *Ahadith* relating incidences of Muslim women offering prayers in the mosque. The Prophet, upon whom be blessings and peace, himself said, 'Do not prevent the female servants of Allah from offering their prayers in the mosque, but let them go in a decent, moderate way.' There are many variations of this statement, all of which confirm the right of a Muslim woman to offer her prayer in the mosque. For example, the Prophet is reported as saying, 'On many occasions I intend to prolong the prayer – then I hear a child crying and I shorten my prayer in order that the mother can attend to the child.'

In another *Hadith*, one of the female Companions of the Prophet, upon whom be blessings and peace, said, 'I learnt *Surah Qaf*,' *Surah* 50, 'directly from the mouth of the Prophet during *Jumu'ah* prayers.' It seems that we have forgotten this great tradition. I recall a joke in this connection. I once visited a beautiful, newly built mosque in Sheffield. In the *wudu* area for males there were about forty ablution taps for men, but only four in the women's area. I remarked, 'People accuse Muslims of marrying four wives. So for each male tap we should have four taps for women!'

Unfortunately, many people are narrow-minded and unaware of the circumstances prevailing in this country where we should provide much greater and better facilities for Muslim women to pray in *Jama'ah* and supplicate in the mosque and generally enrich their spiritual lives.

Q : *Our local mosque is on the verge of civil war. The young, myself included, have become disaffected with the present leadership's narrow-minded, parochial, keep-power-at-all-costs attitude. The mosque is mismanaged, educational methods are Victorian, and the committee bans all youth activities out of fear of losing its iron-fisted grip. Some of the young are now intent on taking 'physical action' following a committee decision to get us banned from standing for election. The mosque is in the wrong hands and we feel that, as the Hadith states, we should in the first instance prevent wrongdoing with our own hands. Please advise.*

A : Unfortunately, you are not alone – this particular problem is widespread; it runs through the heart of Islam in Britain. Before I say anything else, please do not resort to 'physical' means. Whatever the problem, violence is certainly not the answer. Getting physical, far from improving the situation, could do intolerable damage.

I'm sure that the present committee – if they are as you describe them – will resort to equally ruthless means in quelling any 'rebellion'. Equally, as the mosque's elected office bearers, they could take out a court injunction forbidding you or your friends from entering the mosque. Any ensuing legal battle would only be a miserable waste of the community's scarce resources. And it encourages the image of the Muslim community as a warring and trouble-making one.

Instead of getting 'physical' – and I know exactly how you feel – why don't you consider being a bit more patient and mature and press your case with the less 'agro' members of the committee, the ones who are most likely to listen to reason. Surely they can't all be 'power hungry' as you said! Remember, if they are old, they may well be insecure and feel threatened by your aggressive tactics – which will only make them more stubborn and determined to fight you and keep you out.

Why not work with them rather than against them? Tell them that you are their sons and daughters. Tell them that you don't want to push them aside. Convince them that there are certain things about young people in this society which you understand more than them. Persuade them that your involvement will attract more young people to the mosque. If you still don't get anywhere, then don't give up hope. Often it is useful to involve national bodies in the role of independent arbiter. Choose an organisation that commands the greatest respect. I'm sure they will be happy to oblige.

But under no circumstances, please, contemplate using violent means. Too many of our mosques have gone down that road. And you, the young, should know better and lead us into genuine consultations within the community to solve our problems in the manner most preferable to Allah and his Prophet, blessings and peace be on him.

Muslim Groups

Q : *Do you think it would be worthwhile spending time with the Tablighi Jama'at? I ask because although they participate in a few bid'a, as far as I know, they also carry out a lot of work in the way of Allah.*

A : If the brother asking this question has the time to do it, there is no objection whatsoever in joining the Tablighi Jama'at. However, it is disliked to say things like 'they participate in a few *bid'a*', unless he can be specific about the practice. We have to stress the positive aspects of their work – although if there is anything which is not acceptable it is fair enough to put it on the scale with the authentic traditions to see whether it is a *bid'a* or not.

Q : *Al-Firqat'un-Naajiyah, 'the Saved Sect', are those such as the Ahl'ul-Hadith, etc., but what if there were some Muslims of other sects, such as the Bareilwis who to the best of their ability and knowledge were following the Qur'an and Sunnah; would these people burn because they are not from al-Firqat'un-Naajiyah? I ask this because I have noticed some of my Muslim brothers looking down upon other Muslims with the attitude of: 'I'm from the saved sect and you are not.'*

A : Here I will quote from one of the standard old text books about the Muslim sects, called *Al-Farqu Baina Al-Firaq – The Differences between the Sects*, by Abu Mansur Al-Ifra'ini. He lived in the 5th century AH and wrote about the Islamic sects. In section 5, chapter 1, of his book he talks about the 'Saved Sect' and he says: 'These are the people of *As-Sunnah wa'l-Jama'ah*: The *first* group are the *Mutakallimun*, the theologians, who have accepted the attributes of Allah, *subhanahu wa ta'ala*, and who have not made any resemblance between Allah and His creation, nor do they deny any of His attributes; and who are free from other *bid'a*, innovation, and other sects which are out of Islam.

The *second* group are those people who are the *Imams* in *Fiqh* who have accepted the qualities of the first group. Again, they have accepted the attributes of Allah, *subhanahu wa ta'ala*; and they have not followed the Mutazilites; they have not given any shape to Allah, *subhanahu wa ta'ala*, nor do they deny His attributes; they have believed in the resurrection and the questioning in the grave, the message of the Prophet, the *Siraat*, the Bridge over Hell leading to Paradise, and the intercession of the Prophet, upon whom be blessings and peace, on the Day of Judgement.

'The *third* group are the people of *Hadith* who are steeped in this science and able to distinguish between what is authentic and what is fabricated, between what is good and what is weak. The *fourth* group are the grammarians, those who have been writing books on grammar and Arabic language, and who follow in the way of the previously-mentioned groups. The *fifth* group are those knowledgeable about the recitation of the *Qur'an* and its explanation, without imposing points of view unacceptable in Islam.

The *sixth* group are the Sufis and the mystics – those who reach the stage where they are able to taste some of the supreme Reality; those who have kept good manners and know that they will be questioned about their hearing, sight and thoughts; those who have followed the first group concerning the attributes of Allah, *subhanahu wa ta'ala*. The *seventh* group are those who are within the boundaries of Islam where they are standing to protect the Muslims from the armies of their enemies encroaching on Islamic territory – they are the *Mujahidun*, those who are following again, the *Sunnah wa'l-Jama'ah*. The *eighth* group are the ordinary folk in the major cities of al-Islam where the *Sunnah* is well-established, even though they may not be able to distinguish what is in it – but they are in the land where the *Sunnah* is well-established. These are all considered to be those who will fill Paradise, *Hashqoo al-Jannah*.'

This is one of the statements of one of the great Muslim scholars as far as the Saved Sect is concerned. It embraces a wide spectrum of the Muslim community. Sheikh Jamaluddin Al-Qasimi, when he wrote a section about Al-Mutazilah – sometimes translated as 'the Rationalist School', and Al-Murji'ah – those who say that once you have faith, you are not affected whether you do good or bad, said: 'All these sects are *Mujtahid*, diligent, and no one doubts that. It is approved by all Muslim scholars that any *Mujtahid* has his own excuse, even though he is to be rewarded, even though he may commit a mistake – and once there is no sin on the *Mujtahid*, how can we use bad names for him?'

The *Ummah* has been divided into sects and weakened by people abusing and insulting each other. We have to do what gathers us together as Muslims; we have to argue in the best manner and if there is anything wrong we have to correct it, in the way that Allah, *subhanahu wa ta'ala*, has taught us, through the *Sunnah* of the Prophet, upon whom be blessings and peace. Al-Muqdili said, 'I am not a Mutazilite; I am not an Asharite; I do not accept that I am attributed to any group except Islam, Allah and His Prophet, blessings and peace be on him, but I consider all of these groups to be my brothers, and I consider them as helpers to reach the truth.'

This is the Islamic, compassionate attitude which should be adopted by those who talk about *bid'a* – innovation, *shirk* – associating forms with Allah, and *kufr* – rejecting the truth, and who want to exclude everyone except themselves from the mainstream of Islam.

Q : *Many 'Muslims' I know often rudely cut people out of conversations by speaking in another language. I find this really hurtful and offensive. What can I do when I find myself in this situation?*

A : Cutting out people from a conversation by switching to a different language is bad manners, disrespectful and very offensive. The Prophet, upon whom be blessings and peace, directed us to speak in a decent and respectable way, taking into consideration the feelings of others when we are sitting together, talking and conversing. People who did not do so – according to a *Hadith* of the Prophet, upon whom be blessings and peace – made him very sad. The scholar Ibn Hajr, in explaining the *Hadith*, said that it is wrong to alienate people from conversations; but he also pointed out that newcomers to a social gathering should not barge in and interrupt the conversations of others either, for this is equally disrespectful to those who may have been having a private conversation.

Marriage

Q : *What is the Islamic ruling on segregation between men and women? I have come across conflicting views on the matter. Some people tell me* *that men and women must not see or talk to each other at all unless they are married or among close family. Apart from total segregation, leading to a breakdown of understanding between men and women in society, this rule is also difficult to enforce as it breaks down as soon as you get out on the street, board the bus, take a lift, talk to teachers, etc. Can you please clarify?*

A : The practice understood today as 'total segregation' was not observed in the early days of Islam. It is a characteristic of Madinan Islamic societies. During and immediately after the Prophet's time, male and female members of the community did not conform to a system of blanket separation. In *Imam* Ash-Shafi'i's book *Al-Umm*, the scholar writes that it was acceptable for a woman to offer her prayers in front of a man. 'During congregational prayers, I dislike women who stand in the rows alongside men, or even in front of them', said the *Imam*, but added, surprisingly, that, 'their prayer is correct'.

Once 'Umar ibn al-Khattab, the second *Khalifah*, found men and women performing *wudu*, ablution, from the same wash-basin, although he immediately told them to separate; just imagine, here were men and women making *wudu* in the same place. It is clear from this incident, and from *Imam* Ash-Shafi'i's writings, that there were many practices in the early days which did not have a sound basis from the Islamic point of view. Nonetheless, cultural elements soon took over, and certain societies became well-established along segregational lines.

But speaking about today, and in particular, men and women can meet and talk, provided that the woman observes decent *hijab*, and provided that there is no intimacy between them. Men and women can meet or work in group surroundings – they cannot get together on their own. While observing basic Islamic rules, both sexes should be careful not to get too familiar with one another, for such 'friendliness' could later lead to situations which are totally unacceptable from an Islamic point of view.

Q : *As a new Muslim, a convert, I am often bewildered when fellow Muslim women and men insist on addressing each other as 'sister' and 'brother'. This practice becomes even more bizarre when Muslim 'brothers' advertise in newspaper marital columns seeking to marry 'sisters'. Can you please tell me the origin of these terms. Were they in use at the time of the Prophet, blessings and peace be on him?*

A: Addressing fellow Muslims as 'brothers' and 'sisters' is a practice which has roots in the *Qur'an*. According to *Surah* 49, *Al-Hujurat – The Private Apartments*, verses 9-10 : ***'If two parties among the believers fall into a quarrel, make peace between them: but if one of them transgresses beyond bounds against the other, then fight against the one that transgresses until it complies with the command of Allah – and if it complies, then make peace between them with justice, and be fair: surely Allah loves those who are just and fair. The believers are but a single brotherhood, so make peace between your brothers; and fear Allah that you may receive mercy.'*** 'Brother' and 'Sister' is an honorary description and a decent way for Muslims to address one another. However, there is one exception: in the case of married people. Abu Da'ud related a *Hadith* in which the Prophet, blessings and peace be on him, expressed his displeasure at a man who used to refer to his wife as 'my little sister'. The Prophet strictly forbade him to address her in that way in future. 'Is she your sister?' the Prophet is said to have asked the man.

It is worth looking a little closer as to why the Prophet was so displeased: By referring to his wife as his 'sister', the man had ventured perilously close to a forbidden pagan custom which the Prophet was determined to stamp out. *Dhihar*, a pre-Islamic one-sided system of divorce, biased totally in favour of the husband, was a tradition which the Prophet had outlawed. Under *Dhihar*, a husband simply had to say: 'Thou art to me as the back of my mother,' to be free of any responsibility towards his wife – who, on the other hand, was still bound to him, as she could not leave his home or contract a second marriage. After abolishing such an iniquitous custom, the Prophet, blessings and peace be on him, did not want to see it re-enter by the back door *via* husbands conveniently referring to their wives as their 'mothers' or 'sisters'.

The subject is mentioned in the *Qur'an* in *Surah* 58, *Al-Mujadilah – The Woman who Pleads*, verses 2-3: ***'If any men among you divorce their wives by Dhihar,*** (by saying they are as their mothers) ***– they cannot be their mothers: None can be their mothers except those who gave birth to them – and they indeed use words both iniquitous and false; but truly Allah is all-Pardoning, all-Forgiving. As for those who pronounce the word 'Dhihar' to their wives and then wish to take back the words they have uttered – they should free a slave before they touch each other. This you are admonished to do – and Allah is aware of all that you do.'***

Q : *Is there a minimum age at which Muslims can marry, assuming they are in a Muslim country?*

A : There is no minimum age. The *wali*, guardian, of the children, male or female, has the right to conduct a marriage agreement on their behalf, as long as there is an interest for both parties. Suppose there is a young girl whose father has passed away and she is being looked after by her grandfather, and suppose there is a young boy of a similar age in her family, and her grandfather wishes to see that she will be in a secure home in the future, (i.e. a home within the family which he already knows), then he has the right to betroth her to the boy.

However, we know that a young girl may not he given to her husband until she is physically and emotionally able to have a physical relationship with her husband. The Islamic attitude towards the family is to protect what is, after all, the nucleus of the society – and we have the concept of the extended family, where young newly-weds can be supported and looked after within the family environment. It is the western concept of a family unit – one man, one woman and a couple of children – standing by itself which leads to the need to stipulate a minimum age for marriage, when the couple will be old enough to shoulder their responsibilities and look after themselves in life. In an extended family the young couple are protected – something which is missing in the West.

In Muslim countries nowadays, legislation has been passed restricting the age for marriage – normally 18 for the man and 16 for the woman. But even there they are not talking about legality from a *Shari'ah* point of view; it is instead an *administrative* point of view, to cater for changing societies, where migration has been necessary for economic reasons and young people find themselves in strange towns and cities, far away from the security of the extended family.

Q : *In the 1-8 October issue of Q-News, in the pages focusing on marriage, the writer Shohaab Dar quoted a Hadith urging a poor man to marry continually until his wives created some income for him. This seems totally against what I understand about the Prophet's teaching on marriage which is not to use women as an economic prop. Is there any evidence for such a Hadith?*

A : The *Hadith* alluded to in the article you have cited may have been the one concerning a man who used to look after the Prophet, blessings and peace be on him, and who repeatedly complained of being poor. One day, after hearing the complaint many times, the Prophet surprised the man by telling him to, 'Go and get married.' The man was in shock. He could not comprehend the logic of the Prophet's reply. 'I don't understand it,' he is reported to have said to himself. 'I complain about being poor and the Prophet tells me to get married?' Dismissing this response, the man went back to the Prophet and repeated his catalogue of woes all over again. But as before, the Prophet's reply consisted only of the words: 'Go and get married!' When the Prophet repeated the message for the third time, the man got the hint. Marriage he realised, was the route through which Allah was going to help him. It was a good enough omen. The man duly got married and sure enough, the man and his newly-wedded wife were blessed with an income to live on.

This, I suspect, is the *Hadith* which was paraphrased in the article you read – with the exception that the Prophet, blessings and peace be on him, did not urge the poor man 'to marry continually' – but rather he 'continually urged' the poor man to marry!

The answer to your second question is 'yes'; women are *not* considered an 'economic prop' in Islam. But neither is poverty considered an insurmountable barrier to getting married. The *Qur'an* tells us: ***'Marry those among you who are single, or the virtuous ones among your slaves, male and female: if they are in poverty, Allah will give them means out of His Grace – for Allah encompasses all, and knows all things. Let those who find not the wherewithal for marriage keep themselves chaste, until Allah gives them means out of His Grace.'*** (*Surah* 24, *An-Nur*, verses 32-33). These verses, if taken together with the *Hadith* about the poor man who was told to marry, indicate that lack of wealth should not be a barrier to marriage. There is yet another *Hadith* of the Prophet, blessings and peace be on him, recorded while he was addressing a group of young people, in which he described guidelines for those contemplating marriage: 'Get married if you have the means to marry, if you are financially able and willing,' the Prophet told the gathering which consisted of men and women. 'This is better for you as it keeps you chaste and keeps your gaze averted. If, however, you do not yet have the necessary things, then fast, for this will reduce the pressure upon yourself,' the Messenger of Allah explained.

Q : *I am a 28-year-old engineering student and I want to get married. As I have heard that Muslim ladies do not like men with beards, would you suggest that I become clean shaven? Is there anything in the Qur'an or Hadith about this subject?*

A : Don't even think of it! Do not shave off your beard – for keeping a beard is one of the things highly recommended in Islam. The Prophet, blessings and peace be on him, used to say to the men: 'Grow your beards and trim your moustaches.' The Prophetic recommendation was because this habit is a 'natural practice', or *Sunnat'al-Fitrah.* Don't worry about 'Muslim ladies' rejecting your marriage proposals because you choose to follow a *Sunnah* of the Prophet. I am sure there are many decent, good Muslimahs who will gladly say 'Yes' for precisely the same reason.

Q : *Does Islam allow a woman to take off her hijab before a prospective marriage partner? Every time a prospective partner and his family come to my house to propose marriage, I am told to remove my hijab to show him how I look without it. Is this Islamic?*

A : It is not acceptable for a girl to remove her *hijab* every time someone comes to propose marriage. If people insist you remove your head-covering, try and explain to them that the person coming round is not yet your husband. He may want to marry you, but until he does, he is just another man, a *non-mahram* man, one who must be suitably attired before a lady, as must the lady when she is in his presence. For you this means that the *hijab* must remain in place. If the man has shown an interest in marriage then presumably he recognises you from your face. Your face and your hands are about as far as he is permitted to be able to see.

One of the Companions of the Prophet, upon whom be blessings and peace, came to the Prophet, asking for the hand of a woman from the Ansar, (the Muslims of Madina who had chosen to share their land and property with the Muhajirun, the Muslims fleeing to Madina from persecution in Makka). The Prophet asked the Companion if he had seen anyone he liked. When the Companion replied he had not, the Prophet told him to go and look, 'for it will be much better for your future life.'

While men are prohibited from looking at a girl's hair face-to-face, some Muslim scholars, however, have allowed men to look at decent photographs of *un-hijabed* women. According to these scholars, you can send your 'prospective marriage partner' photographs of yourself dressed modestly with your hair uncovered.

The status and nature of a photographic image, according to Islam, is still unclear – and the subject of much research and debate among scholars. But this group of scholars has argued that as pictures are, at their most basic level, the results of a collision between light and different chemicals recorded onto special paper, a decent photograph of a woman not in *hijab* should be allowed. Other scholars, however, counter with the opinion that a photo of a live being is more than just chemistry. If a person in a photograph is not suitably dressed, then the picture should not he allowed to enter the public domain.

Q : *My sister recently started wearing hijab, and prefers to keep photos of herself prior to this away from non-mahram friends. However, she was told recently that it is all right to show these photos. Is this correct?*

A : No, it is not correct, and the sister is right to keep away photos that depict her before she dressed in the proper Islamic way. Photography itself has only been accepted recently, since the invention of the camera, because there are numerous *Ahadith* stating that Allah Almighty curses those who take up the profession of depicting animate subjects. Printed materials are allowed in the homes of Muslims, but only if they do not represent particular individuals. Unknown people can be depicted, but not actual people who will be recognised for who they are.

Really, pictures should not be shown to non-*mahram* males unless it is a case of someone seriously wishing to marry her, in which case photographs, with *hijab*, may be exchanged. Apart from such a situation, this person is absolutely right to keep these photos away.

Q : *Can you tell me if it is Islamic for two people to get engaged before marriage? How long should an engagement last and what are the 'rules of engagement'? Are couples allowed to 'go out' to get to know one another before marriage?*

A : Getting engaged is a social custom: it is a way for a prospective couple and their families to get to know one another and prepare themselves for their new life. As a custom it is not unique to any particular society, and it was widely practised in the time of the Prophet, blessings and peace be upon him. Evidence for this can be found in a *Hadith* of the Prophet in which he forbade a Muslim man to propose to a girl who 'had already been spoken for'. Today, this girl would be considered as being engaged.

The length of an engagement really varies according to individual circumstances. Prospective couples may want to delay a wedding while they prepare their home; they may need to find out more about each other, understand one another, make plans for the future, etc. – but whatever the reasons for waiting, it should not be for too long. A prolonged delay is often a sign that one or even both of the prospective partners are running away from the responsibility of marriage.

During this 'getting-to-know period' it is, nonetheless, crucial that the prospective couple follow the appropriate Islamic guidelines for unmarried couples at all times. Putting it bluntly, this means that un-chaperoned, private meetings are not allowed. It is often helpful to remember that an engagement is a promise of marriage; it is not marriage itself. That, *insh' Allah*, comes later. Muslims who live in this society, where norms, traditions and customs run contrary to Islamic teachings, often find it difficult to come to terms with Islamic rules and guidelines, particularly when it comes to ideas about marriage and family which are quiet different to Western ways. Our 'rules of engagement' may be different, but, unlike the West, so far we have managed to keep the family intact.

Q : *Is it permissible for me to go out for lunch or dinner with my fiancée?*

A : A proposal of marriage is a mere promise. It may be fulfilled, it may be broken. The honour and good name of the girl and her family are at stake. It is not fair for her and her family, once a person has proposed, for her to start going around here and there with him, and then perhaps to suddenly find herself on her own – if, for example, the young man was not satisfied with her.

What is acceptable during the betrothal period is for you to see the girl concerned in the presence of members of the family. The *Hadith* of the Messenger of Allah, blessings and peace be on him, as reported by Al-

Mughira ibn Shu'ba, when he informed the Prophet that he had proposed to a woman, is that the Prophet said: 'Did you look at her?' He said: 'No.' The Prophet said to him: 'Better look at her. This will make for a successful marriage.' But apart from that, there should be no running around together.

Q : *Is it alright for a Muslim to meet a prospective partner in a public place where there is no possibility of them being alone, in order to find out if they are compatible?*

A : Even though the setting may not involve something which is *haram*, nevertheless the honour and integrity of the girl in question is at stake. For if there is no promise to the family that they are going to get married, that dating may be abused, particularly if it is allowed to take place very often. The barriers of shyness will break down and there will be a lot of talk in the community about the respectability of the girl, which may affect her marriageability later on. Without the promise given to the family that the suitor is a prospective husband to the girl, a *Hadith* of the Prophet allows the man to look at the girl and *vice versa*, to establish whether they are compatible. It is better for the meetings to be chaperoned.

Q : *Is it a Sunnah or recommendation to marry one's cousins, or is the reverse true – marry from afar to produce strong progeny?*

A : It is not a *Sunnah* or a recommendation to marry one's cousin, nor is the reverse true – to marry from afar to produce strong progeny. This whole question is left to social customs or norms. I am told by a Muslim scholar from a traditional tribal society that a man has a social right upon his female cousin and that she is to be offered to him first. No one may propose to her until he has expressed his wish not to marry her. In a way, within the Arab, particularly tribal, society, they consider marrying within the family more honourable, more protective – keeping the lineage pure and well-established.

However, there is a statement which is attributed mistakenly to the Messenger of Allah, blessings and peace be on him, 'Marry from outside the family, otherwise your offspring will be weak.' In fact this, or something similar, is correctly attributed to 'Umar ibn al-Khattab when saying to the family of As-Saib, 'Your offspring are becoming so thin and weak. Marry outside your close kin.' In discouraging this kind of marriage, Al-Ghazzali in his *Ihya al-Ulum ad-Deen* says, 'Familiarity and close family ties weaken the sexual desire in both of them. As a result, children become weak.' This is not a good reason. For surely, when partners marry, after a few months they become familiar – there may be nothing new to attract, as they know each other inside out, but the natural desire is there. However, research nowadays is showing that marriage between close relatives leads to the accumulation of negative inherited qualities. For scientific reasons, therefore, it may be advisable to marry from afar.

Q : *Can a girl or boy choose her or his partner?*

A : Traditionally girls were the passive partners in such matches. The possibility of meeting, becoming acquainted with or familiarising oneself with the male partner-to-be was not widely available. It was left to families, who knew one another in static immovable communities, to arrange such a proposal. Al-Islam has given each party the right to see the other in a family setting. If they like one another, the match may go further and marriage preparations proceed. One of the Companions of the Prophet, blessings and peace be on him, told him one day that he had proposed to a woman. The Prophet said, 'Have you seen her?' He said, 'No.' He said to him, 'See her. For this will bless your marriage with success.'

The same is true as far as the girl is concerned. The Messenger of Allah, blessings and peace be on him, has given the girl the right to express her views about the proposed person. He said, 'The permission of the virgin is to be sought. And if she does not object, her silence is her permission. As for the one who is divorced or the one who is widowed, no one has a say with her.' That is, she has to express very clearly her desire in accepting or rejecting. This is the traditional old-fashioned way.

Nowadays girls go to schools and proceed to universities. They meet with boys in classrooms, Islamic societies and at universities up and down the country. They get to know one another in a decent moral environment. They are mature, well-educated, cultured and outspoken. These factors have to be taken into consideration. Once a decent, good mannered, Islamically committed young Muslim attracts the attention of a like-minded Muslimah, their parents have to be reasonable. Of course, they are interested in the happiness and success of the marriage of their son or daughter, but they have to realise that they are not buying or selling commodities. Their care, compassion and love for their children should not make them extra-protective or act as a barrier between their children and their children's future. In the words of the *Hadith*, 'If a person with a satisfactory religious attitude comes to you to seek your daughter in marriage, accept that. If you do not, there will be great mischief on earth and great trouble.' At the same time, young people who are blessed with education have to show patience and understanding and should argue their case in a rational and respectable manner.

Q : *What should one look for in a partner?*

A : It is very difficult to give general guidelines, as people are individuals and as such have different priorities when selecting a life-long partner. However, a *Hadith* of the Prophet, blessings and peace be on him, has given us some clues as to what is to be desired most in both men and women. Because it is usually the male who proposes, the *Hadith* is addressed to the male would-be suitor. He said, 'A woman may be sought in marriage either for her beauty, nobility, wealth, or religious inclination. Seek the last and you will be the more successful.' The same holds true for the female in her choice of a partner.

However, the *Hadith* does not exclude beauty. It is one of the qualities satisfying and protecting from the hungry gaze. If that is required in the young woman, it is required in the man too. Al-Qurtubi reported the Prophet, blessings and peace be on him, as saying, 'Do not give your daughters to the ugly or nasty-looking, for they desire of men what men desire of women.'

The wife of Thabit ibn Qays said to the Messenger of Allah, blessings and peace be on him, 'My face and his face will never look at one another.' He asked her, 'Why?' She said, 'I looked at him coming in the company of his other friends – and he was the shortest and the ugliest.' The Messenger asked her, 'Will you return to him the dower which he has given you?' She replied, 'Even if he asks for more than it, I shall give it to him.' The Prophet told the husband, 'Take what you have given her and release her.' He did.

The age difference between potential partners should not be too great. It is not fair to give a young girl to a man who is twenty or thirty years her senior. If she, for one reason or another, accepts – or if he accepts, then it is their choice. But they should be aware of the future of their relationship and the implications of such a marriage. A grey-haired man once passed by a young black-haired girl and he proposed to her. She looked at him and said, 'I accept, but there is a snag.' He enquired what it was, to which she answered, 'I have some grey hair.' The man passed on without a word. She called out. 'My uncle, look at my hair!' She had hair as black as coal. He said to her, 'Why did you say what you did?' She answered, 'To let you know that we do not like in men what they do not like in women.'

Marriage is not for fun or experience. It is a life-long relationship. For that reason, any factor detrimental to the relationship should be avoided as much as is possible. Highly educated males and females should seek partners with a similar educational background. Cultural and family background is very important. Common language is an essential way of communicating. Such things help the two partners to understand, communicate and relate to one another and are factors of stability and success – as are financial independence and the ability to provide a decent acceptable level of maintenance. Again, this is a way of ensuring that outside influences do not spoil an otherwise happy life. All ways and means should be considered, giving a solid basis for a new human experience which is expected to provide a framework for a happy, successful and amicable life.

All this has to be considered within the context of Muslims living in Britain today. A Muslim woman is not allowed to marry a non-Muslim man. A Muslim man has to think very seriously indeed before marrying a woman from the People of the Book – and conversion just for the sake of marriage may not be a genuine reason. In a non-Muslim country, a Muslim man has no legally recognised right to bring up his children as Muslims, and this Islamic obligation upon him could be very difficult, particularly if love gradually dries up and the relationship begins to show signs of strain.

The questions of common language, background, education and age, etc., are meant, in an ordinary stable context, to maximise the chances of success and stability in a very important Islamic institution, that of marriage. However, considering the particular position of Muslim communities living in minority situations, young Muslims, male and female, are exposed to all sorts of challenges – be they cultural, linguistic, racial or social. The most fundamental question when choosing a partner is a religious one. As far as language, background, or social position are concerned, these are not significant factors that absolutely must be fulfilled before a marriage can take place – indeed such considerations may not be relevant to young Muslims living in Britain, as they have a common language, English, and the social positions of their families in their countries of origin may well be equalised when living in Britain. If the prospective partner is of good character, with a strong religious inclination, and the two young people are happy and feel compatible with one another, other considerations are not of such importance.

Q : *Can a parent refuse a proposal from a good Muslim for his daughter on the basis that the suitor is not of the same race or caste?*

A : There is no concept of caste in Islam. Racial background is a fact of life. The *Qur'an* considers the differences of race, colour and language as signs of the creative ability of Allah: ***'And of His signs is the creation of the heavens and earth and the difference in your languages and colours – here indeed are signs for men of knowledge.'*** (*Surah* 30, *Ar-Rum*, verse 22).

In *Surah* 49, *Al-Hujurat*, verse 13, is the most universal declaration of human equality and brotherhood: ***'O mankind! We have created you from a male and a female, and then made you into nations and tribes so that you might know one another. Indeed the most honourable among you in the sight of Allah is the one who is most pious.'***

There is a wealth of *Ahadith* quoted by Al-Qurtubi in his commentary on this *Qur'anic* verse in which the Messenger of Allah, blessings and peace be on him, condemned outright any racial discrimination in the Islamic community. For that reason we come across many examples of people who, from a racial viewpoint, were not considered equal to Arab women marrying among the high tribal classes. Bilal married the sister of Abd'ur-Rahman ibn Awf. Zayd was married to one of the noble ladies of the tribe of Quraysh, and so on.

But customs die hard and no sooner are they abolished, than they start to re-appear again. Salman al-Farsi once proposed to the daughter of 'Umar, the *Khalifah*. He accepted. His knowledgeable, pious son and a great Companion of the Prophet was upset. He complained to 'Amr ibn al-'Aas. 'Amr said, 'Leave it to me and I will get him to retract from that.' When 'Amr met Salman he said to him, 'Congratulations! It has come to my knowledge that the Commander of the Faithful has humbled himself and accepted to give you his daughter in marriage.' Salman felt slighted by this insinuation and retorted, 'By Allah, I will never accept to marry his daughter!'

Al-Hajjaj, the brute of the Umayyad era, married the daughter of Muhammad ibn Ja'far. Abd'ul-Malik, the Umayyad king, was furious. He said to Muhammad, 'You have given one of the noble Qurayshi women to a slave from Thaqif?' and he ordered Al-Hajjaj to divorce her. So this social attitude is very difficult to abolish outright. It does not make any difference whether the parents are well-educated or unlettered.

In the new environment of living in Britain the situation may ease gradually. However, young educated people who find themselves locked in such situations have to be patient and use every rational argument to advance their case. Failing that, I advise them to read my article, *Guardianship in Marriage*, [available from Amanah Publications, 841 Barkerend Road, Bradford BD3 8QJ].

Q : *Should children deliberately set about altering the views of their parents or relatives by marrying in a manner which they know is allowed but frowned upon by the others?*

A : This should be the last resort, if they really are very emotionally attached to one another. Marriage is a solemn, important bond. It cannot be played about with as a means of changing die-hard customs. The marrying couple will be the first victims of such a defiant gesture. I am saying, if they really love one another – so that this love may sustain them until they are able to change the attitude of their parents – then well and good, although, it will not change the attitude of the whole community. However, it would be suicidal to jump into this type of relationship just to change people. It may prove that the couple do not have the common cause to sustain this gesture of rejection. They themselves may reject the attempt. The consequences of such actions can be far-reaching.

Q : *What are the rituals of marriage? What are the sacred or important ones?*

A : There are no such rituals in an Islamic marriage. It is a simple form of expressing the commitment to live as husband and wife. The procedure is as follows: There is a young man wishing to get married, and a young woman who is ready for marriage. Their families know one another and so the man's family approaches the woman's family – the opposite is also appropriate. If there is acceptance, the two persons have the chance of seeing, talking, exploring – in a chaperoned, not in a private manner – with one another. If they choose to settle down, some gifts may be exchanged and a date set for the announcement of the match and working out of marriage preparations. The families may arrange the civil ceremony first, then go to the mosque or house where the formal Islamic agreement may take place:

The woman's guardian, usually the father, will say to the would-be-husband, 'I give you my daughter,' (or, 'the girl in my guardianship'), 'in marriage in accordance with the Islamic *Shari'ah*, in the presence of the witnesses here with the dowry agreed upon. And Allah is our best witness.'

The young man, or his father, will reply by saying, 'I accept marrying your daughter,' (or, 'ward') – giving her name – 'to myself,' and repeating the other words. Thus, the marriage is concluded.

It is good Islamic practice to announce the ceremony, to hold it in a mosque and to have some form of entertainment. In the words of the Prophet, blessings and peace be on him, 'Declare this marriage, have it in the mosque and beat the drums.' This used to be the way of establishing this great, sacred relationship.

Q : *What is dowry and who gives it to whom?*

A : The question of dowry is one of the rights of a Muslim woman as part of the correct contract of marriage. The *Qur'an* states in *Surah* 4, *An-Nisa*, verse 4: ***'And give the women their dowries as a free gift, but if they are pleased to offer you any of it, accept it with happiness and with wholesome pleasure.'*** Dowry is defined in legal text books as 'the wealth to which the wife has a right from her husband as a result of the contract of marriage after consummation.'

So the dower is to be given by the husband to his correctly wedded wife. It is enjoined by the *Qur'an*, the practical example of the Messenger of Allah, blessings and peace be on him, and the consensus of the Companions of the Prophet. There is no specific minimum or maximum. The customs of the community play a great part in deciding the agreed amount to be given as dower. In the past, families would ask for a dower which reflected their social status. After the spread of education and the maturity of age of both husband and wife, families began to relax this custom, taking into consideration that young people who start work after graduation do not have much money to offer for the girls they are going to marry. Families have come to the realisation that dower is a symbolic gesture. It is good to start building their family life without incurring a debt which may ruin their happiness and future prospects. If both husband and wife are working, the families may prefer that the young couple build their life from scratch together, rather than burdening them with a hefty dower which they cannot afford.

It is not Islamic to ask the woman to give a dower to the husband. This is not a noble thing to ask a woman. The Islamic requirement is not because the man is going to 'buy' the woman – it is to express his love, care and the dignity of the woman. Whatever expresses these sentiments, great or small, is considered to be an acceptable dowry, simply because it expresses these feelings.

Q : *Is it necessary to also have a civil marriage?*

A : It is important to have a marriage registered with a civil authority so that it may be recognised. There are many legal implications as a result of such a registration. Firstly, it is a recognised form of marriage in this country. An Islamic marriage, in the narrow sense, is not recognised in this country. A civil marriage – if it is attended by the guardian of the girl and at least two male Muslim witnesses – amounts to a correct Islamic marriage. It is only the social aspect which leads to another ceremony in a mosque with an *Imam* officiating, although these things are not required Islamically.

Secondly, without the civil marriage, the spouses' entitlement to inheritance, pension and legal documentation are not accepted by the present authorities – so for the sake of legality it must be registered. Even in Muslim countries nowadays they have made it an administrative obligation to register marriages. This is to validate and recognise all rights and duties that arise from the marital relationship. So, if for nothing else, it is a must for the sake of the children.

Q : *Weddings these days seem such costly ventures. Is one required to spend huge sums on a wedding?*

A : Weddings are a social expression of the occasion of marriages. Moderation is the Islamic concept in all aspects of a Muslim's life. Weddings should not be ostentatious, nor are they supposed to be expressions of pride and competition. It is not fair for the parents or the young couple to start their life together debt-ridden as a result of an occasion which lasted a couple of hours or a little longer. Expenses in all steps leading to marriage should not be a burden. Big cars, fancy wedding costumes, big parties, expensive hotels or halls – all such expenses should be avoided. But at the same time, it should not be a dull and gloomy occasion. It is an occasion of great joy and happiness and should be celebrated as such.

The most important element is the *walima* – the wedding feast. It is the *Sunnah* so that relatives, friends and acquaintances may come to share the joy of the occasion, to give thanks to Allah and to entertain needy people within the community. This was a pre-Islamic custom which Islam accepted. It was the responsibility of the husband or his family. The Prophet, blessings and peace be on him, once saw some coloured perfume on Abd'ur-Rahman. He asked him about it and Abd'ur-Rahman replied, 'I got married.' The Prophet told him, 'Make *walima* with at least one lamb.'

The Prophet himself made a number of *walimas* each time he got married. The *walimas* differed according to his financial position at the time. The best *walima* recorded was that of Zaynab. Nearly three hundred people were entertained and fed meat and bread. On other occasions the Prophet asked his Companions to bring whatever food was available. The important part is the coming together, sharing the happiness, and publicising the new relationship in a moderate and inexpensive manner.

Q : *Are secret marriages allowed, e.g., at universities where girls or boys marry without parental consent, knowledge or approval?*

A : The word used in the question, 'secret', is anathema to the concept of marriage which is a relationship built to secure peace, happiness and tranquillity. There are many rights and obligations resulting from the agreement of marriage. These include the honour and integrity of the woman concerned, her family and relations and most importantly, offspring. In so many instances, even with use of precautions, women get pregnant. How can they face this situation? Where lies the blame? And what if the young couple tire of one another after taking what they want from one another? Who loses in such situations? That is why Muslim scholars frown upon secretive arrangements even though other basic formalities have been satisfied. They argue that the *Shari'ah* has made it mandatory to publicise marriage in every available way. They quote a number of statements of the Prophet, blessings and peace be on him, to that effect. For example the statement: 'There is no valid marriage without a guardian and two male witnesses. Any arrangement short of that is invalid, invalid, invalid.' Another statement quoted by the Hanafi texts: 'Any marriage not attended by four people is not a marriage, it is fornication. They are: the suitor, the guardian and two witnesses.'

Scholars differentiate between two types of what is known as common marriage. 'Common', here, stands in contrast to 'well-documented' marriage. The first is when marriage takes place without being officially recorded, but it takes place within the family, is known about among friends and neighbours, but for other reasons it is not registered. Maybe the couple are drawing unmarried benefits or whatever. This is an acceptable religious marriage even though there are unethical motives behind it.

The other type is exactly the one referred to in the question – when the two parties agree to keep it secret. They ask two friends to witness the marriage with the understanding that they do not talk about it. And they do not, I repeat, they do not register it. This does not amount to a secure, tranquil marriage. It is simply satisfying their physical need. The comment of a scholar, who was a judge before taking the chair of the Islamic *Shari'ah* in the Faculty of Law, Cairo University, is: 'We do not condone, nor accept such an arrangement. It is far from the real concept of marriage. Families' and girls' honour should not be treated so flippantly. In my life as a judge I have come across so many miserable, depressing cases resulting in acrimonious disputes. Allah's *Shari'ah* has to be respectfully followed. Any so-called legal fictions in this particular matter must be shunned.' – ***'And Allah says the Truth and He guides to the right way.'*** (*Surah* 33, *Al-Ahzab*, verse 4).

Q : *Due to a complicated series of family disagreements preventing him from getting married to the girl of his choice, a cousin of mine has decided to tie the knot 'on the quiet', i.e. by not telling his parents and* *other close relatives. The wedding is to be witnessed only by one male and one female relative from the bride's side. He says that he must do things this way to keep his family united. I would like to know whether his methods are allowed in Islam.*

A : This man has no excuses whatsoever to get married 'on the quiet' as you describe it. As I mentioned in the recent paper which I wrote on marriage two weeks ago, no one has the right of guardianship over a man once he becomes mature. He can marry any girl of any status or wealth. Islamically speaking, there are no restrictions on him announcing publicly his wedding. It also appears as though the question of witnessing marriages is linked to the issue of wedding in secret. However, to clarify the position from the Hanafi point of view, one female and one male witness to a marriage are not enough. According to *Surah* 2, *Al-Baqarah*, verse 282 of the *Qur'an*, two male witnesses – or one male and two female – are required.

Returning to the first part of the question, I cannot over-stress that when a man comes of age, then no one has the authority to override any decision he has made. If he is facing opposition to his desire to get married, he needs to take a stand. I understand that prevailing social habits put girls at more of a disadvantage than boys. But, if a girl follows the Hanafi opinion, then she too can contract the marriage herself, there is no need for a guardian.

Q : *Both my sisters are of marriageable age, and are attracting many rishtey, marriage proposals. However, my father cannot agree to any of the proposals because he says he spent all his money on my wedding, dowry and all the elaborate arrangements and functions, and is waiting until he has saved up some more. While my father saves up, I feel that the girls will get too old and the proposals will dry up. If I argue with my father he says that Islam encourages big weddings because it is important to announce it to as many people as possible. Is this correct?*

A : Your father is not right. There are many *Ahadith* of the Prophet, blessings and peace be on him, in which Muslims are encouraged to get married as early as possible so that they may establish a stable family relationship. There are other *Ahadith* in which the Prophet has said, 'The best of marriages is that which doesn't cost alot.'

These two narrations sum up concisely the Islamic position regarding delaying marriages for the reasons you describe. Besides, it is not Islamically acceptable for parents to throw big, extravagant parties at weddings anyway. This may be a social phenomenon which reflects a certain culture, but it is wrong. The Prophet, blessings and peace be on him, never wedded in this way – the very best he ever did was to feed his guests with bread dipped in gravy when he married Zaynab. Otherwise dates and barley was the normal wedding fare.

There is another *Hadith* of the Prophet, blessings and peace be on him, which says that if a man of good religion and character comes to you seeking the hand of your daughter, then give it to him. Failure to do so will cause much ruin and discord on this earth. For you will be exposing young people to succumb to temptations which will deflect them from the right course. I would advise your father not to wait for lots of money. I am aware of many families who, having agreed to a wedding, to having it registered, and to having it solemnised in the mosque, then quibble over dowries and payments for trivial arrangements, often with very bitter consequences.

If someone of good character asks your father for the hand of your sister, and you know that he will be able to look after her, to maintain her, and to provide decent accommodation, then don't wait for a big party – let the wedding take place! The simplest way is the Islamic way.

Q : *Can one regard – with the exception of Jews and Christians – followers of other scriptural faiths such as Hindus, Sikhs, Buddhists, Jains and Zoroastrians as 'People of the Book'? If yes, then is marriage possible with their women?*

A : There are two criteria which qualify an individual or a nation to be known as belonging to the People of the Book. Firstly, they should have a Scripture and secondly, the Scripture has to have been revealed to a Prophet as mentioned in the *Qur'an*. As such, only Jews and Christians satisfy these two criteria, which is why Muslims are not allowed to marry outside the three 'Abrahamic faiths'. Jews and Christians believe in the existence of God, in the life to come, in the moral code, and that they will be requited on the Day of Judgment. Other faiths do not qualify as such. The Prophet, blessings and peace be on him, when replying to a question about a Muslim's relationship with a Magian – a Persian from pre-Islam, said that they should be treated as People of the Book, but, 'Do not marry their women or eat their meat.'

Q : *Assuming that Sunnis can marry Shi'as, as both are Muslims, what happens to the children? Which fiqh should they follow?*

A : This is a very critical question. I remember the number of people who were upset when I answered this question recently in an Arabic magazine. But this is no time for complacency. We are talking about ourselves. While not wishing to pass judgement on this issue, or on the Shi'a community, from my experience at the Islamic *Shari'ah* Council, I know that such marriages lead to a lot of tension.

Muslims marry for good. They marry for a stable successful, happy relationship. A common background – cultural, social and religious – makes for the success and stability of families. In the Islamic *Shari'ah* Council, we have an unbelievable number of cases where a Sunni/Shi'a union starts to go wrong, often within the first few years. She wants to take the children to the Hussainiyyah Centre – he disagrees and wants to take them to the local Mosque, etc., etc. There is a lot of tension and quarrelling.

My advice from the beginning is for people to be very, very careful. Love, which everyone harps on about, is, to say the least, a fragile and confusing emotion which, unfortunately, does not have a long shelf-life in most instances. We have all heard of honeymoons. But which moon after that? Onion moon, or pepper moon? Unless people have a deep understanding of one another, families are bound to be torn apart. My advice for people contemplating such a union – again, I am not passing judgment – is to think twice, three times, four times, before entering into any kind of relationship. Judging by the case load which we have at the Islamic *Shari'ah* Council, there could be many troubles ahead.

Q : *I have fallen in love with a Hindu boy at my school. I know I cannot marry him because he is not a Muslim, but I feel terrible if I spend one minute away from him. I cannot live without him. What should I do?*

A : Your plight seems to be the direct result of the drawbacks of having undergone a mixed education at a sensitive period in your life. In Islam, opposite sexes do not mix: there is no 'going out', nor is there any 'dating'.

These things are unacceptable from the Islamic point of view. However, I am fully aware of the effect on young people such as yourself of always being told, 'No, no, no!' I know that alternative pastimes that are Islamically acceptable have to be provided. You rightly understand that marriage to a non-Muslim is out of the question. But if the boy loves you, cares about you and is ready to accept and understand the Islamic point of view – if he is ready to learn about Islam and then accepts Islam out of his own personal volition, not as a licence to gain acceptance from your family – then all well and good. But remember that those who become Muslims of convenience run into trouble later on. These marriages rarely work. Also, legally, if he later abandons Islam, the relationship is then null and void.

So you must tread carefully. Your plea that you 'cannot live without him' is, in my opinion, a sign of immaturity. There is little point in getting emotional, as life cannot function on the basis of whims and fantasies. Emotions always subside, leaving in their wake the stark reality of ordinary life. Excess emotions damage and threaten the stability of family life. Both of you must understand that your traditional backgrounds value greatly the importance of family life. If you venture beyond the limits of acceptability, you will be in danger of losing support from friends and family within your community. In short you will have to cope on your own. So, I would advise you to approach this issue with maturity. Keep a level head and bear in mind always the implications of whatever actions you choose to take.

Q : *My friend's sister who is 17 wants to marry a non-Muslim who is 22. Will this marriage be valid from the Islamic point of view? If not, can the girl marry him if he converts to Islam?*

A : That will be no marriage – we cannot call this a marriage for the simple reason that a Muslim woman cannot marry anyone but a Muslim man. For Muslims there should be no discussion about this at all. Allah's command is clear. It is mentioned in two places in the *Qur'an*: the first is in *Surah* 2, *Al-Baqarah*, verse 221, which says: ***'Do not marry disbelieving women until they believe – indeed a female slave who is a believer is better than a disbeliever even though she attracts you. And do not give believing women in marriage to disbelieving men until they believe – indeed a male slave who is a believer is better than a disbeliever even though he attracts you.'*** The second reference is in *Surah* 60, *Al-Mumtahanah*, verse 10, which, referring to the union of Muslim women to non-Muslim men says, ***'they*** (Muslim women) ***are not lawful for them and they*** (non-Muslim men) ***are not lawful for them.'***

And by the way, the matter is not resolved by the non-Muslim simply uttering the words of the *Shahadah*, because – and I will quote another *Hadith* of the Prophet, blessings and peace be on him, which says: 'Actions will be judged by their intentions.' If someone reverts to Islam for the love of a woman, then that is the criterion upon which his Islam will be judged – i.e. he didn't become a Muslim for God, but for a woman. I know of many unhappy instances where one partner 'reverted' to Islam to get married, but when the marriage didn't work out, they filed for divorce – not just from their estranged partner, but from Islam itself.

I know this is a great challenge facing young Muslims in this country. They go to school together, to college together, and they work together. So naturally they get attracted to one another. One way out, as I see it, is to get our youngsters 'attuned' to the idea of getting married at an early age as opposed to 'going out'. For that, mechanisms have to be devised for marriages to take place within communities whose children go to school together and who meet one another regularly. But this has to be done in a pure and sincere way. 'Importing people from abroad', alas, is not the best way of doing things.

Q : *I have been attracted to a girl for a very long time and we both agree that we should get married. However, the problem is that although she is Muslim she is West Indian, whereas my family is Pakistani. My family will not even consider the possibility of marriage. Should I ignore them and go ahead with the marriage, or pander to their prejudices and look for someone else?*

A : This is not an Islamic problem. There is no racial barrier to marriage in Islam. The point is that the person concerned does not need the consent of his parents. If he is well-established and able to look after himself and the girl, he can get married. We are no longer living in a static society, and strict family bonds may no longer be relevant in this new situation.

However, the questioner sounds a little hesitant and appears not to have the moral courage to break with the wishes of his family. Love between the couple at the moment may be very strong, but he must also consider that later on his marriage may affect his integration into the Muslim community. After one or two years, when the initial attraction has worn off, will he still he able to protect his wife and children in the face of a hostile environment? Once there is love, this is what is important from the Islamic point of view. But it is also a question with wider implications which should not be overlooked. All eventualities should be discussed and carefully thought out.

Q : *I am a 24-year-old Muslim man. I have been writing to a 34-year-old Muslim woman whom I met while on holiday in India with my parents. We both want to marry but my family is against it. They say that her previous marriage – which ended in a childless divorce, and the ten-year age difference are two reasons why I cannot marry her. My parents are religious and it is possible that if I referred to Hadith and Qur'an, I could persuade them. What do you advise?*

A : Parental consent for your marriage is not required for the union to take place, particularly as you yourself are mature and responsible. Similarly, there is no objection to a younger man wanting to marry a lady who is 10 years older than him. Of course, you must be able to satisfy yourself that the person you want to marry is decent and respectable and a woman of morality. The best example I can quote here is the Prophet, blessings and peace be upon him, who married Khadijah, may Allah be pleased with her, who was 15 years older than him. Needless to say, the marriage was happy and successful.

Having said that, and given recent experience, I would advise caution. Let me explain. Last week a Muslim lady who is 15 years older than her husband came to see me. She complained that her husband would often abuse and hurt her, and threaten to divorce her. Then, he would come to his senses and apologise profusely, promising never to do it again – only to repeat his actions again at a later date. It is quite clear that he had not taken his responsibilities seriously, in contrast to his older and more mature wife, who had much higher expectations of their marriage. This is an obvious example of a mismatch. Women mature more quickly than men – hence both have to tread with caution when entering marital relationships where there is a significant age gap.

Q : *The Imam at my local mosque gave a speech in which he spoke out against imitating English weddings. In particular, he said that wearing a wedding dress was forbidden. Is this true?*

A : I don't know where he gets the authority to ban wedding dresses – I mean a wedding dress that is Islamically acceptable. It is alright to wear a wedding dress of whatever colour, shape or size, even if it emphasises the beauty of the wearer.

What the *Imam* may have been condemning is the extravagance involved in spending huge amounts of money on a fashionable wedding dress that will only be worn once. In the early days of Islam, it was encouraged to lend beautiful clothes and other items to those who were going to get married. 'A'isha, may Allah be pleased with her, borrowed a necklace from one of her sisters on the occasion of her marriage – which is analogous with the custom today of hiring a wedding dress. From the Islamic point of view, this is beautiful occasion in the life of a woman and a man, and they are allowed to make themselves look beautiful for it, just as *sayyidatuna* 'A'isha did when she was preparing for her '*arousa*'. The only objectionable thing is too much extravagance on such an occasion.

Q : *What does Islam have to say about a 'house-husband'? I understand that Islam grants men the responsibility for providing for their families. But can you tell me what happens if, as is increasingly the case in this country, the wife earns more than the husband? How, e.g., should household duties be divided, and can men just stay at home to cook, clean and look after the children?*

A : We are indeed witnessing the signs of the Hour. Yet while the natural duty for a man is to be the breadwinner, I also know of many family situations where the roles have been reversed. Naturally, this state of affairs cannot be condoned Islamically speaking. House-bound men must never give up trying to look for work, even if it means re-training or becoming self-employed, as it is their job to provide for the family.

But if the worst comes to the worst, women are allowed to take on the man's role – if the husband has no objection. The Islamic precedent for this comes from Zaynab, the wife of Abdullah ibn Mas'ud. While Abdullah had dedicated his life to the service of the Prophet, blessings and peace be on him, Zaynab used to earn a good living from spinning and weaving. But she was clearly worried about her husband's well-being, and one day she asked if she could give her *Zakat* to her husband and children. The Prophet, blessings and peace be on him, not only allowed her to do so, but said she would be doubly rewarded – once on account of her paying her *Zakat*, and twice for looking after her next-of-kin.

So we come to the final part of the question, and I am quite amazed that such a thing has been asked. Husbands are duty-bound to cook, clean, do the shopping and help out in any way possible. We need to banish the notion of men expecting to marry hoovers and dishwashers: they are marrying partners. Even the literalist scholar Ibn Hazm says that husbands must cook for themselves. But while Muslim men can cook for themselves, they should not be expected to look after the children full-time on their own. The task of nurturing and educating the young is for the woman. Men are not equipped, both emotionally and physically, to look after babies. Men can never be a substitute for the love, emotional attachment, care and patience which mothers offer.

Q : *Is it permissible for a husband and wife to hold hands in public?*

A : This depends upon the situation. Holding hands is an intimate gesture, indicating closeness between man and wife. Decency, from an Islamic point of view, requires that these acts are performed in private, although from the texts of Islam it is not prohibited.

Q : *I have noticed nowadays that the tendency for Muslims is to marry young, often before they are mature enough to be considered responsible parents. In such circumstances is it permissible for them to use the pill as a contraceptive device? Under which circumstances can they use the pill or other contraceptives?*

A : Let us address ourselves to the question of marrying early first. Let me begin by making it clear that in Islam it is highly recommended to marry young. This is a very important thing to remember. The Prophet, may the blessings and peace of Allah be upon him, is reported to have told young people who were physically fit and financially capable to get married, '... for this,' said the Prophet, 'will reduce your gaze and maintain your chastity.'

The Prophet, blessings and peace be upon him, added: 'If someone is not able to get married, then let him fast – for again, this will reduce the physical pressures on him.' So Islamically it is preferable for young people to get married earlier. Young couples should not worry too much in this regard as the concept of family in Islam does not consist of one man and one woman in isolation – they are part of the extended community. This 'family' also acts as a support group, looking after and caring for the newly wedded couple, which means that young couples are not left stranded out on their own.

On this issue of using contraceptive devices, there is one condition that needs to be fulfilled: Yes, you may use a device, but the decision to do so cannot be left to one party alone. This is not a decision, e.g., to be left to the husband alone – it has to be made by the mutual consent of both husband and wife.

Al-Ghazzali discusses this question in his work entitled *Ihya al-Ulum ad-Deen*. In book two, on *Marriage*, he wrote about *al-azl*, *coitus interruptus* – i.e. withdrawing before ejaculation, to prevent fertilisation. According to *Imam* Al-Araqi, a great traditionalist who used to correct the *Ahadith* in Al-Ghazzali's book, all the *Ahadith* which allow *coitus interruptus* 'are sound *Ahadith*.' The *Ahadith* which refer to *coitus interruptus* being practised during the time of the Prophet, blessings and peace be on him, make it clear that Allah does not object to this act.

I must stress that contraception is permitted, as it is a temporary measure. Sterilisation and vasectomy are permanent measures and are therefore totally prohibited.

Q : *A husband is using contraceptives to prevent a child. His wife wants to have a baby and strongly refuses to have sexual relations with the husband until he stops using preventive methods. The husband already has several children from his previous wife (deceased), and one child from this wife. Is the wife correct in her act of refusing sexual relations, as this may lead to bitter relations between the couple?*

A : The question of contraception raises a great deal of emotion and heated debate. There are a great many scholars who are against it, particularly within sparsely-populated, diversely-resourced countries – while an overwhelming number of scholars, particularly within densely-populated countries, support the call for birth control. However, there is no question about it taking place during the time of the Prophet, blessings and peace be on him, and the reporting of it to him. As Jabir ibn Abdillah is authentically reported as saying: 'We used to practice *azl, coitus interruptus,* during the time of the Prophet, may Allah bless him and grant him peace, while the *Qur'an* was being revealed to him. The *Qur'an* did not order or forbid us.'

The reasons for using family planning vary. That is why it is stated that this is a personal, not a national issue. Those who allow *azl* state that a man has no right to practice *azl* without the permission of his wife – for she, too, has the right to enjoy having children of her own. One of the main natural functions of a woman – and, for that matter, of a man too – is to have children. This is one of the great joys in life, particularly for women. It is a sign of fertility and usefulness, and for this reason many women dread the time of menopause when their periods stop.

So to come to her when she is still in her prime and to use contraception, for the reason that you already have other children from a deceased wife, is an insult to her. She may even feel jealous of the late wife. At the same time, she is not right in denying you your basic right to have a natural physical relationship with her. This is one of the reasons for the permissiveness of the present society in the west, since women's liberation movements consider that such an act without their permission is an act of rape. They push their husbands into committing a major wrong-action and into the loss of fidelity in their marriage.

This issue has to be tackled in a more reasonable, rational way between both of you. If you cannot agree, it is advisable to seek the assistance of close members of both your families to try to reach a common, acceptable ground in this very sensitive area.

Q : *I have heard it said that the concept of rape within marriage does not exist within Islam because the marriage contract itself grants consent. Doesn't this give any wicked husband the right to force himself upon an unwilling wife?*

A : Yes, there is no concept of rape within marriage. The contract of marriage states that the two partners have rights to a conjugal relationship. In a *Hadith* of the Prophet, blessings and peace be upon him, it is stated that a wife should never deny her husband, whenever she is approached. But at the same time, there are etiquettes and decent norms of behaviour to be observed by the husband.

One Muslim writer has said that it is of supreme importance that a husband endeavours to approach conjugal relations with skill, care and understanding. He should not regard his wife as an object for his own fulfilment alone, but as a partner with whom he should seek mutual satisfaction and fulfilment. He should approach her with love and tenderness, and he should always show due regard for his wife's feelings. In the words of a *Hadith* of the Prophet, upon whom be blessings and peace, 'Let not any of you fall upon his woman in the manner a male animal jumps on his female victim. Let there be a messenger to go between them.' He was asked, 'Who or what is the messenger?' The Prophet, blessings and peace be upon him, replied, 'Kissing and endearing speech.'

But at the same time, the wife should show due regard for the feelings of the person whom she has married. We always insist that it is *haram* to have physical relationships outside marriage. If the husband is not physically satisfied by his wife, then she may be driving him to seek fulfilment elsewhere.

Q : *There has been a big debate about wife-beating in the media, provoked by the plot of a popular soap-opera. Does Islam allow a husband to beat his wife if she is not obedient?*

A : Decent, respectable members of society do not beat one another. They respect the honour and feelings of one another. In family life, where the partners are closer to each other, difficult psychological situations can arise where one party loses his or her temper and becomes violent. However, the fact that some of these people beat their children and also smash objects in the house shows that this is a psychological disorder in humans.

There is a misconception about the *Qur'anic* verse in *Surah* 4, *An-Nisa*, verse 34, which speaks about the internal rectification of family splits. The *Qur'an* says, ***'Admonish them in the best possible way.'*** This is a moral attitude meaning that the husband should be well-mannered enough to be able to advise and verbally admonish the wife if she behaves badly towards him. If that does not produce the desired result, the *Qur'an* moves on to the second phase, which is to, ***'Sleep in separate beds.'*** If there is love or affection between the partners, then that will be a reminder of the wrong attitude taken by the wife and normality will be restored. If this fails, then finally the *Qur'an* says, ***'And beat them.'*** This is where the great misunderstanding lies. The Prophet, peace be upon him, explained 'beating' as a symbolic beating – using a *miswak*, a tooth stick. Imagine beating someone with a small piece of twig. There is no chance they will be hurt. The husband is not allowed to even touch any sensitive part of the face or body. It is not a matter of physical punishment or infliction of bodily harm. The beating should not do any harm to the skin or the body. This is very far from the rage into which some husbands fly and lose control – this is excluded totally from the Islamic point of view. That is why the Prophet asked why some men beat their wives as if they were animals, and then crawl back to them for intimate relations afterwards. He said that only bad husbands behave in such a manner.

Q : *I have been an avid reader of these columns since the start of Q-News, and one question which has never appeared in print, but I am sure all adult Muslims are eager, but too shy to ask about, is this: 'Is oral sex between a husband and wife allowed in Islam?'*

A : I dispute the assumption that all Muslims are 'eager, but too shy' to ask this question. This is a question to which I have been trying time and time again to avoid replying, because this is not something to be publicly discussed. Muslim scholars consider discussing such matters in public as disreputable and dishonourable. However, with reference to a book written by Dr Muhammad Abd'ur-Ra'ouf, the ex-director of the Islamic Centre in Washington, who elaborates on conjugal etiquette between man and wife, he says that the liquid lubrication, *madi*, that is discharged by the sex organs when excited, is counted as a polluting and polluted element in Islam. Therefore a Muslim is forbidden to smear any of this on any part of his or her body unnecessarily. The custom of licking the excitable areas with the tongue, as is prevalent in the West, may not only be unhealthy – it is also undesirable on that account. He also feels that it is indeed disgusting, and that this might in the long run plant the seeds of hatred in the hearts of the couple, and might ultimately break their relationship.

However, according to the Islamic point of view, a husband and wife are allowed to enjoy themselves without any restriction whatsoever in whichever way they like, except during a woman's menstrual period. Whilst this lasts, a man is not allowed to have full sexual relations with his wife. Nor is he allowed at any time to enter her from behind, i.e., anal sex. The Prophet, upon whom be blessings and peace, in many *Ahadith* considered the latter to be 'sodomy in a minor way', which is totally prohibited and unacceptable.

So, all in all, we may say that the only prohibited things between wife and husband are sexual relations during menstruation and anal sex. Apart from that, a husband and wife are free to do whatever they like. We have to remember, as one great scholar has said, that, 'There are decent, respectable, honourable people when it comes to these matters, and there are those who are not so respectable – and they also may be allowed to enjoy themselves.'

Q: *After sexual relations with one's wife, is it necessary to take a shower? If so, which parts of the body have to be washed or purified? I particularly want to know whether the head needs to be washed.*

A: Washing after intercourse, *ghusl*, is obligatory for both men and women. Having a *ghusl* implies that water should cover all parts of the body, and as such I do not think that this poses much of a problem for men. But I do acknowledge that the same is not true for women, particularly if it will spoil hair that they have elaborately 'made up'.

To make things easier, women are allowed, during the course of their post-intercourse purification, to throw three cupfuls of water over their hair. A *Hadith* of the Prophet, blessings and peace be on him, confirms this. He is reported to have said, 'I used to take three handfuls of water and throw them over my head and that would be enough.'

Q: *My wife is not in the habit of bathing immediately after marital relations. Sometimes she does not bathe for up to a week, which worries me as she cooks for the family even though she has not cleaned herself fully. What should I do? Please advise.*

A: Answering this question would have been easier for me had you mentioned your wife's religion. Nonetheless, not having had a bath does not prevent your wife from handling or cooking food. There is no difference at all. There is nothing to worry about on that score.

If your wife is Muslim, however, you ought to be worried about something much more serious: the fact that your wife seems to disregard her five daily prayers, which she cannot perform unless she has a *ghusl* after menstrual cycles and after marital relations. This is a very serious matter indeed, as refusing to pray, for whatever reason, is considered an act of apostasy in Islam. Not only should individuals make sure that prayers are offered on time, but they are also obliged to remind family members to follow suit. This is mentioned in two places in the *Qur'an*.

In fact in the *Surah of Prohibition, Surah* 66, Allah commands the believers to enjoin prayers and thus save themselves and their families from Hellfire. So, remind your wife of her obligations until she resumes her prayers. Keep asking her. Remember, according to Ibn Taiymiyyah, a noted scholar of Islam, a Muslim woman who does not pray despite continued reminders can be divorced. Naturally, this does not apply to non-Muslim women, who should, nonetheless, bathe themselves regularly after intercourse and after menstrual periods.

Q : *I am an Indian working in the kingdom of Saudi Arabia. I recently went on vacation back to India where I was told by my in-laws that according to the Islamic Shari'ah a man cannot leave his wife for more than three months. I had a good job in India, but I went to the kingdom to get my life settled so that I could do some business there. My wife agreed and she allowed me to go. How many months can a husband live without his wife? My in-laws are not happy with me, so can you please tell me what the Shari'ah says about leaving a wife.*

A : Your in-laws may be confusing a number of issues here. Issue number one: the physical needs of your young wife; 'Umar ibn al-Khattab was touring around Al-Madina one night. He heard a young woman complaining about the long absence of her husband who had been conscripted into the Muslim army – which meant that she was not being satisfied physically. He asked his daughter, Hafsa, how long a young woman could be patient during the absence of her husband. She replied, 'From four to six months.' So he decided that troops were to be relieved after that period, so that their wives would not be tempted into any wrong. This is what we may call it: a human, administrative arrangement.

Issue number two: is that mentioned in the *Qur'an* in *Surah* 2, *Al-Baqarah*, verse 226, which deals with the unjust attitude of some husbands who may wish to punish their wives by taking an oath of abstention – i.e. by not having physical contact with them – for a period exceeding four months. This is known in *fiqh* as *'ila'*. This has serious implications, since if the person does not rescind his oath, his wife is entitled to be divorced from him.

While your case is not that of the second category, it does resemble the first one. This means that if your wife is not happy to be left behind she has the right to accompany you, or to stop you from going abroad, or to seek a divorce. If both of you are agreeable to the idea that you go abroad to work for a period to collect some funds to set up a business at home, as is the case with most migrant workers, and your wife is living with your family or your in-laws and you trust her, then there is no objection from a *Shari'ah* point of view. But you should not be absent for a long period of time as this may lead to a troublesome situation.

Q : *I recently gave birth and had no option regarding the method of childbirth which was used. I understand that the Qur'an recommended Maryam, peace be on her, to take relief from the shade of a tree before childbirth. Does this mean that Islam encourages more natural child-bearing methods as opposed to the more modern ones that are used today?*

A : The advancement in medicine leading to a better understanding of how human bodies work should not be shunned by Muslims. This is not saying that natural methods are the best – this goes without saying. But Islamically speaking, there is nothing wrong with heeding the words of a specialist advising hospital birth with the aid of a specific technique.

A *Hadith* of the Prophet, blessings and peace be on him, says, 'Oh servants of Allah, seek treatment for all that happens to you, for surely He Who causes the disease has also given a remedy for it.' Giving birth is, of course, a natural thing and not a disease. Natural phenomena should be left to take their course, but there is no Islamic prohibition on using modern methods to ease the experience.

Incidentally, the story of Maryam to which you refer has nothing to do with the issue of child-bearing methods at all. Allow me to clarify: Maryam, peace be on her, was simply sitting under a palm tree when there was no food or water. Allah caused a miracle to occur in that upon His command, the tree began to bear fruit of which she ate.

Q : *Can a husband's sperm be used by his wife for artificial insemination after his death?*

A : Artificial insemination from special banks holding dead men's sperm is definitely not allowed in Islam. The relationship between a man and his wife ends once one of the partners dies. When a husband dies, his wife is given a four-months-and-ten-days period of mourning, in case she may be already carrying the child of her late husband. If she is not, she is free to marry another man at the end of this period – otherwise she must wait at least until the baby is born. From the moment the man is certified dead, and he is put in the grave, the physical relationship comes to an end, and artificial insemination is prohibited.

Q : *As marriage in Islam is a contract between two people, can a wife stop her husband from taking on a second wife, during their marriage, by having a prohibition clause written into the marriage contract?*

A : Muslim jurists are in two camps on this issue – but unlike other instances of disagreement that have appeared in these columns, this time it is the Hanafi school which emerges as the more strict. According to this opinion, a marriage contract should not contain clauses outlawing any tradition which Islam has allowed.

The Hanbali opinion, on the other hand, is more liberal. When a marriage contract is drawn up, according to this school of Islamic jurisprudence, women are allowed to stipulate terms and conditions which protect and reinforce their rights in marriage. Under Hanbali *fiqh*, a newly-married woman has the right to live in her own house or locality, and she is also allowed to stop her husband from taking another wife. As such, there is no opposition to her writing such prohibitions into the marriage contract. Two *Ahadith* of the Prophet, upon whom be blessings and peace, form the basis for this Hanbali rule. The first states: 'The more deserving of conditions are those conditions attached to marriage.' And the second *Hadith* reports the Prophet as saying, 'Muslims are bound by their conditions.'

However, couples intending to marry should bear in mind that the contents of a marriage contract should not be treated like the clauses of an insurance policy. It is true that a well-thought out contract can avoid major potential causes of conflict – such as protecting a wife's right to exercise her choice to go to work, ensuring that she receives a decent dowry, etc. – but the piece of paper itself is no substitute for the good will, tolerance and give-and-take which the couple will have to show each other for their marriage to work. A contract which specifies who does the ironing and who collects the children from school, in my opinion, goes against the spirit of marriage, which is to enjoy each other's company and to bring up children.

Finally, there are some things which no contract is allowed to contain: No husband can expect his wife to constantly cook and clean for him. No wife can insist on a ban on physical relations. And no wife can refuse to carry children.

Q : *In what circumstances are Muslim men permitted to marry more than one wife? I am interested in taking on another wife – my first wife has given her consent – but I am unsure if it is a good idea since polygamy is officially prohibited under British law.*

A : If you're asking my advice, I would say that one wife is more than enough. One is quite a handful for any husband, let alone two. But, if you feel you can provide for both wives, then there is nothing stopping you from taking a second wife – least of all the law in this country. Marriage in Islam does not depend on the registry office – that is just a civil record. One extra wife is no extra burden on a legal system that allows you to have 10 girl-friends and 15 common-law spouses.

People take on second wives for a variety of reasons. The first wife of one person I knew actually encouraged her husband to marry again, as she found it very difficult to satisfy fully his demanding physical needs. Generally speaking, the ability to marry more than once at a time acts as a useful vent for society to keep a check on infidelity and creeping immorality. All wives are entitled to full rights. And, unlike the thousands of children born as a result of casual relationships today, children born to second and subsequent wives in Muslim families are guaranteed full inheritance and do not need elaborate multi-million-pound state institutions. But whatever your reasons to marry twice, Islam makes it clear that you must be able to provide for both women and all the children. The *Qur'an*, in two instances in *Surah* 4, *The Women*, clearly says that men should refrain from marrying more than one wife, '***... if you fear that you will not be able to deal justly with them...***' (*Surah* 4, verse 3).

Q : *I am a married man with three children but my relationship with my wife has been on the rocks now for some time because we feel that we have fallen out of love for each other. My wife and I rarely speak although there is no acrimony or conflict. We are both clearly unhappy. Is this sufficient grounds for a divorce?*

A : People mistake passion in the early stages of marriage with love. Love in the later stages of marriage means mutual consideration, respect, care and compassion. We do not expect passion to last for ever. Aptly enough, people call the first few months of a marriage the honey-moon period. After the honeymoon months, there are many more months in which there is less and less honey and more and more bread, chilli, garlic and onion. Without sustaining the commitment to tolerate one another, we cannot expect any marriage to last very long. A man once came to 'Umar and said, 'Oh Commander of the Faithful, I want to divorce my wife.' 'Umar asked the man why. He replied, 'Because I am no longer in love with her.' 'Umar said to him, 'Are family ties built only on love? If houses and families were to be broken on the grounds of so-called lost love, then no marriage would continue.'

This means that there are other ties holding the couple together, such as the children. Who is going to look after them? We have to understand that family commitment in Islam is a lifetime commitment. It is a contract or agreement with a sense of permanence. But if the marriage deteriorates and becomes acrimonious, then Allah allows divorce as a last resort, saying that He will care for both the partners. Nevertheless, passion is not a firm ground for the establishment of a happy, successful family.

Q : *I would like you to advise me on how I should tackle a friend of mine who leads a double life. During the week he is the dutiful husband to his Indian-born wife and loving father to his two children. But come the weekend, he goes out to night-clubs and sleeps with other women; his wife thinks he has gone on business trips. I've tried talking to him many times,* *but he tells me to mind my own business. But I can't help feeling sorry for his family. What else can I do?*

A : Advise this person. If he refuses to listen, cut off all ties with him, but on no account should you divulge his secret to anyone else. Talking about allegations of infidelity is very serious. To make public accusations of this sort you need four reliable witnesses to the act of fornication. If, as you say, he ignores you, then cut off all ties with him.

Parents and Children

Q : *In most Muslim cultures, a woman having given birth stays home for 30 to 40 days. Does this practice have Islamic legitimacy or is it a tradition embedded in culture?*

A : Women are not allowed to perform Islamic ritual acts immediately after the delivery of a baby because of the bleeding period. During that time a Muslim woman is exempted from religious observance. She is free – there is no obligation on her, for instance, to offer prayers or to fast. This is done purely so that a Muslim woman can feel at ease during such special circumstances. Now what does this mean? It certainly does not mean that she should be kept at home. She is entirely free to go where she wants from the moment she leaves hospital or home. She can go to hospital, study, whatever, as there is no restriction on her movement during this period. Of course physical relationships are not allowed during this 40 to 50 day period, until the bleeding stops. Even if the blood has stopped for 24 hours, she is free to resume her normal life, after taking a full bath, unless or until, the bleeding resumes.

Q : *Recently a Muslim friend of mine gave birth to a baby boy and named him David. She says she deliberately avoided Arabic names like Da'ud because of her own bad experience of growing up in Britain with a 'foreign' name. My friend's name is Ruqayyah and she tells me that as a child, teachers would make a big thing out of her funny name . As an adult, she thinks she was discriminated against by employers, who were convinced that she would not fit in with the company's image and would alienate clients and colleagues alike. Is it Islamically correct to do what she did?*

A : There is no argument, Islamically, over choosing David instead of Da'ud. Both names do refer to a Prophet of Islam – therefore using David as an alternative is acceptable intrinsically. Generally speaking, parents can choose any name for their children so long as this name does not identify the child as being a slave to anyone other than Allah. However, I would take issue with your friend since she appears to be choosing 'David' in preference to 'Da'ud' in order to conceal her newborn son's background and religion. I advise her not to do this. She is embarking on the slippery road which leads towards losing her own and her son's identity.

It is important for Muslims in this country to make their identity and presence clear to others. This is something I have repeated time and time again in this column: We should not be ashamed of being Muslims. It is wrong to try and obliterate someone's history just to 'fit in'. The *Qur'an* clearly mentions in *Surah* 41, *Surah Fussilat*, verse 33, that the Muslim should declare clearly his or her faith in Allah: ***'And who is better in speech than the one who calls to Allah and does good and says, "I am surely one of the Muslims."'***

Q : *For some reason, my mother openly favours her youngest daughter over myself and my other sister. I understand the importance attached to the status of motherhood in Islam, yet, despite trying all possible ways, I have failed to win her love and affection. My life is thoroughly miserable and I fear the only solution to this problem is the break-up of our family – my worst nightmare. Can you advise me, using references from Qur'an and Hadith, how I can deal with this intolerable situation?*

A : I would advise both you and your mother to read *Surah Yusuf* in the *Qur'an*, *Surah* 12. This *Surah* deals specifically with the consequences of favouritism within a family and the hatred, rancour and conspiracies that occur when parents deal unequally with their children.

Excessive love for the youngest child in a family is natural and nothing new. But it is up to the mother to be able to deal justly with her other children and to demonstrate with total sincerity that her love for one child does not imply hatred for the others. If, however, a mother does love one of her children more than the others, she has to question herself as to why she does this. Love for the last-born is more the norm than the exception and is a well-documented phenomenon of parental love. There are many Arabic proverbs which talk about the immeasurable love and affection directed towards the youngest child. 'The last child is a pure sweet,' says one proverb. But it is the responsibility of the mother, and the father, to ensure that the 'pure sweet' is not enjoyed at the expense of making the other children in the family bitter.

Q : *I treated my mother badly during the last few years of her life and only realised the errors of my ways once she had passed away. I would like to know if there is any way in which I can ask for her forgiveness besides regularly reciting Surah YaSin from the Qur'an. Can I ask, for instance, her ruh, her soul? Sometimes my mother appears to me in my dreams. But I don't know whether this is her ruh or if it is the work of the devil?*

A : Your guilt-laden admission is a good positive thing and it could, in itself, be the first step towards your eventual rehabilitation. Theoretically, it is possible to be forgiven for mistreating a parent, even if the chance to serve them in life has passed – but you have much to do. Reading from the *Qur'an* and reciting *Surah YaSin* helps, but if that is the sum total of the effort you are prepared to expend in this task, then I'm afraid you are asking a bit much. Reciting *Surah YaSin* for the dead, while full of *barakah*, is a bit like asking for forgiveness on-the-cheap. No, you need to do more – we all need to do more for our parents and elders.

A man who had been dutiful to his parents while they were alive once came to the Messenger of Allah, upon whom be blessings and peace, asking if there was anything more he could do to guarantee forgiveness for himself. The Prophet is reported to have told the man to give and perform charity in the name of his parents, to keep in touch with and help out other members of his parents' family, and to do the same for members of their circle of friends. I suggest you follow this example by giving charity in your mother's name and by looking after her friends and relations. By so doing, you may be able to gain the forgiveness in death that eluded you throughout your mother's life.

Q : *What is the Islamic way of referring to one's in-laws? My parents-in-law want me to call them by the Urdu equivalent of 'mother' and 'father'. However, I feel that such a term of reference should be reserved only for one's natural parents. Can you advise?*

A : In trying to answer a question like this it is difficult to extract general rules. From reading the question one could deduce that the Urdu-language custom of referring to one's parents-in-law as 'mother' and 'father' appears to be nothing more than a term of respect. If that is the case, then there is no harm in it at all. The Prophet himself, upon whom be blessings and peace, referred to as 'mother' Umm Ayman – the lady who looked after him following his mother's death. But it is important to note that he said to Umm Ayman, 'You are my mother *after* my mother.'

As I mentioned earlier, to refer to someone other than one's own natural maternal parent as 'mother' is perfectly acceptable if used as a term of respect. But if it is done to spite or belittle one's own parents – as has been known – then this is completely forbidden. Such an act, according to the Prophet, blessings and peace be on him, is tantamount to rejecting one's parents and is forbidden in Islam. An expression of respect, however, does not amount to such a rejection and is perfectly acceptable in the Islamic faith.

Q : *Increasingly I am coming across unmarried Muslim mothers and their offspring who are seeking help, both spiritually and materially – i.e. help with baby clothes, prams etc. I would like to know how they should be treated according to the Shari'ah – e.g., should one point out to them in an intelligent manner where they've gone wrong first, and then help them with their baby's needs?*

A : It is an Islamic duty, as you've rightly mentioned, to point out their mistake. It is very important to explain to young Muslim girls going astray in this society that what they are doing is, in the final analysis, against their interests in this world and in the Hereafter. These girls should be encouraged to make a good *tawbah*, sincere repentance. If you feel that the girls are honest and sincere, and that they know that they were in the wrong, then it is your duty to help them in any way you can. If you cannot, then it is better to give *Sadaqah* to those who are pious and sincere.

I would like to remind you of the *Hadith* of the Prophet, blessings and peace be on him, about a member of the community who during one night went and gave *Sadaqah*, charity, to a person whom he understood to be in need. The following morning, when word began to spread that the *Sadaqah* had been given to a prostitute, the donor lamented at what he had done.

Nonetheless, he continued giving *Sadaqah* until, following another case of 'mistaken identity', it was pointed out to him that he had in fact once donated to a thief, and on another occasion to a rich man. Distressed, he went to the Prophet to ask what to do. The Prophet, blessings and peace be on him, told the man not to worry, as Allah would reward him for his good intentions. Who knows, said the Prophet, the woman to whom he had given money in the beginning might stop going in to prostitution; the thief might stop stealing; and the rich man might even take a leaf out of his book!

Adoption and Fostering

Q : *I know that according to the Shari'ah, adoption is frowned upon, but non-Muslim families are fostering/adopting Muslim babies born to unmarried Muslim girls: shouldn't we encourage responsible Muslim parents to adopt/foster?*

A : I would like to take issue with your choice of words in this question: 'frowning' is not an acceptable word to be used when describing the *Shari'ah* position on adoption. The *Shari'ah* prohibits adoption altogether. The *Holy Qur'an* says: ***'... nor has He (Allah) made those whom you call*** (your sons) ***to be your*** (real) ***sons – that is only your statement from your mouths. And Allah states the truth, and He shows the way. Name them after their own fathers – that is more correct in the sight of Allah. And if you do not know who their fathers are, then (call them) your brothers in religion and your wards.'*** (*Surah* 33, *The Allies*, verses 4-5). This *Qur'anic* passage clearly prohibits the practice of adoption. Children must keep their identity and personality and are the sons or daughters of their natural parents only. On the other hand, fostering is perfectly acceptable and is a meritorious act. Looking after young people in this manner has to be encouraged and commended. If, however, two people have had a child out of wedlock and the couple, having seen the error of their way, have corrected their relationship by getting married, then their child will always be referred to as their own son or daughter, and not as someone who has been fostered.

Q : *I am a social worker with 10 years experience in child care. Several Muslim couples have approached me to adopt a child because they* *are either childless or unable to have more children. As a practising Muslim, I find this a very difficult issue to deal with. I believe that adoption, as set out in British Law, is unlawful in Islam. Can you please clarify the position as there are many Muslim couples in the UK who are not familiar with the Shari'ah position and who may be doing something against their religion.*

A : Fostering and adoption are two very different ways of looking after children who no longer live with their natural parents. Briefly, the relationship between a child and his or her 'adoptive' parent is, legally, the same as that between a parent and his or her natural child. Foster children, on the other hand, are not treated as real sons and daughters. Their 'guardians' are, among other things, asked that the children keep their natural family name. While couples in the West often prefer adoption to fostering, to compensate, e.g., for childlessness, Muslim couples must be clear that this practice is forbidden in Islam. Islam gives all children the right to know the identity of their natural parents, family history and religion: a fact conveniently ignored by many couples in their zeal to absorb adopted children into their new families.

Adoption, as understood by the West, was a common pre-Islamic phenomenon – but it was soon outlawed by the *Qur'an* during the early Islamic period. The *Qur'an*, in the last verse of *Surah* 8, *Al-Anfal – The Spoils of War*, verse 75, highlights the difference: ***'... and kindred by blood have a higher claim on each other according to the Book of Allah.'*** This was directed to the Prophet, blessings and peace be on him, to refer to his 'adopted' son Zayid as 'Zayid ibn Haritha' after his natural father, as opposed to 'Zayid ibn Muhammad' after his 'adoptive' father. Children, according to Islamic Law, have only one pair of parents: their natural parents.

The second reference is in *Surah* 33, *Al-Ahzab – The Allies*, verses 4-5, which are very clear in prohibiting acts of adoption. Allah Almighty says: ***'Allah has not placed two hearts inside the body of any man; nor has He made any of your wives whom you declare to be Dhihar*** (by saying they are as your mothers – see page 86) ***their mothers, nor has He made those whom you call*** (your sons) ***to be your*** (real) ***sons – that is only your statement from your mouths. And Allah states the truth, and He shows the way. Name them after their own fathers – that is more correct in the sight of Allah. And if you do not know who their fathers are, then (call them)***

your brothers in religion and your wards. And there is no wrong in any mistakes which you make in this – only in what your hearts deliberately intend. And Allah is always Forgiving, Most Merciful.'

These two *Qur'anic* verses prohibit the practice of child adoption. Obliterating the personality of the child and changing his name also does the same to religious matters as well. That is not acceptable, especially once a person reaches the age of maturity – he cannot sit with women and daughters on his own. Fostering with the aim of looking after and caring for a child is something that is highly recommended in Islam, and something which every capable Muslim should consider.

Q : *In answer to a question on fostering and adoption you claim, quoting the Qur'an, that adoption is unlawful and prohibited. However, the verse you refer to simply says that a child should retain its own name. As adoptive parents are not obliged to change the names of children in their care, why should Muslims be barred from adopting? Is there any Islamic reason?*

A : Let us first define the question clearly. What we are talking about here is adoption in the legal sense, with all its ramifications. A child – adopted legally – becomes the same as a natural child, in every sense of the term: he becomes a part of his new family. Legally, the child can inherit in the same way as his adoptive brothers and sisters; he is even forbidden from marrying them as they are now considered the same as blood relations.

No doubt, you will always find considerate, well-intentioned parents who will allow adopted children to retain their identity. But, I am afraid, a few good adoptive parents are no assurance for an adopted Muslim child who can legally be deprived of his name, his history, and his beliefs. We certainly need more good people. But, more importantly, we need legislation that will protect a child from many not-so-good adoptive parents who have taken Muslim children in their care, only to obliterate their past life.

Q : *In the same question, you say that once a person reaches the age of maturity he cannot sit with members of the opposite sex. I know that during the time of the Prophet, upon whom be blessings and peace, men and women sat with him in the mosque, and women often taught in the* *mosque to both men and women. Can you give a Qur'anic reference for your contention that men and women cannot sit together?*

A: Mixing of the sexes is a topic under debate, and I personally do not take the 'restrictive' view on this issue. However, let me remind you that we are not simply discussing male-female relations here: we are discussing the issue of adoption. Therefore, let us, please, keep the discussion in its context.

From an Islamic point of view, an adopted child, upon reaching maturity, is not allowed to mix freely with his adoptive family in the way that natural family members can. The reason is simple: Not being blood related, this person is not *mahram* for his adoptive mother and sisters. He cannot sit with them informally in the same way he would with his natural mother and sisters, i.e. without *hijab*, because, unlike a natural son or brother, he is allowed to marry and have sexual relations with them. Remember, a mother is not expected to cover herself in front of her son, or her husband's father or husband's children. As she knows she cannot marry them, the possibility of a physical relationship does not become an issue.

The *Qur'an*, in *Surah* 24, *An-Nur*, verse 31, states precisely who can sit informally with whom. Any combination of grown up children and their adoptive parents, brothers and sisters, is not included in that list, which I shall quote for you: ***'And tell the believing women that they should lower their gaze and guard their chastity; and that they should not display their beauty except what must ordinarily appear; and that they should draw their veils over their bosoms and not display their beauty except to their husbands, their fathers, their husband's fathers, their sons, their husband's sons, their brothers, their brothers' sons, their sisters' sons, their womenfolk, the slaves whom they own, male servants who have no physical needs*** (eunuchs)***, and small children who are not aware of a woman's nakedness; and that they should not stamp their feet to draw attention to what is hidden of their beauty – and turn to Allah all together, oh you who believe, so that you may be successful.'*** The Islamic rules of intermingling are designed to make family life happy, relaxed and comfortable – but family members should understand the boundaries. Wives also cannot sit freely, i.e. without a *hijab*, with their brothers-in-law and *vice versa*.

Finally, I shall quote a *Hadith* of the Prophet, upon whom be blessings and peace, about an allegation concerning the brother of his wife Sawda. A woman claimed that he had been born as a result of extra-marital relations with Sawda's father. Even though the allegation remained unproven, the Prophet asked Sawda to observe *hijab* in front of her perhaps half-brother. Of course I accept that women prayed in mosques during the time of *Rasulu-'llah*, upon whom be blessings and peace – but that is not the issue in this case.

Hijab

Q : *During my three years at University, I have come to witness many changes in the behaviour of young Muslims. Of significance was the wide-spread acceptance by Muslim females of the Hijab. Unfortunately, the enthusiasm of the younger generation is not shared by the older. I have a friend who passionately would like to wear her Hijab. Her obstacle is her parents. They refuse to allow her to fulfil this Islamic requirement as they see it as 'fundamentalist'. How would you advise her to appease her parents as well as carry out her Islamic obligations?*

A : What you have described is sad. Unfortunately it is a phenomenon that seems to be recurring not only among British Muslims but throughout the Muslim world. Therefore it is important for us to try and understand the issues involved and to deal with them appropriately.

As a Muslim parent, I am baffled by anyone who would deny the rights of a child to practise his or her Islamic duties. Fundamentally, the problem is the combination of both ignorance of the essence of Islam and also a deep insecurity about self-identity in a secular and hostile society. You will find that most people who would deny their children a visible Islamic identity have false notions of what makes the secular society around them tick: normally such people are more worried and concerned about being 'accepted' by their neighbours, work-mates, etc., than their own being or the Hereafter. These are the kind of people who would do anything to be like the 'Jones' next door: they change their names, their hair and skin colour if necessary, and even what Islam says, to please another human being. The daughter of a close friend of mine, a senior physician and Dean of the Faculty of Medicine in a leading hospital, has been pleading with her parents to allow her to wear the *Hijab* – but to no avail. Her mother is determined that the girl remains bare-headed. Most probably there is no room for a 'woman-in-*hijab*' in the circles in which they move.

Wherever I go, more and more young women, particularly at universities, are taking up *Hijab*. Yet so many parents are placing barriers and hurdles in their way. To be honest, I cannot understand such belligerence and intolerance. *Hijab*, let me make this clear, is not a matter of 'either/or' – it is an obligation and must be adhered to. Do these kind of parents question Allah's command that a Muslim woman must cover herself appropriately? If that is the case, then I have nothing to say.

My advice to your friend emphasises damage-limitation in order to avoid constant rows at home: Tell her to obey her parents while in the house, but once she leaves to go to college, she should waste no time and wear her scarf. Always remember the *Hadith*: 'There should be no obedience to whatever constitutes disobedience to Allah.' Whatever you do, I pray that your friend never abandons the *Hijab*. May Allah help her in her struggle.

Q : *Should a woman cover her head when the Qur'an is being recited?*

A : I am aware that some Muslim sisters go out to Islamic functions without a *Hijab* and when the *Qur'an* is recited they cover their heads. But they are under an obligation to cover themselves not only when the *Qur'an* is recited, but whenever they step out of the home.

Q : *Does Islam dictate the exact style of hijab which a Muslim woman has to wear? Recently my daughter has taken to experimenting with wearing a variety of hijabs from different Muslim cultures, some of which I believe are not Islamic. Can you tell me which hijab styles are allowed so that I can advise my daughter accordingly.*

A : The only rules which apply to *hijabs*, and dress for women in general, are that the clothing must not be transparent in any way, and that it should not reveal any part of a woman's curvature. Clothes should be loose-fitting. In addition to the universally agreed Islamic principle that a woman should cover her whole body, except her face and hands, a woman must not wear the same clothes as men. Once these basic criteria are satisfied, there is nothing to stop Muslim women from following or preferably creating their own dress styles, which of course includes *hijab*.

Q : *Is it Islamic to wear a sari if I wear it in such a way that no part of my body or hair shows?*

A : There are two basic Islamic requirements for a woman's clothing. They should not be so tight as to reveal the contours of her body, but should be loose fitting; and the material used should not be flimsy – i.e. see-through. Only the hands and face of a woman should be seen. Whatever type of clothing a woman wears should conform to the above-mentioned criteria for it to be acceptable from the Islamic point of view.

Q : *Is the jilbab – the long, single-piece, Arab-style garment – compulsory dress for Muslim women? Or are they allowed to wear other dress forms so long as their attire meets Islamic requirements?*

A : There is no such thing as formal Islamic dress, Arab or non-Arab. You don't have to wear a uniform in order to become a Muslim. You simply need to watch out for certain requirements. Once they are satisfied, wear what you like. Just to remind ourselves, we need to remember a few basics: the first requirement is that the clothes should not be transparent; secondly, they should be sufficiently loose not to project or enhance the contours of the body. Some parts of the body, however you try, will always be difficult to totally camouflage. For instance, a woman's chest. This means it is important for her to avoid excessively tight clothing for, if anything, they are uncomfortable and make her look very unnatural.

Q : *Is the voice part of a woman's aurah, private parts, and if so to what extent are women allowed to talk to men?*

A : This is indeed a strange question, for if you look into the *Qur'an*, *Surah* 33, *Al-Ahzab*, verse 32, which is talking about the goodness of the Prophet's wives, blessings and peace be on him and them, Allah says: **'*Oh wives of the Prophet, you are not like any other women. If you fear God then do not speak gently, lest he in whose heart is a disease may be drawn to you, but speak honourable words.*'** The *Qur'an* is saying that the Prophet's wives are basically not like any other women – and they stand as the highest example. Allah did not forbid them from talking to men in a decent, respectable manner. Muslim women are allowed to talk in this way. Supposing we have a Muslim and Muslimah attending university together and they have a study problem. There is no harm in them discussing it and exchanging ideas in a respectable manner and within an acceptable environment.

Clothes and Jewellery

Q : *I am finding it increasingly difficult to buy loose-fitting clothes in the shops that fit my 'larger-than-average' size. Is it permissible for big women to follow the advice of fashion writers and go out and buy men's clothes? – the size range is much wider and the quality is so much better, and not all men's clothes look masculine, like orange shirts and pink sweaters. They are also, relatively speaking, cheaper.*

A : Clothing and apparel need to be chosen bearing three things in mind: bodily contours should be safely hidden away; the body should stay well covered – everything except for the face and hands for women, and at least from the navel to the knees for men; and men and women should develop and observe distinctly separate dress styles. Once again, the *Hadith* of the Prophet, blessings and peace be on him, is quite clear: he cursed those who imitate the opposite sex in speech, dress and mannerisms. If you know that something is meant for the opposite sex, it is better not to wear it. I know that people will find this difficult to accept today, in a society which has turned menswear and womenswear into one and the same thing – but it is better to be safe than sorry.

Perhaps I could use this opportunity to 'remind' you of an old, yet extremely useful Islamic tradition that seems to have gone astray: that of tailoring and dressmaking. By making your own clothes, you can set your own standards of craftsmanship while at the same time, you will not be restrained by what is available 'off the peg'. Cut and tailor your own clothing, in whatever shape you choose. The Muslim world is rich in its variety of women's fashion and you will, I'm sure, have no shortage of styles from which to choose. You could also inspire and influence other women facing the same problem.

You mentioned seeking the advice of the fashion world – the non-Muslim world I presume. Do remember, whatever advice these fashion writers may give, they certainly do not take Islam as one of their criteria in judging the suitability of the clothes on offer to their readers. The US $4 billion clothing industry in the West has its own sales force and its own business logic. The fashion industry is there to make money, not to cater for Muslim needs and tastes. So, as in many other things, we have to seek our own advice from what the *Qur'an* and *Hadith* teach us.

Q: *A friend of mine, quoting a Hadith, told me that Islam forbids men to wear the colours yellow and red. Is this so, and are there any other colours which men are prohibited from wearing? And are there any colours not allowed for women to wear?*

A: There is only one colour which scholars and commentators consider to be prohibited in Islam and that colour is saffron. According to a sound *Hadith* recorded by *Imam* Muslim, the Prophet, upon whom be blessings and peace, once found one of his Companions, Abdullah ibn 'Amr – not to be confused with ibn 'Umar – dressed in a saffron-coloured garment. According to the tradition, the Prophet first asked Abdullah whether his mother had told him to dress that way, then he ordered the Companion to take it off.

As far as Islamic opinion on the acceptability or otherwise of the colour red is concerned, some scholars have thought that, like saffron, red too was disallowed. This ruling, however, has since been cast into doubt. The only recorded evidence against wearing red – even as a horse's bridle – has been attributed to the Companion Abdullah ibn 'Umar. All other traditions, both written and orally transmitted, however, point to the contrary. Asma', the daughter of the Prophet's Companion who later became the first of the four rightly-guided *Khalifs*, Abu Bakr, queried the Abdullah version. And there are many *Ahadith* in which Companions report seeing the Prophet dressed in red clothes. In one particular tradition, one Companion said that he saw the Prophet one night, blessings and peace be on him, dressed in a red garment. 'I looked at the Prophet and then at the moon', the Companion is reported to have remarked. 'By Allah, the Prophet looked much more impressive!'

In fact *Imam* Nawawi, the great 5th Islamic century Shafi'i scholar, in his own *fiqh* textbook, went as far as to say that Muslims are allowed to dress in all colours and that there are no restrictions. However, Al-Bayhaqi, a noted authority on the Shafi'i school of thought, pointed out that this opinion may have more to do with the fact that *Imam* Shafi'i was not aware of the *Hadith* forbidding the wearing of saffron. Besides, Al-Bayhaqi added, *Imam* Shafi'i is on record as saying: 'If my point of view differs from a *Hadith* of the Prophet, may Allah bless him and grant him peace, then disregard what I have written or said and follow the *Hadith* of the Prophet.'

Q : *What are the origins of the use of the colour green to denote all things Islamic?*

A : I don't really know. However, there is a *Hadith* of Prophet, upon whom be blessings and peace, in which he says: 'The best colour for clothes is white – wear them and shroud your dead in white.'

But then, the Prophet used most colours – except saffron – in the clothes he wore. A Companion has reported seeing the Prophet in a red garment. When he entered Makka, the Prophet, blessings and peace be on him, was sighted wearing a black *aimama*, turban. In fact black was the colour favoured by the Ottoman Turks at the time of the Turkish *Khilafah*.

As for green, it is a colour favoured by Sufis – but as for its origins as an 'Islamic colour', I'm afraid I can't explain that, other than to mention the *Hadith* that states that there are three things that you can look at for as long as you like: running water, the colour green, and the face of a *mumin*.

Q : *Does Islam encourage men to wear jewellery? Did the Prophet and his Companions ever wear jewellery? I have often seen men wearing a special type of ring. What is the significance of this ring? Are Muslim men allowed to wear ear-rings?*

A : On the whole, Islam does not encourage men to wear jewellery. While jewellery is not totally banned for men, there are clear do's and don'ts concerning the nature of what men are allowed to wear. The general rule is: with the exception of rings, if women wear it, then men can't. Men can wear rings – but not ear-rings, pendants, neck chains, bracelets, etc., i.e. items that are known to be worn by women.

When it comes to clothing and accessories, Islam does not encourage men to copy women, nor women to copy men. Furthermore, men are not allowed to wear gold in any form, but gold-plated items are permitted in some instances. Similarly, there is no ban on men wearing rings made from other precious metals like, for example, platinum. Rings that have been decorated with gemstones are, similarly, allowed for men. However, while men are allowed to wear precious stones and metals, the Islamic jurist *Imam* Ash-Shafi'i said that it is better if men stick to wearing ordinary silver rings. Wearing precious metals and stones, according to Ash-Shafi'i, was often a sign of extravagance – which is not an Islamic attribute.

In answer to your other question, the Prophet, upon whom be blessings and peace, did wear a ring made from silver which had the inscription '*Muhammad, Messenger of Allah*'. The ring is considered by most scholars to have been his personal identification stamp, a sort of seal or insignia, and not necessarily an item of personal beautification. There is a minority opinion among some Islamic scholars that heads of state and other people who hold office should wear rings to signify their status in the way that the Prophet did, blessings and peace be on him.

Hair

Q : *I am a male, and I keep my hair long (at the moment it rests on my shoulders). Sometimes, in mosques, people, swear at me under their breath and yet I believe that the Prophet, upon whom be blessings and peace, also kept his hair long at times. Am I right? (P.S. I also keep my beard to distinguish me from the ladies!)*

A : This young man is following the *Sunnah* – and the others who swear at him are not aware of the *Sunnah.* In *Al-Mughni,* by Ibn Qudama, he said, 'It is better to keep your hair rather than remove it.' *Imam* Ahmad ibn Hanbal was asked about this and he replied, 'This is a good *sunnah*, and if we could do it, we would do it ourselves.' Then he related: 'The Prophet, upon whom be blessings and peace, used to have a big *Jummah.* There were nine Companions of the Prophet who had long hair – and '*Jummah'* means what comes down to our shoulders.' Al-Bara'a, one of the Prophet's Companions said, 'The hair of the Prophet, upon whom be blessings and peace, used to touch his shoulders.'

Q : *It is haram for women to shave their hair, but is it haram for them to cut their hair into all kinds of trendy styles?*

A : The Prophet, upon whom be blessings and peace, said, 'Allah has cursed *As-Saaliqah wa'l-Haaliqah,*' the one who raises her voice, wailing at the death of a person, and the one who shaves her head because of the death of one of her relatives. So this *Hadith* is directed at shaving the head as a result of the death of someone. It is prohibited for a woman to imitate the haircut of a male. During the Abbasid period there were girls known as

'*Ghulamiyaat*' – 'Boys', because they imitated young boys in their manners and attitude. If there is a specifically male hairstyle, females are not allowed to imitate it. So, we have two things which are *haram* for women: 1) shaving the head, and 2) imitating male haircuts. Apart from this, a Muslim woman is free to cut her hair as she sees fit.

Homosexuality

Q : *Islam is often said to be the religion best suited to human nature and capable of fulfilling all needs both in the present and in the future. Since sexual need is among the strongest of human needs, then why does Islam deny true homosexuals (those who feel sexual attraction only to members of their own sex) the opportunity to fulfil this need? And if this is so, can Islam still be considered to be capable of fulfilling all human needs?*

A : When we speak about Islam as the religion which is best suited to human nature, we mean healthy meaningful nature, which fulfils this purpose in this life, whether in satisfying basic needs, or as regards its moral ideals, or its sense of responsibility – that is the meaning of the religion most suited to human nature. It is not suited to any deviant or sick type of behaviour within human society – and as such, if we speak about homosexuality, we need to ask ourselves what sort of role does it perform in life? Is it only a matter of physical pleasure? – but this needs to be transformed into a beneficial and harmonious way of expressing our relationships in this life. As far as homosexuality is concerned, it does not fulfil the real basic need of human society. If you reflect on male and female sexuality, it has a purpose; it fulfils a need which is beyond satisfying physical desire. It replenishes the earth with offspring – and not only in human society, but for all earthly creatures. Those who indulge in homosexuality do not consider the immoral implications of what they are doing. During the menstrual period, Muslims are forbidden to have physical relationships, as the *Qur'an* says so. This is natural. Homosexuality is an act of humiliation upon the person who is jumped upon. This person loses all dignity and respect. It is against human decency and manners. It has to be treated early – if a person has been spotted, he needs to be treated in a rational way to make him more suitable to fulfil, appreciate and enjoy the qualities which Allah has given him.

Q : *I am writing to enquire about a problem I am having with being a good Muslim. This problem is the one thing that I find very worrying, yet at the same time it is not something I can ask my Muslim friends or teachers about. I found out at the age of 18 that I was homosexual, that is, I have no desire towards women or marriage. At the same time I have no desire at all to have children. What does the Qur'an have to say about this? I know from hearing people talk in the mosque that homosexuality is disapproved of in the strongest possible terms, but I feel I do not have a choice in the matter. It is something my body feels is the right and normal thing. I enjoy being a Muslim. Since I converted to Islam, my life has improved considerably. I have spoken to various psychiatrists about being homosexual, but they all say that there is nothing wrong with me. It is just the way I was made. My Muslim friends tell me I should get married, but if I did I would just end up making some poor young girl very unhappy. The thought of having sex with a woman to me is horrible. Is it possible to be a good Muslim and to remain unmarried?*

A : The question of homosexuality is mentioned in the *Qur'an* and is condemned, as you put it, 'in the strongest possible terms'. It will be enough to quote you one single passage from *Surah* 7, *The Elevated Places*, verses 80-84, which reads: ***'And (remember) Lot, when he said to his people, "Why do you do this disgraceful act which no other creature before you has ever done? – for surely you approach men with desire rather than women; you are certainly an excessive people!" And there was no response from his people, other than their saying, "Turn them (the believers) out from your town, for surely they are a people who aspire to purity!" So we delivered him and his family – except his wife, who was one of those who remained behind (being a disbeliever); and we rained down a rain on them – so see what the outcome was for the guilty ones!'*** However, psychologists are, in the main, secular in outlook. They are not interested in the moral or religious dimensions of the issues they discuss. I tend to accept the point of view that it is the environment surrounding the person which affects his basic inclination and behavioural patterns. Still, there are a few individuals who walk and talk in a feminine manner.

Islam recommends marriage for those who have the physical need, to avoid falling into fornication. Persons like yourself who have an aversion towards physical, sexual relationships with the opposite sex, are not under any pressure to get married. As you put it succinctly, you 'would just end up making some poor young girl very unhappy'. As for your question about the possibility of being a good Muslim while not getting married, the answer is: yes, absolutely – particularly in your case. You are classified in the category of people for whom marriage is not good. You will be rewarded spiritually and psychologically once you feel you have been able to ward off such temptation, and you will enjoy your Islam much more.

My advice is to keep this matter between you and Allah, *subhanahu wa ta'ala*, and to resist any temptation of falling into this dirty thing. Keep away from the places where such things are acceptable or encouraged. If it becomes known within the circle of your acquaintances, it will become bad indeed. We, as Muslims, would not tolerate such a thing. I ask Allah to strengthen your resolve, to protect you from weakness and temptation, and to give you spiritual and moral power to help you in your self-discipline.

Q : *How should Muslims perceive and treat Muslims who are gay? What can one do when a 'gay' Muslim is proud of what he or she is doing and refuses counselling?*

A : Firstly, they should be advised that it is totally against Islam, as it is against the other Abrahamic religions. We have to see that such a person receives psychological treatment. Commenting about this issue recently, an Arab producer came across many Muslim psychologists who were falsely promoting the view that this is a natural inclination. It is a psychological disease which must be treated as such.

I remember in this connection one of the letters sent to Q-News a couple of years ago by a Muslim who said he was gay and wanted advice. I told him to cut off his connections with gay people and places, and to find decent companionship. Happily enough, he wrote back to say that Allah had sent him some good, decent friends who had helped him to find out about the *deen* and to keep away from gay people.

If, however, someone says he is proud to be gay, then we must show him the clear *Qur'anic* condemnation of such behaviour – and if he persists, tell him that he has no right to call himself a Muslim.

Q : *My cousin freely admits to being homosexual. This appears to cause him no concern, even though his parents are worried sick that be may never* *be able to marry and have children. We are a very close family and fear a split caused by a potential feud. Can you advise? How can we persuade my cousin to give up his current behaviour which we assume he did not freely choose? If he refuses, or says that he is incapable of marriage, what can we do as a family in practical terms? How can we explain his behaviour to other members of our family and to our community?*

A: The issue at hand is not one of face-saving measures for the family. What the family will think should be the least of your worries. What should be of greater concern is the consequences of your cousin's actions in this life, and in the hereafter. There is ample Islamic evidence to show that homosexuality is unacceptable. There are many *Ahadith* which call for dealing with homosexuality in very severe terms – the same way as for sodomy and adultery.

Socially speaking, it seems to me that this young man has been neglected by his family for a long time. The wording of the question suggests that the family may have been aware of the boy's errant, deviant behaviour from an early age, but chose to turn a blind eye until he grew up. Ideally, any homosexual tendencies should be dealt with as soon as they are detected. Your cousin should have been taken to see a psychologist, someone who could have helped correct his behaviour. There are many such tendencies in the human personality which, if identified early on, can be addressed, using moral and religious guidance.

Everything in this life has a bearing on the life to come. This is why your cousin's family should worry more about his afterlife and less about his diminished marriage prospects. It must be made clear to your cousin that homosexuality is against the natural pattern of life for a Muslim.

Education

Q: *In the wake of the James Bulger tragedy should Muslim parents ban videos for under-age children?*

A: It is not fair to generalise. As Muslims, we are asked to bring up our children in a specific way – a way which encourages goodness, truth, decency and honesty, and which discourages lying, hatred, hypocrisy and dishonesty. Our children are our responsibility and we will be called to account on the Day of Judgment to explain our child-rearing techniques. It is essential, therefore, that we think carefully before exposing our children to products and institutions whose long-term effects we cannot predict. Parents must not act on impulse, and they must not give in to a child's each and every whim.

The question refers to videos. Videos in themselves are a neutral commodity. They are not bad in themselves. But we can make them much worse if we use them unwisely. Regulate your children's video and television hours. Do not treat the video as a child-minder, or as a substitute parent or teacher. Video-watching need not mean viewing horror movies. There are many, many good programmes available. At the end of the day our duty is to ensure that our children grow up into good, responsible adults and not evil monsters.

Q : *My father has banned us from watching television at home because he says it is the moral equivalent of having a sewer running through the living room. But there are so many programmes that I find are not immoral and very educational so I sneak out and watch at a friend's house. Am I doing the right thing?*

A : No, you are not doing the right thing. Your father, too, is not doing the right thing. Television is a tool. I agree that there are so many nasty, dirty programmes which are immoral and unacceptable. But at the same time there are educational programmes, historical programmes and religious programmes, and you should argue in a rational way with your father to let you watch them. Islam is a religion which caters for all aspects of our lives and we should not live a boring, dim life. That is why entertainment is all right too.

Once, Handhala, a Companion, told *sayyidina* Abu Bakr, may Allah be pleased with both of them, 'Look, I am becoming a hypocrite. When I am with the Prophet, blessings and peace be upon him, I feel high in spirit, but when I go home to my wife and children, I go and forget all about that and I indulge in games and playful things.' Abu Bakr replied that the same happened to him. So they went to the Prophet, blessings and peace be upon him, to relate their anxieties. The Prophet told them, 'If you were to keep up the same height of spirit continuously, angels would shake hands with you very clearly, face to face, in the street.' This implies that a human being needs to be entertained to avert routine and boredom. Also, when some of the Companions were asked about the Prophet, blessings and peace be on him, they said that when they were talking about the things of this world, the Prophet used to be like one of them, entertaining one another with decent talk.

Q : *Is it lawful for Muslim parents to send their children to school knowing that they will be taught things unacceptable in Islam?*

A : Are we going to condemn our children to ignorance? Have we provided them with any alternative where they will be able to study and progress in their educational development? We Muslims must come out of our collective hole and stop imprisoning ourselves in our homes. There are enough allowances to go into schools, study the curriculum and raise objections if anything is felt to be against Islamic teachings or our way of life. There are many books prepared by educational organisations in Britain outlining parental rights and showing how they can lobby for their children's educational rights. There are many ways of influencing what is happening in our schools: as a governor or as a member of the Parent/Teacher Association, for example. Through that we will be able to protect our children from influences which are not conducive to a moral, upright way of life. Until such time as we provide alternatives, and this is a long way off, we must send our children to local schools and protect them as best we can.

Q : *My five year old son is to begin his formal schooling in September. He has a wide choice of primary schools and I am told that both the Church of England and the Catholic schools in our area are very good. However, I am reluctant to send him to either of these places, for I am afraid he may move away from Islam. But then our local state-run primary is a very bad school, full of awful teachers and playground bullies. What do you suggest I do?*

A : At Christian schools they dedicate themselves to one thing: to instil good, moral, Christian values in their pupils. While appreciating this, we Muslims should understand that while these schools seek to embody good morals in their pupils, their very existence is justified solely from a commitment to a solid education in the Christian faith. This is their religious responsibility; it is why they have invested colossal sums of money in the thousands of Church schools that exist in this country today. As such, a Muslim child will not be safe in these circumstances. Islam puts great emphasis on the formative period of a Muslim child. This is the period when he or she needs to learn about his or her own faith – not about some other. And unless he or she is given a solid grounding in Islam, they will not be able to adhere to it in the future.

It is clear that Muslim children in non-Muslim schools are susceptible to influence from the overtly Christian ethos of such schools. And parents must, therefore, choose from among state schools for their children because these schools tend to be religiously neutral. How can we let our children go to schools which say they do not merely instruct and educate, but want to shape the future of those that study within their walls? Remember that the initial school-going period is very crucial in the development of a child.

Once his or her mentality, heart and emotions become directed in a non-Islamic direction, the chances of losing the individual for ever is extremely high. Those educationalists who advise Muslim parents to send their children to Church schools are, in my view, mistaken. I agree that we should support schools which instruct children in moral discipline – but there is a difference between educating a child in moral discipline and changing wholesale his or her concept and vision of life.

Q : *We are deciding which school to send our young girl to next year. There is a good Muslim school not too far away, but a better, longer established private school is quite close by. Both schools teach the same National Curriculum and are single-sex, but the Muslim school teaches Islam too. Our fear is that if we send our child to the Muslim school she may under-perform. Is this a justifiable reason for not sending her there?*

A : The only thing we can provide our children with in this country is education. We are not so wealthy as to be able to leave them vast amounts of wealth. The education which is the key to their future life is at the same time shaping children's moral attitudes. The school is considered to be one of the most important and influential institutions in life. Thoughts are formulated on the grounds of what is received at school through teachers and other children. I know that this matter is becoming some sort of competition between mosques and Islamic societies. At the same time, not so many of those involved in setting up and running Muslim schools are themselves qualified. As such, they lack the basic necessities to instruct children. Such schools have to be very seriously looked at, because they do not impart the education needed by our children.

After saying that, however, I would very strongly recommend that the children should go to a Muslim school. This is because the other schools are either absolutely secularist or denominational. In these circumstances, the Muslim school is the natural place to go – where Muslim manners, attitudes, faith and practices are learned, and where Muslim children all have a common point of view. The Muslim school is the natural choice.

Recently, when talking about unfaithfulness within the family, a religious leader seriously questioned a religious community which we had thought was supporting us in the stance against permissiveness. Now, it seems, such religious communities are working to pull down the walls which stand between permissiveness and decency. That makes it very difficult indeed for Muslim children to be brought up in such an environment. This is because we are not studying only in order to occupy the highest offices or posts in the country, or to establish ourselves as middle class people while forgetting about our culture and faith – we are here either by accident, or by birth, or by necessity. Our faith comes first, and this is nurtured only in the environment of the Muslim school. The shortcomings which some of our youngsters face in these schools should be rectified by the active role of the family. It isn't just a matter of dropping them off at the doorstep of the school and forgetting about them: the family must play an active role in seeing that their children are progressing. We are faced with challenges from all sides.

Q : *One of my friends has sent his teenage daughter to the United States for education. Considering that Islam bans females from even travelling alone, I advised my friend not to let his daughter go or stay abroad alone. However, he says he has given her enough Islamic education for her to be able to take care of herself in any environment. Is this acceptable from the Islamic point of view?*

A : Your friend may have some relatives in the States where his teenage daughter may be accommodated and looked after, as is the case with a good number of young girls who are increasingly coming to study in the West and stay with relatives. He may be thinking that he has given her a solid Islamic background which will enable her to weather any moral storm. After all, education is the only way to raise the status of our children. All these thoughts may be floating in the mind of your friend.

But believe me, your friend has taken a big gamble. People who live in the West with their children who are being educated in the system here, are frightened to death day and night for the safety of their children. Muslim educationists tell tales which would raise your hair about what happens in schools. Sex education materials were described recently by the Secretary of State for Education as pornographic and obscene. Research papers by a Muslim researcher within the community on girls between the ages of 16 and 22, tell amazing stories of their skipping lessons, going to discos and dating. The sad truth was that their teacher, when asked about their arriving back home late, covered for them by saying that they were doing homework back at school.

The moral challenge facing young boys as well is even greater. The least that can take place is that they may get to know a young Muslim girl and then get married against their parents' wishes. It is dangerous indeed.

Q : *Is co-education allowed in Islam?*

A : Co-education may be allowed up to the age of 9 or so. After that, it is not acceptable for an Islamic society to allow such free mixing. Up until recent times, education in the West was in single-sex schools. Only when socialism became the vogue and socialist ideas began to penetrate all levels of the social system did things begin to change. Educationists who were infected with such ideas began to experiment with the younger generation. But even in such societies, religious organisations still insisted on having their own single-sex schools for the children of their own faith. Sadly, these schools are sometimes short of pupils – but, happily, Muslim girls have found a haven in such schools where some of them at least find a safe place to study.

Muslim countries which blindly imitate outside educational systems have begun to implement such educational policies to the detriment and loss of their younger generations. What is good for the secularist may not be good for a society built on faith and decent values.

Q : *Is it permissible for a Muslimah to leave home without a mahram in search of worldly knowledge?*

A : This question may be related to the *Hadith* of the Prophet, blessings and peace be upon him, which says that a woman may not travel the distance of 3 nights or one day and one night without a *mahram*. This was in order to preserve the integrity and honour of Muslim women. In the circumstances of the day, people were travelling on their own, without any protection, through the desert – and as such they were liable to be harmed or molested. The Prophet, upon whom be blessings and peace, was taking this into consideration.

Today, people travel in large groups in trains, in coaches and in planes. It is as if a whole village is on the move together. There is no fear of molestation. And the Muslimah can find safe accommodation with other sisters in the same situation. Therefore, the circumstances of women have changed. Moreover, there are reports of the Prophet's wives travelling without *mahrams* after his death to perform *Hajj*. They were accompanied by 'Uthman ibn 'Affan and Abd'ur-Rahman ibn Awf – who were not *mahrams* to them. No one objected to their travelling like that.

When Adi ibn Hatim, a new convert to Islam, was talking to the Prophet, blessings and peace be upon him, the Prophet said to him that one day al-Islam would spread throughout the peninsula, so that a woman would travel from Yemen to the House of Allah un-chaperoned and unmolested. Ibn Hajar, the commentator on al-Bukhari's *Sahih* said that this was a great blessing and not something to be rejected.

Q : *As my research involves handling haram meat, should I refuse to carry it out?*

A : It is absurd to suggest that handling *haram* objects is itself *haram*. If that were ever the case, how would people collect rubbish, handle dead carcasses and work in sewers? No, there is no justification whatsoever to support claims that it is *haram* to handle *haram* meat.

Q : *I am a student of Arabic whose first language is English. Will you please recommend an Arabic-English-Arabic dictionary and tell me where I can buy it?*

A : There are so many dictionaries available that it is virtually impossible to list them all. The book I have in front of me is, perhaps, the most accurate and comprehensive work in existence: The Arabic-English Lexicon by Edward William Lane – published by the Islamic Texts Society, of 22A Brooklands Avenue, Cambridge, CB2 2DQ – is indispensable to me. At £150, perhaps, it might prove a little too costly for the average student. When it comes to dictionaries, I always say that it would be better if the student or reader took some time out and visited one of the many shops in London and sampled for him or her self the immense choice on offer. There are plenty of shops in the Bayswater area of the West End of London, such as Dar al-Dawa bookshop at 97 Westbourne Grove, London W2. Alternatively, there is the Islamic Welfare House at 233 Seven Sisters Road in North London (literally one minute away from Finsbury Park Station on the Victoria Line).

Q : *I am seriously thinking of leaving my seven-year course at a well-known Dar'ul-Uloom which I began two years ago. When I joined, I was under the impression that we were to be taught Arabic and Islamic studies. Had I known that we were to be taught Urdu, non-stop for two years, I would never have joined. My teachers tell me that this is necessary for us to be able to read the religious text-books which are in Urdu. Does that mean that there are no books in Arabic? Do you think it is time to revise the syllabus before the trickle of people leaving Islamic institutions turns into a flood?*

A : Your teachers are correct in one sense: a mastery of the Urdu language is vital if you are to progress through the *Dar'ul-Uloom* syllabus. That is not to say that there are no books in Arabic, for Arabic is Islam's source language and many non-Arab scholars, amazingly enough, have made important contributions to Islamic scholarship in Arabic. But teachers at *Dar'ul-Ulooms* in Britain have chosen to use Urdu as the medium of instruction. On your second point, I would agree: the syllabuses do need revision, but unless people like yourself stay the full course this will never happen. All courses of study need to be re-evaluated in order to take into account the changing needs of the community. Even Al-Azhar University does this. But this is a task for well-educated people like yourself. The present crop of *Imams* and teachers are incapable of bringing about this much needed change.

Islamic institutions in recent years have acquired very bad reputations, but this was not always the case. Islamic universities were citadels of science and medicine as well as *fiqh* and language. Twenty years ago, Stewart Sutherland, then Professor of Philosophy at King's College, London, told a group of priests that they would be incapable of meeting the needs of their parishes without further education and training. If that was his advice to leading graduates from schools of divinity, I would hate to think what his advice would be to our present day *Imams* and leaders!

Q : *It has always been my ambition to become an architect, but my parents want me to enrol at a Dar'ul-Uloom, an Islamic boarding school, for seven years and study to be an 'alim, a Muslim scholar. They tell me that I can always study architecture later on in life, but that I'll never get a second chance to study Islam. But, equally, I don't want to go to Dar'ul-Uloom and possibly wreck for ever my chances of doing architecture. Many of my friends who went to Dar'ul-Ulooms have ended up doing pointless jobs. I am really confused and afraid. Can you please help?*

A : My sympathies go out to both your parents and yourself. The matter confronting you is not a unique one and is common among many people. It is a delicate issue and needs to be handled with a lot of sophistication and in a holistic manner. There is nothing sinister at all about the matter which is fundamentally a superficial conflict between parental love and concern and an individual's preference and choice. Your parents' insistence that you attend a *Dar'ul-Uloom* college is based on their concern that their son receives a good, deep and decent Islamic education that will make their child an exemplary Muslim individual in his conduct in life. In other words, they wish their son the best in this world and in the Hereafter. But your dissatisfaction with your parents' choice reflects a desire – equally acceptable and noble – of wanting to prepare yourself for life in modern times within which you can secure a reasonable income and hence establish and provide for yourself and your family, *insh'Allah*.

If your parents are rich enough and have made some provision for you and your family's financial needs, then their decision to send you to a *Dar'ul-Uloom* is the best one, and it would be highly commendable if you followed their decision. *Dar'ul-Ulooms* are part of an age-old tradition for Muslim families wishing to dedicate one of their children to the service and in the cause of Islam. However, the reality of today, as you mention in your letter, is that the lack of employment for *Dar'ul-Uloom* graduates from Britain is very high. Part of the problem is the fact that their employment chances are hindered because their qualifications are not recognised as proper graduate qualifications – even though many of them spend twice the length of study that an average British university graduate spends. An additional problem is the poor pay and conditions of those *Dar'ul-Uloom* trained *'Alims* who do find work in British mosques. I am quite sure that current rates of pay – defined with overseas-trained personnel in mind – will certainly not support a person in your category.

In conclusion then, I would like you to have a word with your parents, asking them to let you go and study architecture – with the promise that at the same time you will try very hard to educate yourself about Islam, starting with learning the *Holy Qur'an*. Try and acquire Islamic knowledge in all your spare time from those who are more knowledgeable within the local community. If possible, try to register for part-time studies with the nearest suitable Islamic institution. Go and study architecture but don't forget your Islam. I am sure that if you present your case in a sensitive and intelligent manner, then your parents will finally understand and even help you in your striving.

Q : *I am contemplating early retirement from my job as a chartered accountant, and being – al-hamdulillah – reasonably fit, financially secure and healthy, would like to devote the rest of my days to helping Muslims in any way I can. Which project, cause, or country do you suggest I go to and why?*

A : I would advise this person to undertake three progressive courses of action. First, he should enrol at the *Dar'ul-Uloom al-Arabiyyah al-Islamiyyah* in Holcombe, Bury, for an intensive course in *Aqeeda* and Islamic *Fiqh*. The *Dar'ul-Uloom* is a proper Islamic educational institution, and a course undertaken there will make this brother conversant with the basic Islamic point of view in matters which he is likely to come across in his future work. His previous occupation will have taken him away from good, sound, Islamic knowledge, and this needs to be re-instilled. The *Dar'ul-Uloom* course is essential for the task which I am going to suggest to this brother to undertake.

Next, he should go and spend some time with the Tablighi Jama'at. This exercise is also very important, as it will refresh and develop within him a sense of community and living with Muslims. The Tablighi Jama'at experience is, in addition, very good for learning to spread the message of Islam. It is good for *da'wah*. It inculcates a sense of humility in the person who goes in the way of Allah. It trains a person in communication skills and endurance in the face of hardship, and it teaches one about how to put others before oneself.

After this basic training, the brother should then prepare himself and plan extensively a project for which we have very few qualified people available. This task will centre on safeguarding the rights of Muslims: the Muslims of Britain. We have no organisations that help oppressed Muslims in Britain. This brother will, after finishing his earlier re-training, be in a unique position to start something along these lines, and this will be a much sharper focus for his dual skills than if he went to a non-European Muslim country. Being culturally prominent and educationally authoritative, the care and support of the Muslim under-class in this country will be a great and worthy crowning effort for his life.

Employment

Q : *Is it allowed for a woman to be employed when she has male relatives (husband, father and brothers) who can give her all the financial support she needs?*

A : Islamic society needs woman teachers, doctors, nurses, midwives and women in so many other professions. It is agreed that Islam encourages the education of females as well as males. In this day and age we cannot have double standards by saying that Islam encourages the education of women – and then turning around and saying that they are not allowed to work. After all, education nowadays costs a lot of money which is paid for by the Treasury of the state. It can be considered as a national asset. To educate women to a high degree, and then say that they are not allowed to seek jobs, is to waste nearly one half of the educational budget.

Women are needed in society. What is needed is to safeguard their honour and integrity and to provide them with jobs suitable for them, in an environment which is decent and clean, while avoiding incitement in manner or dress and free, uncontrolled mixing. Apart from that, I do not see why they should not be given the chance, as the early Muslim female Companions were given, to serve the nation of Islam.

Q : *I am in the process of applying for jobs but I am concerned that at interviews the employer may discriminate against me because I wear hijab. Is it allowed for me to take it off for the duration of the interview?*

A : At the time of reading this question, *Al-Sharq'ul-Awsat* carried a big feature on the predicament of *hijab*-wearing working woman under the heading: '*Hijab* is a Barrier to Jobs'. It was looking at the case of a qualified nurse in Germany who could not find a single job in any of the hospitals because she was wearing *hijab*. Even in Muslim clinics they did not give her a chance for fear of alienating their customers. This is a narrow-minded, prejudiced attitude against the Muslim population of Europe. What does the *hijab* do to frighten people away? They call it 'fundamentalism', but fundamentalism in *our* view means sticking to the basics of *our* faith. In fact, it is *secular fundamentalism* which is against the presence of Islam in Europe.

I wouldn't advise this girl to take off the *hijab*, because she will face the same difficulties once she starts working and then wears the *hijab*. Moreover, usually there is a probationary period for most new employees during which any excuse can be dragged up to sack them.

Muslim communities have a duty to protect the Muslim individual by collectively explaining that the *hijab* is not a threat to any person, but a dress of modesty and decency, not dissimilar to the head-covering worn by nuns. It shows the honour and respectability of women, and we should make it clear that it is an important part of *our* faith. We are not aliens, but part and parcel of society. Europe is increasingly becoming home to more and more Muslims, and it is a requirement of Islam that women cover their heads. This is not a threat, but a revival of one of the great expressions of decency and humility, as also shown by those who have dedicated themselves in the Christian Church to the service of God.

Q : *I have been asked by a young Muslimah at a secondary school about Islamic views of nursing as a career. The training, of course, would be in this country. Please advise/inform on this topic.*

A: There is a great need for Muslims to take up medical careers, whether as doctors and nursing staff, or as ambulance-personnel and paramedics. The Muslimah should be encouraged if she wants to take up nursing. However, if *Casualty*, the television series, is anything to go by, she should prepare herself for a lot of stressful, sometimes embarrassing and often highly-charged situations in her chosen career.

Q: *I was interested to see you recommending nursing as a career for a Muslim woman in a recent edition of Q-News. Could you please advise on what a hijab-wearing sister who wants to be a nurse should do about the uniform, which usually consists of a short-sleeved, short-skirted dress worn with a belt and a silly hat, or even no hat at all. Also, what about dealing with male patients? General nurse training involves bed-bathing and catheterising male patients. Is this alright?*

A: Nursing uniforms can be suitably 'modified' to conform with Islamic requirements. But if for some reason hospital and health authorities are inflexible on this issue, it can be taken up by representatives of a Muslim medical organisation. Most employers are committed to equal opportunities policies and, as such, would not like to be seen to be discriminating against their Muslim employees.

The question of female nurses attending to male hospital patients, and *vice versa*, is an old issue and has had much attention from Muslim scholars. My opinion is in line with a leading scholar who says that there is no harm in such an event. Writing in *Al-Mughni*, in a section dealing with the issue of 'contact with strangers', the scholar Ibn Qudama says that 'strange' men and women can look at forbidden parts of the body for 'strictly medical reasons only'. Ibn Qudama quotes an instance where female medical attendants, wanting to see whether two young boys had reached the age of maturity, were allowed to see whether or not the boys had grown pubic hair.

Non-Muslim Relatives and Festivals

Q: *As a recently-converted Muslim (three years ago), I have had several problems with my Christian relatives regarding weddings and funerals. Should I attend or not? What is the correct Islamic stance on such issues?*

A: Muslims are encouraged to stay on reasonable terms with non-Muslim relations. The Prophet, upon whom be blessings and peace, stressed this when Asma', the daughter of his Companion and later the first *Khalifah*, Abu Bakr, refused to accept gifts from or entertain her non-Muslim mother when she came from Makka to Madina to visit her. Asma', who insisted on keeping at arm's length from her mother, only relented when the Prophet reassured her that accepting the gifts and entertaining her mother were far from being un-Islamic.

The *Qur'an* reiterates this in *Surah* 29, *Surat'ul-Ankabut*, verse 8: ***'We have enjoined on man kindness to parents – but if they try to make you worship anything of which you have no knowledge along with Me, then do not obey them. You will all return to Me, and I will tell you all about what you used to do.'*** Thus while *Surah* 29, verse 8, of the *Qur'an* tells man to be kind to his parents, it also sets limits by making it clear that parents are to be disobeyed if they try to convert you away from Islam or encourage you to engage in un-Islamic or anti-Islamic activities.

Activities in which Muslims should not take part would include ritual acts and rites from non-Islamic religions. Going to a wedding or a funeral is not banned in itself, however, so long as you remain an observer and do not get swallowed up into any religious or cultural tradition. Try as much as possible not to sever completely relations with your parents and relatives. Such an attitude will, in the least, show your parents that you belong to a very tolerant way of life.

Q: *To what extent is a Muslim convert allowed to participate in his non-Muslim parents' Christmas celebrations?*

A: He or she is allowed to entertain them and is allowed to be entertained by them. He or she is allowed to take gifts to them. The only prohibition is that he or she should not participate in the ritualistic aspects of the celebrations and, of course, in those acts – like drinking alcohol or eating pork – which go against the teachings of Islam.

Q: *Is it wrong to give Christmas presents? My Christian neighbours always give me presents at this time of year, but I always hesitate until the last minute before reciprocating the gesture, in case I may be guilty of doing something which is un-Islamic. But if I stopped giving them presents, they might feel offended. What should I do?*

A: There is nothing wrong in Muslims giving Christmas presents to friends, acquaintances, neighbours and work colleagues who are from the Christian faith. Such an act shows that you care about them and are concerned for their welfare. A story from the life of the Prophet, upon whom be blessings and peace, illustrates beautifully the Islamic acceptability of giving and receiving presents from non-Muslims. The story tells of how Asma', the daughter of the Companion, Abu Bakr, one day went into shock when her mother came bearing gifts. Now, ordinarily, a visit from a mother ought not to pose any problem for a daughter – only Asma's mother was not a Muslim. Asma' at first politely refused to entertain her mother and would have nothing to do with the presents. It was only when the Prophet reassured her that Muslims should have no problem with taking and receiving gifts from non-Muslims that Asma' backed down.

I would, however, advise just a small note of caution when selecting what to give to your Christian friends at Christmas time. Remember, you are a Muslim and as such, Christmas does not mean the same to Muslims as it does to Christians. Islamic and *Qur'anic* historical records both of his birth and of the events leading up to the departure from this world of the Prophet 'Isa, may blessings and peace be upon him, are quite different to those which inspire modern Christianity. It is not advisable, therefore, for Muslims to give as a Christmas present a gift that has anything to do with the Christian version of the Christmas story, or any item which is part of the Christmas festival itself. So your Christmas presents list ought not to include things like Christmas trees, crackers, crucifixes or toy cribs. But please, do not think that by handing over a gift at Christmas, or by dropping a card through the letter-box, that your obligation towards your neighbours, etc., is over for the rest of the year. Muslims have a duty towards their neighbours – to know them, to be kind to and concerned about them, and to help them whenever the need arises – all the year round. Also, if you're going to give them a Christmas present, please don't forget to give them something for the *'Id*.

Q: *Can Muslims celebrate the birthdays of their loved ones in general?*

A: This has nothing at all to do with the faith of al-Islam. These are social attitudes which have nothing to with *bid'a*. There are so many things which have been invented since the life of the Prophet, blessings and peace be on him, which have nothing to do with worship – so that the question of whether they are *halal* or *haram* doesn't arise. The tables at which people eat now were not around in the time and place of the Prophet. Neither was the device by which the later *Ummah* sifted its flour to make it more refined. Towels and handkerchiefs weren't around either. The celebration of a birthday, usually of a child, is a joyous occasion for the family in which they come together and have a good time. It is one way of cementing relationships within the family, just like a wedding.

Q : *It has been suggested to me by members of a prominent Islamic group based in my local mosque that sending 'Id cards is tantamount to committing a bid'a, that it is too close to the Christian tradition of sending Christmas cards, and that it has no basis in Islam. Is this correct?*

A : The attitude of such people is not only narrow-minded but also totally illogical. If we were to follow this line of reasoning to its logical end, then we Muslims should start telling fibs, stop praying and, as far as possible, be nasty to people. Why? Because telling the truth, praying and being nice to people would all have to be considered *'bid'a'* because they are all 'Christian practices'! How any sane Muslim can believe such total nonsense begs belief!

Muslims need to be especially careful when using the *bid'a* label against any practice. It is not so simple a matter as to pronounce *haram* any cultural tradition which is different from what was practised at the time of the Prophet, upon whom be blessings and peace.

Offering salutations and congratulations have always been integral to the life of a Muslim. So, if today we are unable to give *'Id* greetings in person to each and every one of our friends and relatives, there is nothing stopping us from sending greetings by post or by telephone.

Social Integration

Q : *What is fundamentalism? Who are Islamic fundamentalists? Are they members of some Islamic sect or cult? Are you an Islamic fundamentalist?*

A: If you look into the *Oxford Advanced Learners' Dictionary* you will find the word 'fundamentalism' defined in the following ways: 'someone who forms a foundation'; 'something of great importance to a particular point under discussion'; 'something which must be learned first and which all else depends on'; and finally, 'the maintenance of the literal interpretation of the traditional beliefs of a religion'.

Fundamentalism implies adherence to essentials; clinging to the basics. Muslims are thus, by definition, fundamentalists. Today secularists, especially the liberals who control the media, despise this word because they are not prepared to be bound by nor are they ready to accept the authority of revealed knowledge. They feel threatened by people who possess faith in God. This is why they have turned 'fundamentalism' into a dirty word. This is their insidious way of trying to discredit a religion which is being followed by one fifth of the world's population. – Let them!

As for us Muslims, we have the two main sources of our religion: the Book of Allah and its interpretation in the *Hadith* of the Prophet, blessings and peace be on him. So long as a Muslim follows these two, he or she will be rightly guided, and will remain a fundamentalist. So, yes, I hope that I too am an Islamic fundamentalist.

Q: *What are the obligations of Muslims living in any kafir non-Muslim country? And are we supposed to comply with the law of the land even if this law conflicts with the Shari'ah?*

A: Before I go any further in answering this question, I would like to say that I totally disagree with Muslims – this questioner included – who, while thoroughly enjoying the benefits of living in the West, have the gall to turn around and refer to its non-Muslim inhabitants as *kafir*. Not only is such a term inaccurate, it is also indecent, rude and totally wrong. Yes, the *Qur'an* does describe non-Muslims as *kafir* – but had you bothered to read the context of this description you would have realised that '*kafir*' is a theological definition, used primarily during academic discourse only, and is not meant for everyday use – for which the correct *Qur'anic* phrase is 'People of the Book'.

The *Qur'an* makes it crystal clear that Muslims are obliged to behave impeccably towards non-Muslims. It is true that we often have major disagreements with them, but piling on terms of abuse is not the same as having a difference of opinion. Disagree where you have to, but do it with civility, not rancour or abuse. There is, of course, an underlying reason for all this – for which I would refer you back to *Surah* 6 of the *Qur'an*, *Surat'al-An'am*, verses 107-108: ***'If it had been Allah's plan, they would not have taken false gods – but We did not make you to watch over them, and you are not responsible for them. And do not revile those to whom they pray instead of Allah, lest they wrongfully revile Allah in their ignorance.'*** Note the last sentence. If you, as a Muslim, lose control and all sense of proportion, then, tell me, what is there to stop a non-Muslim from responding by abusing and insulting all that you hold dear?

On to the second part of your question: I will begin by pointing out that Muslims enjoy innumerable freedoms in many western non-Muslim countries. Freedom to speak, to think, to associate with whom they like. Freedoms which people in many Muslim countries only dream about. Here in Britain, for example, the authorities do not prevent us from performing basic religious obligations. We pray, we fast, we hold Islamic meetings without the threat of being followed, abducted or detained. And at another level we are not forced to drink, to womanise, or to enter into contracts that are against the Islamic point of view. Where our world-view differs from the law of the land, the safest course of action is to opt out as a conscious objector – again, an opportunity to choose which is almost non-existent in most Muslim countries.

Q : *The British Army is currently on a drive to recruit Asians. Given the demography of the Muslim population in this country, this will inevitably target Muslim youngsters. If a Muslim signs up, he will have to swear an oath of allegiance to the Crown. What is the Islamic position of a Muslim serving in non-Muslim forces? Has it ever historically been permitted?*

A : We are part of this nation. Once we are given our homes in this country and are free to practise Islam here, it becomes our duty to try to safeguard this country. It is our moral, national and social duty to participate in the process of defending the country. If this country were to fight against a Muslim one, we would have the choice of opting-out and becoming conscientious objectors.

Q : *If one accepts that Islam is a social religion, i.e. one that isn't merely practised in private but which plays an integral part in one's conduct with others, how can it correctly be practised when the society is non-Muslim?*

A : Islam is a most tolerant, most flexible religion. An Islamic society guarantees freedom for both Muslims and non-Muslims to practice the religion of their choice, free from intimidation. A Muslim is not allowed to bully, harass, heckle, ridicule or boycott anyone – even parents who may not be Muslim – into accepting the faith. The *Qur'anic* verses relating to this could not be clearer. In the *Holy Qur'an*, *Surah* 31, *Surah Luqman*, verse 14, Allah says: ***'And We have enjoined upon man concerning his parents – his mother carries him with weakness upon weakness and his weaning is within two years – be grateful to Me and to your parents: to Me is the journeying.'***

Similarly, neighbours and relatives – regardless of their beliefs – are to be accorded respect. Muslims are ordered to be good to neighbours and to those who live locally. Again, we can turn to the *Qur'an*, *Surah* 60, *Surat'al-Mumtahanah*, verse 8, which demonstrates how Muslims should treat those not of the faith: ***'Allah does not forbid you – as regards those who have not fought you because of your deen, nor driven you out of your homes – from dealing kindly and justly with them: for surely Allah loves those who are just.'*** This applies to those non-Muslims who are decent and respectable and who do not wage wars of hatred against Muslims. Of the latter, Allah has this to say, in the following verse – *Surah* 60, verse 9: ***'Allah only forbids you from making friends with those who have fought you because of your deen, and driven you out of your homes, and helped to drive you out.'***

This means that when we deal with non-Muslims who are decent and respectable and not hostile to Islam or Muslims, then we are duty-bound to treat them in a kind, compassionate and respectable way. Of course, Muslims are not supposed to 'turn the other cheek' when they are confronted by those waging war against them – whether cultural, social or physical. In the multi-cultural societies of the West, the priority for Muslims is to practise every aspect of Islam that they know, and to speak about their faith in an intelligent, decent and sensitive way. They are on no account to attempt to impose Islam on anybody: ***'There is no compulsion in the deen,'*** says the *Qur'an* in *Surah* 2, *Surat'ul-Baqarah*, verse 256.

When it comes to non-Islamic practices, remember that other people do not force Muslims to drink or engage in illicit acts. It is up to the will of the person concerned to be aware, and to be able to judge the situation on its merits, and to respond in the best and most suitable way. The Prophet, upon whom be blessings and peace, had a non-Muslim servant. One day the servant fell ill, and so the Prophet gathered some Companions together to go and visit him. In another equally well-known tradition, the Prophet is reported to have stood up when the funeral procession of a non-Muslim passed by. All these examples teach us that as Muslims we have a duty towards other human beings, regardless of their faith. For those Muslims living in the West, it is very crucial that we know what is expected from us and behave and act accordingly.

Q : *Your reply on the captioned subject in Friday's (October 22nd, 1993) Gazette was realistic and factual. Western culture also has plenty of other very, very seriously questionable aspects such as: gambling; cheating, through the lottery; insurance and banking based on exploitation; lack of respect for parents and elders; incest – more than 70% of reported rape cases are within the family; illegitimate births – every 4th child is born to an unmarried mother (not counting births through adultery); abortion and other child abuse; abandoning of elders in the family; selfishness; monopolies in technology – thereby amassing wealth and depriving the majority of the people of their right to share in the bounties of Allah; women labour – women are forced by circumstances to work; women and child abuse of a variety of types; and lack of true and real knowledge about Allah and the universe, thereby leading the masses to their eternal destruction – this is a very, very important short-coming if people could only realise!*

A : Following up on your comments on the western way of life: You can go on enumerating these practical vices without end, but unless you try to dig out the roots of these vices you will not be able to address these social and moral problems in a correct, sound, basic way.

The modern, non-Islamic society is secular in outlook. This secularism, which basically is concerned only with the life here on earth, affects all their legislation. When you ask about their source of legislation, they will say it is the human institutions, which are the parliaments. There are no more basic values to grant some sort of permanency to and in their society. It is relativity which is the norm. When there is a change in social behaviour, their legislation will reflect that. So they will legalise abortion, because the 'freedom' of the woman – who votes, counts more than the life of the unborn foetus – who cannot vote. They will lower the age of consent for homosexual acts from 21 to 18, because the homosexual lobby is vocal in its campaign, and so on. Once the basic permanent factor that has been preserving the fabric of the society all through its history – religion, or faith – is removed from the arena of legislation, then everything is subject to relativism and values change in accordance with the vogue of the time. The *Qur'an* says: ***'And those who disbelieve enjoy themselves, and eat as the cattle eat – and the Fire shall be their abode.'*** (*Surah* 47, *Surah Muhammad*, verse 12).

Politics

Q : *Is it permissible for Muslims to participate in local and general elections in this country, either as candidates or as voters?*

A : If we are going to live in this country, and want our voice and point of view to be heard, then we must play a positive role in the life of the community here. Excluding ourselves will show that we do not believe in our existence here; if that is so, then we must migrate back to our countries of origin.

Assuming that we all agree on the first option, we must take part and show that we are always interested to hear and support those parliamentary candidates and parties who support 'Islamic issues'. If a decent committed Muslim man, aware of the wider issues, is able to put the interests of the Muslim community across in an objective way using any of the established political parties as a vehicle, then I would say all right, go ahead and present the Muslims' case. And I know that there are many people who are strong in their religion and culture who are doing just that. We must work within the system with a full commitment to the prosperity of the country in which we are living. If we cannot do that, then we must leave.

Q : *Can a woman be the head of a Muslim country?*

A : This is a contradiction in terms. If it is a Muslim state it should not go against the authentic *Hadith* of the Prophet, blessings and peace be on him, who said, on hearing that the Persian Empire had elected a princess to be their Empress, 'No people shall succeed who put their affairs in the hands of a woman.' It is only during the weakness and secularisation of such societies that a woman may become the ruler. This shows the senile nature of such societies. When Egypt was ruled for a short period by a woman, the Abbasid *Khalifah* sent a message saying: 'If you cannot find a man to rule you, we are ready to despatch one to you!'

Q : *In Islam it is not permissible for women to rule over men. But in India brave women such as Razzia Sultan and Chand Bibi have passed who ruled the country splendidly while they still observed purdah. Can women rule?*

A : When the *Hadith* mentioned that the nation which submits its rule to a female will not succeed, it was not addressing itself to a particular example where a woman may be much better than a man. The *Hadith* was general in outlook. When a society becomes so emasculated, or so secular, that anyone can rule it, then there is no difference between a male or a female. It has happened and it will happen again, as long as clarity of Muslim thought and action is not widespread. But these are not the good times in the history of either al-Islam or other nations which opt for such systems. The *Hadith* sets the general rule – the exception does not change this. And Allah knows all.

Q : *Does Islamic Law permit rule by a female? If not, why?*

A : There is a *Hadith* of the Prophet, blessings and peace be upon him, in which, when told that the Persian Empire was headed by a female, he said that people ruled by a woman will not succeed. It has been extrapolated from that *Hadith* that a woman cannot be the head of a Muslim state. However, there is no clear statement to say that women are prohibited from becoming Head of State. Traditionally, the head of the Muslim state has been a male, and when the constitutional writers within the Islamic state discussed the qualities that a ruler should have, they usually included that the ruler should be a male. This is really a matter of precedent. In human history, the leadership role has been associated with fighting and conquest, which are better suited to a male.

Nowadays, we are seeing many women becoming heads of state, even within the Muslim nations. We need to go back to the conditions that were established in the early days of Islam regarding who should be head of state. It was said, in those times, that the head of state should be from the tribe of the Quraysh. This was adhered to during the Umayyad and Abbasid periods, which did not last long. Thereafter, during the Turkish Khalifate, the Muslims were ruled by non-Arab rulers. If we can take our lead from this, we can say that traditionally and historically, leadership has been the domain of the male, but there is no clear prohibition on women taking up the role. This is a case of legalising a *de facto* situation. The recommendation that the Quraysh should lead was later left off, and there are no absolutely clear-cut *Hadith* governing this matter.

What we can say, though, is that it may not lie in the interests of women to be arguing about whether or not they could become head of a Muslim state at a time when we in the Muslim world do not have any democratic procedure by which we can choose a ruler. So this is a hypothetical question. Once we have a free Muslim society, with an educated class of women, who uphold the *Shari'ah* in every way, then the question would seriously arise. In this situation, the possibility should be there, but not before women, and men, have fulfilled the obligations of their home lives.

Q : *The Babri mosque affair, like the Rushdie issue, unleashed a lot of emotions within the world-wide Muslim community. But do you think it was right to create such a fuss, which led to so many deaths, over the demolition of a mosque that wasn't even being used? The Indian authorities have quietly been bulldozing mosques for years, but no one said anything then. So why all the noise now?*

A : What alternative do we have? Are we going to sit idle and let our sacred Islamic monuments be demolished without taking any action whatsoever? Yes, we react emotionally to such incidents, but our emotions are not in vain. They are a message to the afflicted to say, 'You have not been forgotten!' Also they stir up the thinking community within the Muslim nation to formulate future policy regarding the safety of our Islamic heritage from the forces that want to crush it. Emotion is all that we can display until such time as we become united – which we are moving towards. The fact that so many different schools of thought got together to express their anger and frustration about the Babri mosque demolition – or previously, about a man who had abused and insulted the Prophet, upon whom be blessings and peace – shows that the Muslims remain a nation with a soul and heart and are unlikely to sit idle and let acts that defile and attempt to destroy what they hold dear take place with impunity. At the moment our action might not be totally rational, but it is certainly a prelude to a future where there is more thought not only about how to react, but also about how to initiate actions in the defence and maintenance of our Islamic identity.

Q : *I have been watching with horror the Bosnia situation get worse, and worse, and worse. Muslim Aid and Islamic Relief are not the answer. Lorry-loads of baked beans and spaghetti for victims of ethnic cleansing amounts to a sell-out. Why can't we stop the ethnic cleansing in the first place? While Muslim governments remain idle, is there anything concerned Muslims can do? I feel so ashamed.*

A : I myself, like you, am puzzled by the attitude of the Muslim world whose first responsibility is to look after and support the people of Bosnia. We hear about billions of dollars being spent on armaments throughout the Muslim world – over the last two decades we have spent over US$250 billion in arms purchases. All this is now rusting because it is sitting idle – taken out only to be used against the Muslim people themselves. This is one of the most frustrating and disgraceful signs of the weakness of the global Muslim community at the moment. When we are incapable of fixing that deep wound in the heart of every Muslim – the occupation and desecration of the first *Qiblah, Al-Aqsa*, by the Zionists – how can you expect us to do anything else, whether in Bosnia, Somalia, Tajikistan, etc., other than to fatten and feed them so that they can be further humiliated before they are slaughtered in front of television cameras, watched by the entire world?

But why just blame the Muslims? Let us take Western society to task. During the Gulf War, all of them ganged up and destroyed a Muslim country. Of course they had a good excuse – but just what was the excuse? A dictator who failed in his bid to stem the tide of Islam in his neighbouring country suddenly jumped into Kuwait. What happened? The whole of western society taught him a lesson by dividing and then destroying a great Muslim nation. Why can't the leaders of the 'new world order' do the same to the Serbs? I'll tell you why: their motives are nothing but self-interest – Bosnia-Herzegovina has no oil, and the idea of a Muslim state in Europe remains an anathema to a West which has never stopped behaving as if a Crusade is going on.

Unfortunately the hands of Muslims like yourself and myself are tied. There is very little we can do of our own accord. I just pray that those young people who have the ability and determination will find a way to provide some help and support and even engage in attempts aimed at stopping the brutal suffering of their Muslim brothers.

Q: *Muslims in Europe are being warned to prepare themselves for a Bosnia-style scenario erupting in places where Muslims constitute significant minorities. Is such scare-mongering permitted in Islam? Or should we make provision for the worst, but hope and work for the best?*

A: As long as Muslims are considered third-class citizens of the West, unwilling to rock society's secular fabric, they will continue to be tolerated. For how long no one knows. But the moment the Establishment feels that Muslims are beginning to tread on their toes, trying to be respectable citizens of the West, but at the same time elbowing them from high places, I do not know what the fate of these Muslim communities will be. We have seen the work of the National Front in this country, in France and more recently in Germany. We cannot close our eyes to these plain, bare facts. Similarly, we cannot say that what has happened in Bosnia cannot happen elsewhere. We do not like to scare-monger, or to harbour undue despair, but we must be ready for any eventuality. The only way to protect the Muslim community in the West is ...?

Q: *What is the position of a hunger-striker in Islam? Is a fast to the death, for an Islamic cause, considered suicide or is it shahadah?*

A: The hunger-strike is a recent development; it is the latest weapon in the arsenal of the oppressed in their fight for liberation against their enemies. Islamically speaking, however, this is one weapon which we

Muslims are forbidden to use. The basis for this prohibition lies in a verse in *Surah* 4, *Surat'an-Nisa*, verse 29, of the *Qur'an* where Allah says: **'... *and do not kill yourselves – surely Allah is Most Merciful towards you.'*** This verse applies to any fast-to-the-death as, indeed, it does to other forms of suicide. So, in answer to the first part of your question, yes – a hunger-strike to the death is considered suicide and is, therefore, forbidden.

It is often argued that hunger-strikers do not die in vain; that at the very least, their death serves to highlight a particular cause. This, nonetheless, does not necessarily legitimise what is essentially a suicide. According to Islam, only that life which has been taken on the battlefield, or in a battle-field situation, qualifies for *shahadah,* martyrdom.

Hunger-strikers are often compared to suicide bombers, such as Muslims from the Lebanon who drive jeeps packed with explosives straight into Israeli military bases. However, suicide bombers and hunger-strikers are, in fact, two very different things. If a Muslim feels that throwing himself against enemy lines or against an enemy target will benefit his side, this is allowed, as the action is considered positive and will almost certainly cause serious damage to his opponents. A hunger-striker, on the other hand, will benefit no one, least of all himself. The reason for this is that suicide carries a particularly prickly punishment for whoever is foolhardy enough to carry it out. In many *Ahadith* it is reported that on the Day of Judgement those who committed suicide will be handed the implement with which they took their lives and will be told to repeat what they did – for eternity. If they used poison, poison is what they will be made to drink; if they bashed themselves to death with an iron rod ... A man who starved himself to death would, similarly, be made to go without food or drink.

If anyone wants to liberate Muslims from the clutches of those who have encroached upon their land or state, or subverted their moral base, or even undermined or repressed Islam, a fast-to-the-death is not the way to go about it.

Q : *What are the criteria for shahada, martyrdom, in Islam?*

A : Martyrdom in Islam is the greatest action a Muslim can offer for the sake of Allah. It is the highest sacrifice. Once a man asked the Prophet: 'What is real *Jihad* for the sake of Allah?' The Prophet, blessings and peace be on him, replied: 'When it is absolutely for the sake of Allah.'

Believers achieve martyrdom when they are killed fighting in a battle which is clearly defined as being between Al-Islam and its enemies who are attacking and committing acts of violation against the rights of Muslims. The war has to be declared by the head of a true Muslim state, which has been built upon the Islamic *Shari'ah* and which observes the basic Islamic rules; if it is other than that, it is not considered to be martyrdom. According to the Prophet, blessings and peace be on him, 'Those who pass away do not wish to return to this world, except those who are martyrs. Because of the honour, rewards and respect that they receive in heaven, they wish to come back to this world to be martyred again and again, to receive more rewards.

Trade and Commerce

Q: *With so much emphasis in Islamic texts placed on the need for Muslims not to be extravagant with money, would it be correct to deduce that Islam is an 'anti-wealth-creation' religion?*

A: You have deduced incorrectly. Islam is anything but against the creation of wealth. The *Qur'an* speaks at length on the subject in several *Surahs*. And there are many examples from the Prophet downwards of eminent Muslims whose chosen profession was business. However, Islam is clear about one thing: the Islamic notion of what constitutes wealth, and how this wealth should be disposed of, differs markedly from the Western secular perspective. In *Surah* 7, *Surat'al-'Araf*, verses 31-32, of the *Qur'an* Allah says: ***'Oh children of Adam, wear your beautiful apparel at every place of prayer, and eat and drink – but do not be excessive, for Allah does not love those who are excessive. Say: "Who has forbidden the beautiful things of Allah, which He has produced for His servants, and the good things which He has provided?" Say: "Only those who are believers during the life of this world will have these on the Day of Judgement." Thus do We explain the signs for people who have knowledge.'***

So the *Qur'an* says in no uncertain terms that Muslims are allowed to earn as much as their earning capacity allows, but only so long as this is done in a lawful manner and in an atmosphere of social responsibility. So, this means that there is no moral good if a wealthy person enjoys himself while abandoning the needs of others around him. According to a *Hadith* of the Prophet, upon whom be blessings and peace: 'He is not one of us who sleeps after having eaten his fill, while his next-door neighbour goes hungry.' Just as the profit-motive is not the sole incentive for creating wealth in Islam, the act of making money itself has to be carried out in a lawful way. The billions of pounds made by currency speculators and banks creating credit out of nothing – all forms of artificial money – are totally prohibited in Islam.

Q : *Is it Islamic to sell water? I am told that in Islam, water is a commodity that is available free of charge for everyone to use. Is this correct?*

A : The whole issue of Islam's position on the sale and distribution of water has been completely misunderstood. The idea that water should be available on tap to every single household in the land, free of charge, is absurd, wrong and certainly not Islamic. It is true that there are a number of *Ahadith* that can 'loosely' be described as prohibiting the sale of water. But it is clear that these narrations, from the time of the Prophet, blessings and peace be on him, if read to the very end, talk about a specific incident and not the general rule. A careful and proper reading of the relevant *Ahadith* should dispel any notion that water is a free commodity in Islam. I will attempt to provide an explanation:

Most of the *Ahadith* on water appear in *Imam* Muslim's *Ahadith* collection. They are usually summarised as follows, and the first *Hadith* ought to be familiar to those who argue that water is a free commodity: **1)** The Prophet, blessings and peace be on him, prevented the sale of water. **2)** The Prophet prevented the sale of water and of farmland used for grazing. **3)** The Prophet prevented the sale of water to protect nearby herbage.

What perhaps is not always mentioned is that all three narrations refer to an incident in the time of the Prophet involving an agricultural dispute: users of a common pasture had complained that a landowner demanded payment for the use of a nearby well which he owned. Once the Prophet, blessings and peace be on him, had made sure that the water was surplus to the owner's requirements, he ordered him to give it out free for the use of animals grazing next door. Now nowhere in this incident does it say – and nor can anyone assume this – that it is *haram* to buy or sell bottled water; that water must be state-owned; that Muslims are forbidden to pay water rates – or any of the other, largely wild, theories that many Muslims have put forward about water. Providing a 24-hour water service direct to your home costs money. If someone wants to use the service then he or she must pay for it. Similarly, any Muslim who is thinking of investing in one of the newly-privatised water companies should go right ahead and buy shares. There is nothing in Islam against such a thing.

Commenting on these *Ahadith*, *Imam* Nawawi, author of the popular *An-Nawawi's Forty Hadith*, said that the Prophet's instructions for free water applied only to those who might have more water than they needed, and whose wells were the only source of water in a largely barren, desert area.

Q : *There is a Hadith of the Prophet, blessings and peace be on him, which, to paraphrase, says that water, air and wood should not be kept from the people at large. Some people use this to say that public resources such as gas, electricity, water, etc. should be state-owned. Are they correct?*

A : We should not introduce a religious attitude here. The *Hadith* to which you refer is a correct, sound *Hadith* from *Imam Muslim*, in which the Prophet, blessings and peace be upon him, said that a man is not allowed to withhold his water to prevent pasturing. What does this mean? It refers to a situation in which a man owns a well or watering facility, which is surrounded by a pasturing area, and he demands payment for the watering of animals. People couldn't pasture their animals without watering them from that well. So if he prevents the animals from using the water, he is preventing them from pasturing in the area which is nearest to water – and the Prophet, blessings and peace be upon him, disliked that this should be done. That is why Muslim *fuqaha* say that water is the property of the man on whose land the well is, and he is entitled in the first place to the ownership of everything on his land – but the water is free, if it is more than he needs.

Here we are talking about natural things. If water is coming through a river, you are allowed to use it. If electricity was produced by itself, then likewise. But nowadays, the production, purification and distribution, etc., of these basic commodities require labour and capital – and once there are such efforts then they become services which have to be organised to be made available to people. The state is not bound to provide these utilities, but to look after the safety of people and to arbitrate in disputes. It is for the community to arrange these matters in a way which is fair and just to everyone. In the past, people used to fetch water and deliver it for money, and nothing was seen to be wrong in this. Once the Prophet, blessings and peace be upon him, even advised a beggar to go and gather wood to sell, in order to earn a living.

Q : *Can Muslims apply the copyright laws in this country to protect an idea or work being commercially exploited by someone else?*

A : The Hanafi School defines wealth in tangible or material terms. As a result, it is difficult to define any concept of intellectual property rights. But the other three schools, the Maliki, the Shafi'i and the Hanbali, define wealth more widely – for example, the ability of a person to hire his services, which is not material, is considered to be a source of wealth. From that consideration they say that Muslims have the right to protect their inventions or ideas, because they have researched and worked hard to achieve something which may be a source of wealth to them. I have to stress, however, that this is a new *Ijtihad*, and that the author of the comparative work on this issue to whom I am referring states that the early Hanafis considered a wider definition of property, and that therefore there may be said to be a consensus.

Q : *Is it permissible to receive commissions for rendering services as Estate Agents, Marriage Counsellors or Indenting Agents from parties on both sides? What sort of commission percentages are legitimate and reasonable? The current rates on real estate deals vary between 1 and 5% and on rental agreements it is one month's rent. Both parties have to pay these commissions because services are rendered to both parties and documentation is done for both. In the event of problems, both parties are helped according to the nature of the problem. Indenting involves the introduction of foreign suppliers to local customers. Commission is charged only to the foreign supplier and is between 0.25 and 5% depending upon the value and nature of the items sold.*

A : Yes, it is allowed to receive wages or commissions for the services you have mentioned. This is what is known as a *samsarah* – a broker. In Ibn Abideen, Vol. 6, p. 63, we find that Ibn al-Hawi Muhammad ibn Salama was asked about the wages given to the broker. His answer was: 'I hope there is no harm in that. This and many other things were not acceptable – but the need of the people for such services let this be allowed.' In the book *The Fiqh according to the Four Schools of Thought*, Vol. 3, pp. 113-114, in the section on *Hiring*, it states that it is allowed to hire someone to sell goods if he provides a real service in that. The wage to be given should be in accordance with such services, and whatever is the norm and custom in that field.

There is an area where the *Hadith* of the Prophet, blessings and peace be on him, has forbidden the work of the broker, or middle-man, and that is in meeting farmers or producers from the country, who are not aware of the market price of their goods in the city, and selling their produce for them. The *Hadith* is agreed upon – and when Ibn 'Abbas was asked to explain it, he said that the *samsarah* should not be a middle man for such people, in order to stop the inflation of the price of the goods.

The examples mentioned in the question here are common practices, for services which are needed and for prices which are known. There is no cheating or deception. What is mentioned in the question are new developments, falling into what are known as legitimate activities. But there should be no collusion between those who are in the business to deflate or inflate the prices of the services, and the market should be left free. This is what the Messenger of Allah, blessings and peace be on him, meant in the *Hadith*: 'Let people exchange benefits one from the other,' when he was asked to fix prices – in other words, 'Let market forces stabilise themselves in a free way for the benefit of the community.' This part of the *Hadith* also leaves the question of fixing prices, and by extension commissions, to the market. The range of 1 to 5%, or even to 9%, may be acceptable within the trade. This leaves a margin for those who wish to attract more customers by lowering their percentage, as long as the trade is regulated and supervised by a regulatory, fair body. Once such a body becomes suspect, then there is authority to correct the situation, once again in a fair manner.

Debts and Usury

Q : *I have some interest which was credited to my bank account. How can I dispose of this without being wasteful? Are there any organisations which could use it lawfully?*

A : There is a standard *Fatwah* issued by the Islamic Research Academy, Dar Al-Ifta, the Conference of *Zakat*, the Conference on the Islamic Banking System – some in Kuwait, some in Qatar – where it is said that we must collect this interest and disperse it in some way without expecting any reward from Allah. We are not allowed to leave it with the banks, because they are duty bound to give interest left by Muslims to charitable organisations – many of which are using funds against Muslims. The money created through interest cannot be used to print the *Qur'an* or to build mosques, but we are free to give it away in any way for the interest of the Muslim community. However, we cannot use interest to protect our money, to offset it against taxation, for example, or other such things.

Q : *I am an Indian and I am planning to distribute the interest/usury which I receive from the bank among my poor relatives. I know usury is 100% haram for me, even when paid by the bank, and also that I do not expect any reward from Allah for giving it to the poor, but is it halal for them?*

A : In the second Conference on the Islamic Banking System in Al-Kuwait, in 1983, it was recommended that, until such time as Islamic financial institutions became available in Muslim countries, those who were keeping their money in interest-bearing accounts should collect the interest, even though it is a dirty impure gain, and get rid of it by spending it on the general welfare of the community. They are not allowed to use such interest in any way for their own benefit. So it is allowed for you to give the money to those relatives of yours for whom you are not responsible for maintaining financially.

Q : *My building society is merging with one of its former rivals. The merged entity proposes to issue free shares to existing account-holders. Am I allowed to accept them?*

A : It is an economical and financial fact that the work of the building societies is to lend money to those who want to have their own houses. So it is like trading in money like banks. As such, we are not allowed to own any shares in institutions which are basically dealing in interest. As a result of the need to protect ourselves, it is allowed to have current accounts where we do not claim interest on the amount of money we keep there for safe-keeping. Apart from that, ordinary Muslims, like me and you, who have a couple of hundred pounds in the bank, should not dilute their income with any part of the interest – because it is has been defined very strictly in a number of Islamic conferences that the modern concept of interest is the same as the old concept of usury, in a different form. Those who have accounts in building societies should not buy shares in these societies. Neither are they allowed to buy shares in banks, leisure complexes, and enterprises associated with gambling, breweries, etc. These are areas which are totally unacceptable from the Islamic point of view.

Q : *If it is haram to take out a mortgage because interest is haram, how is someone living in the West supposed to buy a house when there is no alternative way of borrowing halal money?*

A : There is no doubt that the mortgage system is an interest-bearing one, and interest is prohibited. So what can Muslims do in order to own their property? The answer to this question arose out of a heated and lengthy discussion at a recent *Fiqh* Seminar in France on Muslims in the West. I will try to summarise here what was said:

Sheikh Mustafa az-Zarqa'a, an eminent *faqih*, had no hesitation in saying that Muslims in non-Muslim countries may be allowed to enter into such transactions, according to the Hanafi school of thought. On the question as to whether Muslims can both accept and pay interest, the Sheikh replied: 'It is not a matter of giving or taking interest. It is the comparison between the pros and cons of the transaction. The final result is better for the Muslims who are allowed to live in the West, for they are in a state of real need. As that need is supported by a great *Imam* like Abu Hanifa, I have no hesitation in saying that they can enter into such a transaction. I also endorse the ruling in *Fatwah* No. 42 by the General Affairs Committee in the Ministry of Awqaf of Kuwait, Ayn 15 Shawwal 1404, which permits such transactions.'

However, certain members of the panel did not agree with this ruling without indicating clearly that interest is forbidden. Muslims are not allowed to undertake such a transaction unless there is a general, strong, real need regarded as a necessity. The 'allowability' should be very strict – until such time as *halal* Islamic financial institutions are set up.

Q : *Last week, I paid the final instalment of my 25-year mortgage, yet I still do not consider myself to be free of debt. You see, as a child, I was for ever borrowing small amounts of money from school-friends – money which, to this day, I have not returned. Am I still Islamically considered to be in debt? If so, is there any alternative way of repaying this money as it could take me the equivalent of a lifetime tracking down all the people I owe? Will I, on the Day of Judgement, be called to account for these monies?*

A : So your conscience has finally woken up! Good. Repentance is good: remember, in Islam it is never too late to correct a mistake. You are faced with a difficult but very important issue – for unless you clear all your debts in this life, the unpaid pounds and pennies will return to haunt you in the Hereafter. The Islamic stance on this matter is very clear: correct the mistakes and transgressions you have made in this life today. Otherwise, in the Hereafter, God will dip into your good deeds to repay those you owed in this life.

The Prophet, may blessings and peace be upon him, once asked his Companions if they could define the meaning of the word 'bankrupt' for him. A few of them must have ventured some suggestions, for the Prophet then went on to say that bankruptcy wasn't necessarily losing all one's money. A bankrupt person, according to the Prophet, blessings and peace be upon him, was that person who left this world with a mountain of good deeds to his credit, but then watched those deeds disappear before his eyes. How? Because they were used to redress an equal mountain of misdeeds committed during his earthly life. So, that unpaid loan, or a rash of temper, or what at the time seemed an insignificant little fib – all worked against him on the Day of Judgement. Even if he was left with nothing left to his credit, the Prophet, blessings and peace be on him, continued, the sins of his creditors and of others who had been wronged by him would be thrown on this man: 'This is the definition of a bankrupt.'

So what can you do? First, try as best as possible to trace your creditors. No matter how small the amounts, they must be repaid. A gift for the equivalent amount might be a more diplomatic way of repaying your debt. As for those whom you cannot trace, pay the equivalent amount to a charity, on behalf of the person whom you owe – but should you chance to meet such a person at a later date, remember, your debt is still outstanding and you should repay it.

Q: *I borrowed SR10 from a stranger 5 years ago. I had promised to return the money to him but I forgot to do so and have since lost his address and do not know his whereabouts. How will I compensate for this?*

A: If you cannot locate the stranger from whom you borrowed the money, you should give the amount as *Sadaqah* in his name. Once you locate him after that, you should still return the borrowed money to him. But remember the saying of the Prophet, blessings and peace be on him: 'Whoever takes the wealth of people by borrowing it, with the intention of repaying it, Allah will help him in repaying it – but whoever takes it with the intention of not repaying it, Allah will destroy him.' (*Al-Bukhari*).

Q: *I have heard that Islam prohibits taking out insurance policies as a general rule. How then are Muslims to allay, or protect against, the damaging consequences of burglaries and car accidents that are endemic in this day and age?*

A: When it is said that Muslims are not allowed to take out insurance policies, it is referring to the territory of Islam, *Dar'ul-Islam*. This is because insurance policies are built upon the concept of what is defined as *gharar*, i.e. hidden or uncertain factors which we cannot foresee. Any transactions that are based on *gharar* elements are prohibited. Insurance policies are *gharar*, and as such are prohibited in Islam. The Ministry of Awqaf in Egypt was asked on a number of occasions – particularly by guardians of the wealth of minors – if it was possible to take out insurance to protect this wealth. In response to this inquiry, a great sheikh told his secretary that if he relayed papers with such questions to him again, he would beat him with them and throw him out of the window!

In the case of cars, however, it is impossible to own and drive a car without having motor insurance, so in that case one cannot avoid it. Since we are living in a land that is not part of *Dar'ul-Islam*, we are not free to decide for ourselves on every matter. Also, insurance policies in this country are not exploitative in the sense that both parties to the deal enter into it willingly and voluntarily. So in a non-Muslim land, a Muslim can take out insurance on anything, with the exception of life-insurance. There is no usury involved in these kinds of transactions.

Q : *If I were to find something valuable or useful lying in the street, for example, money or jewellery, what should I do? Should I just leave it? – but if I picked it up what should I do with it?*

A : Textbooks on *Fiqh* have devoted an entire section on what to do with unattended valuables. The Prophet, upon whom be blessings and peace, is said to have told a Companion who had found a purse containing gold and silver to return to the place where he had picked it up, and announce every day for a whole year that the purse had been reported lost – or until someone reclaimed it, after which it would be his if no one had claimed it.

Rather than Muslims taking on such a huge responsibility, the Companions Abdullah ibn 'Abbas and Abdullah ibn 'Umar both recommended that unattended valuables should be left alone. Nowadays, if you do find something valuable, hand it straight to the nearest police station, giving the time and location where you found it. The police will do the rest.

Competitions and Gambling

Q : *Does Islam permit participation in television-style game shows, lotteries and prize draws – particularly where a person may win a lot of money or prizes without having spent any money or done much work?*

A : Islam may allow participation in game shows, but not in lotteries or, indeed, in prize draws, both of which are akin to gambling.

A participant in a game show or quiz event wins money or prizes by exercising his or her intellectual ability; winning a lottery, on the other hand, depends entirely on luck – which is gambling.

Surah 5, Surat'ul-Ma'idah, verses 90-91, of the *Qur'an* state clearly the Islamic position on gambling: ***'Oh you who believe, surely intoxicants, and gambling, and idols, and fortune-telling are an abomination of shaytan's handiwork – so avoid it so that you may be successful. Shaytan only wishes to excite enmity and hatred between you through intoxicants and gambling, and to turn you away from the remembrance of Allah and from prayer – will you not then abstain?'***

Q : *Should Muslim organisations accept money from the 25% of lottery receipts set aside for 'good causes'?*

A: Money coming out of the lottery is considered illegal gain. Now if the government decides to distribute this money between different charities, without there being any application from Muslim organisations for it, then they are allowed to take it and use it for any good cause – except for building a mosque or printing the *Qur'an*. It must be stressed, however, that Muslims are not allowed to solicit for the money.

Q: *If the proceeds from the National Lottery are to go to charity, does this not make it a halal exercise?*

A: Absolutely not! There are three clear *Qur'anic* prohibitions on gambling. In *Surah* 5, *Surat'ul-Ma'idah*, verses 90-91, drinking and gambling are totally forbidden. If the aim of an exercise is good, then the means to the attainment of that aim must also be good. Furthermore, a *Hadith* states: 'Allah is good and pure and He only accepts what is good and pure.' At the same time, it is prohibited for Muslims to engage in any activity related to the National Lottery, because this would be participating in what is *haram*. Handling and selling the tickets is, therefore, not acceptable.

Art and Photography

Q: *Why does Islam place restrictions on reproducing animal figures, painting, etc., and figurative art in general? And is it permissible to reproduce the naked human form?*

A: At the beginning of Islam, all statues and drawings were prohibited, so that people could concentrate on the reality of the absolute Oneness of Allah, and His transcendence beyond all forms. This practice continued simply because human beings are prone to fall into mistakes. This is why there are many *Ahadith* in which the Prophet, blessings and peace be upon him, warns very strongly against the depiction of complete human figures, saying that those who draw human figures or animals will be severely punished on the Day of Resurrection, when they will be asked to breathe life into the figures they have created.

However, there is an exception to this rule, which is the case of children's toys and printed materials which, even though they might be undesirable, are allowed so long as they are not venerated. But these must be printed images rather than actual drawings. Also allowed is the drawing of human or animal figures in the classroom, in order to understand better how they function.

Q : *Two Fridays ago, an assignment took me to a new mosque in West London to take some photographs. While I was snapping away, a kindly, old gentleman came up to me and told me to stop committing haram acts. 'Photography is un-Islamic, and you must certainly not take pictures in mosques,' he told me politely after quoting a Hadith. What is your opinion?*

A : The subject of imagery has divided Muslim scholars for centuries. And the debate on the Islamic validity of art – drawings and paintings – intensified after the invention of the camera, which some scholars campaigned vehemently to ban. 'Photography is *haram* for Muslims,' they said. But some argue, equally passionately, that this was not the case, and that early cameras and their modern-day successors have an important role to play in Islam.

Essentially, those against photography draw their evidence from a number of *Ahadith* which forbid Muslims to sculpt statues or to draw pictures of living things, including humans, animals and birds. The argument is that painting and drawing living things is seen to be trying to create such things. 'Creation is Allah's domain, and it should stay that way,' say some scholars. This specific argument is taken from a *Hadith* narrated by Ibn 'Umar who has related that painters and sculptors will be asked by Allah on the Day of Judgement to breathe life – without success – into whatever they 'tried to create'. The fear was, say scholars, that painting and sculpting might lead people into idol-worship. In another *Hadith*, 'A'isha, the wife of the Prophet, has related that the Prophet, blessings and peace be on him, could not bear to see pictures of living objects and statues in people's houses. If he was visiting, he would not leave without breaking the statues or cutting such drawings to pieces. However, the *Hadith* with which perhaps most people will be familiar, and one used by scholars opposed to photography, is the one which says that angels never enter houses with pictures of living things inside them.

Yet, surprisingly, it is precisely this *Hadith* which scholars in the other camp make use of to support their pro-photography stance. Apparently, during the time of the Prophet, blessings and peace be on him, two Companions of the Prophet went to visit the Companion who had narrated this *Hadith* and who had fallen ill. When they entered his house, they were horrified to find pictures decorating his curtains. 'Didn't you say that the Prophet forbade such things?' They asked him – to which the ailing Companion replied, 'You didn't hear the whole story. Yes, the Prophet forbade drawings – *except those done on pieces of cloth.*' From this, a substantial body of scholars have deduced that photography, too, is allowed in Islam – and not only simply that it is allowed, but also that it ought to be developed within an Islamic context. That is not to say that there should be no restrictions on its applications. Modelling, for example, is not allowed as it serves no useful purpose. On the other hand, a picture for a newspaper such as *Q-news* does have a useful purpose, as it helps the reader understand what is being said. The *deen*, remember, is ease not hardship.

You also asked about taking photographs in a mosque. This is allowed so long as you do not interrupt anyone at prayer.

Q : *Having just finished a degree in the Fine Arts (photography and video-filming were my main subjects), I often wonder about the Islamic opinion on the use of both moving and still pictures. Is their use just restricted to education and information, or can they also be employed for reasons of 'art'? Can you please give an extensive answer.*

A : While drawing and photography are permitted in certain instances (we will go on to discuss this), there is no justification for any Muslim engaging in sculpture. In one *Hadith* reported in *Sahih al-Bukhari,* Masrouq, a Companion of the Prophet, blessings and peace be on him, who was shocked to find a life-like statue in the room of another Companion, said: 'I remember hearing Abdullah ibn Mas'ud relate a saying of the Prophet, may Allah bless him and grant him peace, 'Surely he who makes statues will be persecuted on the Day of Reckoning.' In another *Hadith*, the Prophet is reported to have said: 'Those who build statues will be punished on the Day of the *Qiyama*, the Day of Judgement, and will be told by Allah to breathe life into their creations.'

Muslim scholars, therefore, have had no hesitation in concluding that all three-dimensional work, whether a picture or a statue, is unacceptable in Islam – except for certain toys, for example dolls and similar toys for girls, contact with which might help them to understand their responsibilities when they grow up.

On the question of two-dimensional work, such as line drawings, works of art, etc., the scholars took more time to deliberate. They were aware of two sound, yet apparently conflicting, *Ahadith* on the issue. According to one *Hadith*, reported by Ibn 'Abbas, Allah will ask artists to blow the spirit of life into their drawings, but they will fail. In another *Hadith*, Abu Hurayrah is reported to have said: 'Allah considers none to be more unjust than those who try to copy His creation.' And 'A'isha, the wife of the Prophet, blessings and peace be on him, said that the Prophet never allowed any cloth into the house if it contained pictures of any kind as part of its design. But, on the other hand, a *Hadith* narrated by Abu Talha clearly allows Muslims to draw and paint objects in two dimensions. According to this *Hadith*, the Prophet is reported to have said that angels do not enter houses which contain pictures drawn on objects other than paper and cloth.

In an attempt to resolve this contradiction, scholars retraced both sets of *Ahadith* and found that the first three – from Ibn 'Abbas, Abu Hurayrah and 'A'isha – pre-dated Abu Talha's narration, which was recorded during the period when Islam had achieved a degree of consolidation among those early Muslims. The first three *Ahadith*, on the other hand, had been narrated at a time when Islam was still battling to eradicate idol-worship – a theme which crops up in all three traditions.

According to the scholars, this explains why these earlier *Ahadith* were so hard on anyone found drawing or painting. Once Islam had become well-established, they concluded, there was no longer a need for such tough measures to continue. The *Hadith* narrated by Abu Talha, therefore, was the one on which these scholars chose to base their final recommendation – that is, that two-dimensional pictures are permitted, so long as they do not hang on walls or other places to glorify individuals, whether alive or dead.

After discussing photography at length, the scholars decided to permit the use of the celluloid image, since its benefits were regarded as outweighing its disadvantages.

Q : *Does Islam allow the display of photographs of people who have died in homes and mosques?*

A: A comprehensive discussion on the issue of photography has already taken place in an earlier edition of *Q-news* (Vol. 1, No. 30, Friday 23rd November, 1992), but to recap, opinion on the issue is divided evenly between supporters and detractors. However, the late Sheikh Muhammad Bakhit, an Egyptian Mufti from the turn of the century and a man known for his immense religious stature, said that photographs were acceptable for practical purposes. This ruling should be considered in the light of the fact that the Sheikh, unlike many of his modern-day contemporaries, refused to manufacture *fatwahs* at the whims and desires of the authority of the day.

However, as regards the question being asked, I do not consider venerating dead persons, like *pirs* and saints, an 'acceptable practical purpose'. In an incident from the early days of Islam, the Prophet, blessings and peace be on him, prohibited pictures in case they distracted him from praying. On one occasion he asked his wife 'A'isha to remove a piece of cloth displaying a bird in its design, saying, 'Take it away, as this is the first thing I always face.'

Sports and Leisure

Q: *I am thinking of taking up sport to keep fit and for pleasure. Which sport would you consider as Islamically correct?*

A: There is a *Hadith* of the Prophet, blessings and peace be on him, in which he says, 'Teach your children how to swim.' Men and women should be separated while swimming. Men should supervise men only, and women should do the same for other women. It is important to dress according to the usual requirements of Islam: women should be covered from the chest to the knees when only women are together, but the outfit should not be cumbersome. For men it is a must that they be covered from the navel to the knee. Among sporting activities, running is also recommended. The Prophet, we know, once raced with his wife, 'A'isha, blessings and peace be on them – and he was able to beat her. On a later occasion they raced again, when she beat him – and the Prophet is reported to have said that they were now equal.

Archery is highly recommended in Islam, together with swimming and horse-riding. Wrestling is also allowed. There was a man by the name of

Rukana who was so strong that no one could move him if he sat down anywhere. He once sat on a piece of cloth and said to the Prophet, 'If you can move me, then I will accept your faith.' The Prophet, blessings and peace be on him, took him by the right hand and lifted him up.

As long as these recreational and sporting activities do not interfere with our livelihood and acts of worship, and also do not lead us into negligence or cause enmity in the community, then they are acceptable.

Q : *My family are football mad. Is it Islamic to follow a football team around Britain, wearing football-team scarves and chanting slogans?*

A : People need some recreation in their lives, and from that point of view football is good family entertainment. But to be 'mad' about the sport is an absolute waste of time, money and energy. This is happening in some Muslim countries as people spend a lot of time discussing, playing and watching football. Those who are here in Britain should be encouraged to have this type of entertainment – but what must be avoided is this narrow-minded approach to teams when fighting breaks out between supporters. If it reaches that point, that is not acceptable. The Islamic way is to be moderate in all aspects of our lives. It is not acceptable for Muslims to dress in football team colours and be obsessed with the whole thing. If this happens, it means we are being enchanted by something which does not have much impact on our spiritual and moral lives. It is an entertainment and should be confined to that.

Q : *I am thinking of starting up a keep-fit class for Muslim women in my local area, but I am a little unsure about the Islamic position on such things. I wonder if it is right for Muslim women to take as role-models the likes of Lizzie Webb and Jane Fonda, whose videos are used extensively. Also, most callisthenics, circuit training and aerobics classes rely heavily on intensely rhythmic, beat-filled music, which I know is discouraged in Islam. What would you advise me to do?*

A : Firstly, if the women need to have such classes, they should be conducted by a decent, respectable, Muslim woman in an environment that has no men around at all. There is no other objection from the Islamic point of view. Actually, looking after one's body and health is something highly recommended in Islam and everybody should do it.

Secondly, beat music which is decent, void of obscene lyrics and which does not arouse base emotions is also acceptable. For somebody really interested, such music is easy to come across, but all those who want to sweat it out should try to remember that it is the exercises, not the music – which is just an aid to liven up what could otherwise be a tedious act – which are important.

Music and Pets

Q : *I am a great fan of Indian classical music, particularly of the Sufi variety. I get great pleasure listening as it makes me feel at peace with my surroundings; it gives me inner strength. Listening to it rejuvenates my love for Islam. But I have heard that music and singing is one of those 'grey' areas in Islam: a subject that forever divides scholars who are unable to agree on the limits of musical enjoyment. I would like to know what you think.*

A : During the time of the Prophet, blessings and peace be on him, music was not banned. In fact, when the Companion, later the first *Khalifah*, Abu Bakr, expressed his displeasure at two girls, who were singing and beating a *duff*, drum on the *'Id*, the Prophet asked him to leave them alone saying, 'Leave them, Oh Abu Bakr – let them know that our religion is not so strict and that there is a wide area for refreshment.' Similarly in Madina, 'A'isha, the wife of the Prophet, had sent a girl to marry an Ansar, whereupon the Prophet asked her whether singers had been sent with the bride – he even began to compose the words, 'we are coming to you,' of a song for the wedding. However, that was when songs and music were of a very simple kind. Furthermore, playing and listening to music was restricted to special occasions and reserved for weddings and for moments of relaxation. Such practices, if still adhered to, are acceptable from an Islamic point of view.

What is thoroughly unacceptable is the music of today, which is suggestive, which is erotic, and which unfortunately consumes every waking hour of today's youth. Modern music – which is indecent, whose lyrics describe intimate physical relationships and the beauty of real people, and which is backed by a plethora of musical instruments – is not allowed in Islam, in accordance with the wealth of literature which has been written on the subject both by Companions of the Prophet, blessings and peace be on him and them, and by scholars.

Q : *Which pets are Muslims not allowed to keep in their houses? Did the Prophet or his Companions have any pets?*

A : Dogs and pigs are the animals which we are not allowed to keep in our houses. I am not aware if the Prophet, blessings and peace be on him, had any pets. Once, however, the Prophet was concerned because the angel Jibril did not appear for several days. This greatly upset him and he asked for the house to be cleaned. In the process it was discovered that a small dog had died in a corner somewhere. When Jibril eventually came to the Prophet, upon whom be blessings and peace, he asked him why he had not made an appearance for such a long time. Jibril answered, 'You know that angels do not enter places where dogs are to be found.' Muslims can keep pets like birds and cats, so long as they are well fed, looked after and properly cared for. A Companion of the Prophet was nick-named Abu Hurayrah, meaning 'owner of the small kitten', after the kitten which he carried down his sleeve.

Q : *I have a Muslim friend who is blind. She relies constantly on her guide dog, an invaluable companion which rarely leaves her side. The dog, naturally, has complete access to all the house. I understand that dogs are not allowed inside Muslim homes, but is there a special dispensation given to guide dogs for the blind? Similarly, how should friends and relatives of the blind and partially-sighted treat guide dogs in their homes? My friend would also like to know what she should do when praying. Is she allowed to touch the animal in between performing wudu and going to pray?*

A : Firstly, let us understand that it is only the saliva at the mouth of the dog which is considered to be unclean. All its body, as long as there is no outside impurity – the hair, the skin and other parts – are considered to be pure. However, in a *Hadith* in *Sahih Muslim*, Vol. 3, No. 3822, in the section on *Hunting*, Abu Hurayrah reports the Messenger of Allah as saying: 'He who keeps a dog which is neither meant for hunting, nor for watching animals, nor for watching the fields, will lose two *qiraat* every day out of his reward.' Now in this *Hadith* the Prophet, blessings and peace be on him, has given us three instances where we are allowed to keep dogs.

The question of training dogs to guide blind people was not around at the time of the Prophet, blessings and peace be on him, but one of the texts, *Nayl'ul-Awtar*, by *Imam* Ash-Shawkani, comments, Vol. 8, p. 146, that dogs can be kept for other reasons, so long as they are clean and pure. We say, therefore, that there is a very clear dispensation given by Muslim scholars to the blind who need to have guide dogs. If the sister is in need of the dog to guide her and the dog is trained, everything connected to the dog is clean and pure.

Q : *Does Islam allow the neutering of animals? My pet cat has become a little over-active of late and I was wondering ...*

A : Neutering or sterilising animals, while not encouraged in Islam, is not completely forbidden either. Abdullah ibn 'Umar, a Companion of the Prophet, upon whom be blessings and peace, reported that the Prophet forbade the neutering of horses and other animals. However, according to another tradition, the Prophet is said to have permitted the sterilisation of an animal so long as the operation is carried out early in its life and not when the animal reaches maturity. In the context of your question, in my opinion, it may be acceptable to neuter your cat, particularly, if you want to prevent the birth of a multiplicity of unwanted kittens.

Magic and the *Jinn*

Q : *After consulting many doctors about his wife's condition, my friend has come to the conclusion that her suffering is due to black magic. He sought advice from some people who gave him charms inscribed with Qur'anic verses. My question is: Is it permissible for a Muslim to believe that an ailment has been caused by 'black magic'? If so, can it be cured by the method adopted by my friend?*

A : Black magic does have physical effects. This phenomenon is recognised in Islam. The Prophet was one person upon whom black magic was tried, and as such, acts of this nature are considered to be *kufr*.

However, this is entirely separate to the question as to whether a Muslim is allowed to seek help from people who claim to be able to treat the effects of black magic. Let me say that the people who claim to cure the effects of black magic invariably tend to be unscrupulous con men who lack sincerity and honesty. Going to them is very dangerous, and a conscientious Muslim is advised best not to. The *Qur'an* is very clear on this matter. Referring to people who follow the people from the time of the Prophet Solomon who ran after knowledge of the occult, the *Qur'an* has this to say: ***'And they follow what the shayatin taught during the reign of Solomon. And Solomon did not disbelieve, but it was the shayatin who disbelieved, teaching people magic, and what was revealed to the two angels in Babylon – Harut and Marut – and they did not teach it to anyone until they had said, "Surely we are only a test, so do not disbelieve." And from these two they have learned how to cause separation between a man and his wife – and they can not harm anyone with it except by the permission of Allah – and they have only learned what is harmful for them, and not what is beneficial for them; and they certainly know that whoever deals in it will not have any share of good in the next life, and certainly what they have sold their selves for is awful – if only they knew.'*** (*Surah* 2, *Al-Baqarah*, verse 102). Similarly, many *Ahadith* also forbid such practices. The Prophet, blessings and peace be on him, strictly forbade the hanging round necks of *tameemah*, (charms or *taveez*). Anyone found doing so, said the Prophet, blessings and peace be on him, 'may Allah not perfect his recovery.'

What then do people who are suffering from black magic do? The answer lies in the teachings of our Prophet, blessings and peace be on him, who said that we should read *Surat'l-Ikhlas*, *Surat'al-Falaq* and *Surat'an-Nas* to protect us from harm. Also, *Imam* Malik relates several *Ahadith* in *Al-Muwatta'* which make it clear that the Prophet permitted writing talismans, using *ayats* of *Qur'an*, as a protection against evil.

Q : *The ghosts that people report seeing are often dismissed as figments of people's imaginations. Is there a case for arguing that these could be the jinn who are mentioned in the Qur'an?*

A : The Prophet, blessings and peace be upon him, has mentioned in numerous *Ahadith* the existence of a parallel kingdom in the Unseen of creatures known as the *jinn*, and there is a whole *Surah* of the *Qur'an* named after these beings. The ghosts that people see could be explained as being *jinn*, because we know that these creatures exist. The people who dismiss them as 'figments of the imagination' are fundamentally materialists, who believe in nothing that they do not know of through their sense-perceptions – but we know that these 'ghosts' could be *jinn*.

Q : *A former neighbour in Pakistan tells me that her house is haunted by jinn: she often hears doors bang when there is no one in the room, and food sometimes gets eaten when there is no one at the table. Do jinn live in ordinary houses with humans? If so, can they be glimpsed or sighted and would we be in any danger?*

A : The experience you describe is quite possible. I recall reading of a similar incident in an earlier edition of a noted Islamic journal, a magazine called *Islamic Research*. According to the article, a family managed to trace missing amounts of money to some *jinn* who, they found out, were actually living with them. There was no other explanation as, apart from the fact that people do not normally steal from themselves, money often went missing when the family went out – even for a short while. The authors confirmed that there are certain *jinn* who inhabit houses with human beings, mentioning an incident from the life of the Prophet, upon whom be blessings and peace, to support their hypothesis.

According to the story, the Prophet asked his Companion, Abu Hurayrah, to keep overnight watch over a consignment of dates to be given out as *Zakat* the following day. During his shift, Abu Hurayrah caught and reprimanded a man whom he found pilfering from the stock. Pleading poverty, the man promised never to steal again and was released. The Prophet, on hearing about the incident the next morning, told Abu Hurayrah that the 'person' was in fact a *jinn* who had lied and would return the next night offering the same story and the same excuse. Before the third night's shift the Prophet decided enough was enough and gave Abu Hurayrah detailed instructions to drive the *jinn* away for good: 'Read the last part of *Surat'al-Baqarah*, read *Ayat'al-Kursi*, the verse of the Throne, and this *jinn* will do no harm to either you or your house,' the Prophet is reported to have said. 'If you ever find a strange animal, repeat 3 times, "In the Name of Allah I ask you to leave." Kill it if it doesn't move. If it is a *jinn*, it will disappear.'

The Prophet was offering his prayers once, when he caught and squeezed a *jinn* which was up to no good. The Prophet was about to tie it to one of the mosque's pillars, when he remembered a saying of the Prophet Sulayman (Solomon, peace be on him), which is recorded in the *Qur'an*: ***'My Lord, forgive me and give me a kingdom the like of which no one else after me will ever have,'*** (*Surah* 38, *Surah Sad*, verse 35) – a prayer which Allah granted, including giving him mastery over the *jinn*. The Prophet therefore promptly let the *jinn* go.

There is a *Surah* in the *Qur'an* entitled *The Jinn*, which says that they come in different types: some are good, some bad, some Muslim, some non-Muslim. There are authentic incidents from the life of the Prophet, blessings and peace be on him, where he taught newly-converted *jinn* about Islam.

While *jinn* are in no way dangerous, and incapable of inflicting physical harm, they are certainly capable of interfering with our lives. People who think that *jinn* are close by should tread with caution and should not dabble in attempts to communicate with them. Reading the four *Surahs* towards the end of the *Qur'an* which begin with the word '*Qul*' – 'Say', in addition to following the advice which the Prophet gave to Abu Hurayrah, is an effective remedy.

I was once doing some research for a radio programme on the subject of the *jinn*. It was summertime, and I was alone in the house, when I suddenly found a black cat in the kitchen. Unfortunately, I forgot the Prophet's advice and immediately reached for the broom handle! I must have been so engrossed in the subject that I forgot there were definitely no *jinn* in my flat.

Q : *While abroad I was taken by some relatives to see a 'religious saint'. The old man merely looked at me and was able to tell my name and some details about events and incidents that have occurred in my life. I was shocked but sceptical. I am also worried about some of the predictions he made for my future. Can you advise?*

A : There is nothing new in this. It is a regular occurrence in rural areas throughout the Muslim world. Generally, people who successfully manage to recount the life history of complete strangers tend to fall into two categories. There is the obvious, common-sense case of the clever clairvoyant who employs a string of private investigators, spies, gossip-mongers and busybodies throughout a particular village who make it their business to poke their noses into people's private business. The 'religious saint' may have been told of your impending arrival by one of his informers who may be close to your relatives. All that remained was for the spy to research into your history and background so that when you finally visited the saint, he could impress you with his bogus powers. The other explanation could be that he was using a *jinn* who had been watching you.

Alternatively, it could also be a genuine person, gifted with such powers. However, it has to be said that genuine people do not advertise themselves in the way your particular 'saint' seems to be doing. They are also extremely rare and hard to find. But, one thing should be made clear: no person, or *jinn*, has the power to know what the future holds for anyone – that power rests only with Allah. If your 'saint' claims to know about your future, then he is nothing more than a crude fraud.

Medicine

Q : *What is the Islamic position regarding choosing the sex of an unborn child? A London clinic claims an up to 60% success rate in gender selection. Can Muslims use this facility to ensure that a child is born with a particular gender?*

A : The Organisation of Islamic Medical Scientists convened a seminar 10 years ago in Kuwait which discussed at some length the implications of modern medical practices for Islam and Muslims. The seminar, attended by no less than 75 leading scholars in their respective fields, discussed in detail the issue of embryology and human reproduction. On gender selection – sorting the father's sperm into X and Y chromosomes and then artificially inseminating the mother with one or the other – there was a difference of opinion. While the majority of scholars agreed that the practice could be used – but only after satisfying strict criteria – others expressed reservations, primarily the fear of one sex becoming dominant.

Personally speaking, a family that is blessed with an equal number of boys and girls should not have to resort to sex selection at all. But a family with a predominance of children of one sex should not be prohibited from trying to have a child of the opposite sex.

Historical analogy for this point of view was provided in a seminar paper written by Dr Abd'us-Sattar Abu Ghuddah who asked participants to consider the example set by the Prophet Zakariyyah, upon whom be blessings and peace, who prayed to God to grant him male heirs, (see the *Qur'an, Surahs* 19 and 21). He would not have prayed for something that was forbidden, said Dr Abu Ghuddah. 'We cannot pray, for example, to kill or to steal – but we can pray for things we are allowed to have,' he added. Thus, he deduced, if we are allowed to state preference in our choice of sex, there is no harm in using Islamically acceptable means to obtain that preference. And therefore artificial insemination, using a husband's sperm, is allowed in Islam. However, we are talking about using gender selection under special circumstances – where, for example, a mother wants a girl after having five boys. Islamic dispensation for this practice should not be used as a licence for mass gender-selection programmes.

Q : *There are press reports that organs from pigs may soon be used for human transplants; pigs' heart valves and skin are already in use. Would there be an Islamic objection to this, since pigs are forbidden as food?*

A : Maintenance of the public interest tends to be the guiding principle behind decisions to accept or reject scientific and medical developments which are not mentioned in Islamic texts. Organ transplantation in general has been sanctioned by Islamic scholars on the ground that such an operation will be in the public interest and does not violate any Islamic principle.

Once this principle has been established – that organs from foreign bodies can be used in humans – there is no specific prohibition on the use of the organs of a pig; the primary consideration would be that of suitability. Naturally, doctors should investigate all other avenues first. If, however, nothing is found and pig organs are suitable, then there is no objection to them from the Islamic point of view.

Q : *I have come across some information about Homeopathy which gave me cause for concern: 1) Homeopathy is based on the principle of 'like cures like' – a substance which produces certain symptoms in a healthy person is the best cure for an illness which produces the same symptoms. The smaller the dose, the more potent is the remedy – so there can be no more than a few molecules in a tablet. Hence there is the belief that the* *remedy relies on a 'spiritual force', and as such is a 'paranormal' or 'occult' (al-ghayb) science. It has also been suggested that many homeopaths may also be involved in 'cult activities', such as Anthroposophy and Scientology. Homeopathy has been denounced by some 'fundamentalist' Christians as being the work of the devil.* **2)** *The preparation of homeopathic substances involves the use of alcohol to dilute and distil the substances used. Can you please advise as to whether it is acceptable for Muslims to seek homeopathic treatment or train as homeopaths.*

A: As far as I am aware, there is nothing about Homeopathy that conflicts with Islamic teachings. In fact, in many ways, Homeopathy is much closer to Islam than conventional Western medicine. Homeopathy, which was invented – or discovered – by the 17th century scientist Samuel Hahnemann, is based on three principles. The first principle is 'like cures like'; the second, 'the smaller the dose, the more effective the treatment'; and the third – and perhaps the most important – that the patient is treated 'holistically' – that is, as a human being who has both a spirit and a body.

This is totally in keeping with Islamic principles which regard body and soul as one, and not as two separate entities – as with conventional medicine, upon which we have come to rely so heavily. A patient can never fully recover using conventional medicinal treatment as they only concentrate on dealing with bodily symptoms – but this only treats half the problem. Remember, conventional medicine focuses on treating bodily symptoms only, and does not bother itself with matters relating to the spirit or to emotion.

That Homeopathy is a holistic form of medicine should come as little surprise to Muslims, as its founder, Samuel Hahnemann, was a Christian who believed wholeheartedly in the need for a moral and spiritual dimension in matters of health. Hahnemann believed that if a person is honest, decent, good and bears no hatred or ill-feeling towards others, then this will reflect on his personality and health. Again, this is hardly strange or alien to Muslims. Spiritual healing is extensively dealt with in the book *Prophetic Medicine* written by the Muslim scholar Ibn al-Jawzi.

So let me reiterate, Muslims should have no cause for concern about Homeopathy. The only worry would be in the preparation of formulations – and the use of, for example, alcohol in remedies. You can always check this with qualified Homeopaths. Certainly there is no alcohol present in the majority of the remedies, which come in the form of powders, granules or pills.

Q : *As a medical student, a compulsory part of my course is to cut up dead bodies. I have heard that it is forbidden in Islam to do these things and to perform post-mortem examinations. Is this so?*

A : Islam stresses the honour and dignity of man – be he alive or dead. Islam emphasises the sacredness of his blood, wealth and nobility. A man should be accorded the same respect after his death as he was entitled to when he was alive. According to the Prophet, blessings and peace be upon him, 'Breaking the bone of a dead person is like breaking the bone of a living person.' The Prophet even prohibited sitting on the tomb of a dead person as this was an indication to the deceased. In Islam respectful behav-iour towards the dead is not confined to Muslims only but to non-Muslims also.

Now let's get back to your question about cutting up bodies for post-mortem examination or for autopsy. Let me begin by saying that this is not considered mutilation or disrespect to the individual. Such operations are allowed because they are always done with the community's benefit in mind. Where, for instance, the cause of death is unknown or is alleged to have occurred in suspicious circumstances, then an autopsy is an essential part of forensic tests carried out to determine the truth of the matter – and as such it does not contravene Islamic principles. Similarly, autopsies carried out by medical students to study internal parts of the body, their relationships and functions, etc., are also allowed from an Islamic point of view, because the knowledge is, ultimately, to the benefit of the community. A research paper prepared by the permanent committee of Iftah under the presidency of the Islamic Research and Iftah concluded that such operations on deceased persons are acceptable in the light of the modern needs of our community.

Q : *Are Muslims allowed to donate their organs after death for medical research?*

A : This question is prompted by recent scientific developments. We do not expect to give a ruling in individual cases, but there are basic or general principles. We know from the *Ahadith* of the Prophet, upon whom be blessings and peace, that breaking the bone of a dead person is like breaking the bone of a living person. We are not allowed to mutilate or disfigure human bodies. This was related to the days in early Islam, when the enemy used to mutilate the dead bodies of its opponents as a sign of revenge and humiliation. What is happening today is for the benefit of the community as a whole, because organ donation is serving a purpose which is needed by the community. Serving the needs of the community is not the same as humiliating the enemy – therefore donating organs is acceptable if it is done for any good medical reason.

Q : *What is the Shari'ah position regarding donating organs after death? Recently there has been a lot of publicity on the need to carry donor cards, yet some scholars in my local area discourage this and say that donating organs is not a good thing to do. But if, like the 10-years-old girl who died recently, I can save the lives of six people by donating my heart, lungs, liver and kidneys after my death, what possible harm could I have done?*

A : Recent scientific advancements in the area of organ transplants and surgery, and even blood transfusion, have been tackled by some leading modern day *'ulama*. After much deliberation, they have arrived at a comprehensive and well-thought out decision on the matter, based on one source – that of the *Shari'ah*. Remember that the main sources consist of the *Qur'an*, *Hadith*, *qiyas* (analogy), and *ijma* (consensus) – plus another six subsidiary sources which can be considered when legislating on matters which have not been referred to at all in the texts of the *Qur'an* and *Hadith*. Public interest is one of these extra sources. In Arabic this is referred to as *'al-maslahatu al-mursalatu'*.

Many great developments in the history of the Muslim *Ummah* have been dealt with under this source category. What does this mean? It means that we have to consider the intrinsic value of the matter we are deciding. Because blood transfusion and organ transplantation are in the public interest, are of benefit, and, have not been specifically banned in the *Shari'ah*, scholars have decided not to object to these operations being carried out – but it was not all that easy. A *Hadith* of the Prophet, blessings and peace be on him, has been recorded as saying, 'Breaking the bones of a dead person is like breaking the bones of someone who is living.' This means that we need to respect the human body, whether it is alive or dead. The fact that we are not allowed to mutilate bodies posed a dilemma for scholars considering the case of transplant surgery. They considered what is the nature of what the surgeons do. They decided that transplant surgery is not 'an act of mutilation', but rather a good service to the Muslim community – and that as such it should be allowed.

Of course the decision to carry out such an operation belongs to the donor in the first instance, and to his or her family if no specific instructions were left behind. If you want your organs to be donated, you can save your family considerable hardship and agony by carrying a donor card to that effect.

Death and Funerals

Q : *A close relative died here, in England, while on holiday from his home in a Muslim country. Instead of burying him immediately, his relatives insisted that the body be flown back for burial. Were they right to do so?*

A : This depends on the family. If most of the family are abroad, then it is right and proper that the body be flown back, so that there are children, grandchildren, sisters, etc., who can visit the grave and remember their dead. But, of course, if most of the relatives are here, then it is definitely better if the body is retained for burial.

Of course Islamically, bodies should be buried without delay, but delays incurred while death certificates are obtained, or while dead bodies are prepared for the return flight, are necessary and unavoidable. These should not be confused with the kind of delay when families hold bodies in mortuaries for weeks, waiting for long-lost relatives to arrive. It is better in such instances that the body be buried straight away.

Q : *Can a Muslim man view the face of a deceased Muslimah?*

A : Seeing the face of a deceased person is related back to the time of the *Khalifah* Abu Bakr who came and uncovered the face of the Prophet after he had died, blessings and peace be upon him, kissed it, and said: 'You are beautiful.' As far as a Muslim man is concerned, males and females may be allowed to view his face. But if the deceased is a female, it will be better only for a blood-related *maharim* to view the face, and not anyone else.

Q : *From my own experience of having given a ghusl, bath, to deceased ladies, their families often make various requests. One woman wanted rose petals sprinkled over the deceased, because this is done in some areas in Pakistan. Others have asked for make-up and pretty scarves. Is this permitted?*

A : If the woman was wealthy enough to have left money for the expenses and circumstances of her burial, then they are allowed, providing they are within the *Shari'ah*. But if the expense falls on somebody else, then they have to be done without extravagance.

When Abu Bakr was about to pass away, he asked his family to wash his old clothes to wrap his body in, and to leave his new clothes for those who were alive and stood in greater need of them. This is the attitude of a person who does not care about how people will see him, but who is looking forward to the future and to how Allah will see him. Muslims have to be humble. However, if someone would like to be shrouded with good material, there is no objection to that. There is an allowance for the face of the deceased to be made-up to look radiant, so that people may not speak badly of the deceased.

We know from so many *Ahadith* of the Prophet, blessings and peace be upon him, that Allah shows many signs on the faces of those who pass away in a state of sin or having transgressed against other people. The Prophet, blessings and peace be upon him, advised the person who washes the dead body not to talk about these features – but if there are signs of radiance or goodness on the faces of the dead, then he encouraged people to mention them.

Q : *Can a woman go to a funeral? It has been suggested that in the times of early Islam women were prevented from doing so. Is this true? Are women allowed to physically enter cemeteries or graveyards?*

A : There are conflicting *Ahadith* on this subject. While one set of *Ahadith* prohibits such practices, another set seemingly goes the opposite way.

Those people who reject the idea altogether quote the following *Hadith* in which the Prophet, blessings and peace be upon him, is reported to have said: 'Allah has cursed those who often go and visit graves.' Another *Hadith* relates an incident in which the Prophet, blessings and peace be upon him, asked his daughter, Fatima, why she had left her house. She is reported to have replied: 'I went to the family of such and such a dead person and I prayed to Allah to shower His mercy on the person.' The Prophet, blessings and peace be upon him, is then reported to have asked whether she went to the funeral and she replied: 'God forbid, how could I do such a thing when I have heard that you have forbidden this?'

However, those looking for evidence to show that women are allowed to visit graves quote some of the following *Ahadith*: According to one tradition, the Prophet, blessings and peace be upon him, is reported – after acknowledging that he had earlier forbade women to visit cemeteries – to have said: 'Now you are allowed to go and visit them, for they remind you of the life to come.' In another *Hadith*, included in both *Muslim* and *Al-Bukhari*, the Prophet, blessings and peace be upon him, is reported by Umm Atiyyah to have forbade women from following *janazah* prayers – '... but,' adds Umm Atiyyah, 'he did not stress it.'

The question then is: What does the believer gather from all this? After much deliberation, scholars have concluded that women can go to gravesides and cemeteries, providing they fulfil usual requirements – in the same way as, for example, they go shopping or visiting friends and neighbours. This, say scholars, is the best method of combining the two sets of *Ahadith* which may otherwise appear contradictory.

Q : *At a recent janazah, I saw a non-Muslim friend of the deceased standing shoulder to shoulder with Muslims during the prayer. Was it right for the deceased's family to allow this to happen? I would also like to know if it is allowed for Muslims to attend funerals of non-Muslims.*

A : The non-Muslim standing in the *janazah* prayer 'shoulder to shoulder with Muslims' was not committing any wrong. His participation in the prayer should not be looked upon as a violation of an Islamic principle, but should be seen as an expression of shared grief with the family of the deceased. Muslims at the funeral, by letting him pray with them, were merely complying with the *Qur'an*'s advice on the way we should behave towards good-natured, well-intentioned and sincere non-Muslims. In *Surah* 60, *Al-Mumtahana – She who is to be Examined*, verse 8, Allah says: ***'Allah does not forbid you – as regards those who have not fought you because of your deen, nor driven you out of your homes – from dealing kindly and justly with them: for surely Allah loves those who are just.'*** Remember that the non-Muslim friend's standing in prayer does not by itself constitute an act of acceptance of the Islamic faith. His 'prayer' is not the same as the prayer of a Muslim, and it will not be judged as such.

As for your second question, I would refer you to the same *Qur'anic* verse in which Allah does not bar Muslims from showing kindness to non-Muslims, especially at times of grief and sorrow. The only thing which we are not allowed to do is to take part in special non-Muslim acts or rituals.

Q : *In a question on attending funerals of non-Muslims you said it was okay to do so as long as one does not participate in any kind of 'rituals'. What then should a Muslim do when – at a Christian funeral – he has to attend a Church service?*

A : He should sit at the back of the Church and not participate in the ritual. There are so many people who do not believe, but they always go to such funerals and services.

Q : *The relatives of a family friend who died last year are angry with me for not joining in their 'mourning marathon'. I attended the funeral of the deceased and went to his house to offer further condolences. However, I refused to join in the perpetual Qur'an recitals, tasbeeh-counting and sumptuous meals, organised for the third, tenth, twentieth and fortieth day after his death, as I think that these are un-Islamic. Did I act correctly?*

A : Your response was correct. It is good to console the family of someone who has died and share their grief in their hour of need, without getting involved in the more extravagant practices as described. Condolences are offered occasionally before, but usually after, the burial. Mourning, according to the Islamic point of view, lasts for three days only. In fact the three day period is designated as 'extra time' for people who were unable to offer condolences earlier, to go and visit the family. The three-day period serves no other purpose. No one should gather at the house of the deceased after this time is up. The 'seventh', 'tenth', 'twentieth' and 'fortieth' days, etc., are all innovations which have no basis from the Islamic point of view.

Outsiders joining relatives in reading the *Holy Qur'an* for the sake of the spirit of the deceased is acceptable to some Muslim scholars, as long as this remains an occasional practice. But setting dates, compiling guest lists and choosing menus for organised mourning sessions in the way described is not allowed. Even the Hanafi *Fiqh* says that it is better for people to disperse after the burial rather than sit in the mosque for this purpose. Offering food at the time of a death is a *sunnah* of the Prophet, upon whom be blessings and peace. However the simplicity and genuineness of the original Islamic precedent bears no resemblance to the pomp and lavishness of its modern-day successor. When Ja'far ibn Abi Talib passed away, the Prophet, upon whom be blessings and peace, asked for food to be prepared 'for the family of Ja'far' – to help the grief-stricken family whom the Prophet knew would otherwise not have fed themselves. Offering condolences itself is a good Islamic practice. The *Hadith* in this respect is quite clear: 'Anyone offering condolences to a Muslim brother or sister will be clothed by Allah in a dress of honour on the Day of al-Qiyamah, the Day of Judgement.'

Q : *There has been a local dispute in which a Muslim community has prevented a Qadiani woman from burying her husband in a Muslim cemetery. Given that Qadianis are consensually agreed to be outside the fold of mainstream Islam, is this a reasonable stance to take, or is it religious bigotry?*

A : This is not religious bigotry. We do not have an excommunicating authority in Islam, but we do have a set of beliefs which are indisputable. Anybody calling into question these beliefs is considered a *murtadd*, an apostate. The finality of Prophethood is established in the *Qur'an* in *Surah* 33, *Al-Ahzab*, verse 40, where Allah says: ***'Muhammad is not the father of any man among you, but he is the Messenger of Allah, and the Seal of the Prophets – and Allah is always Aware of everything.'***

The Prophet, blessings and peace be upon him, himself confirmed this when he said, 'I am the last of all the Prophets. There will be no prophet after me.' Thus the finality of his Prophethood is an act of faith to which every Muslim must submit.

Those who dispute this belief with arguments, even though they may be couched in Islamic terms, have been declared non-Muslims by all the scholars and research academies. As such, they have no right whatsoever to be buried in a Muslim cemetery. This is not bigotry. It is part of the Islamic way of life, in which only Muslims should be buried in an Islamic cemetery – to the extent that where a non-Muslim woman is married to a Muslim man, and she passes away during pregnancy, she is not to be buried in a Jewish or Christian cemetery, because she was carrying a Muslim child; nor is she to be buried in a Muslim cemetery, because she herself is not a Muslim. She has to be buried somewhere 'neutral'.

Q : *The eldest son of a family died, leaving behind: a father; a mother; one wife, with no children; one brother, married with a daughter and a son; another brother, unmarried; two sisters, each married with a daughter and a son; and two more sisters, both unmarried. How should his estate be distributed?*

A : The division of the estate should be in this way:

The wife will have one fourth of the estate, according to the *Qur'anic* verse, **'... and in what you leave, their (wife/wives) share is a fourth if you have no children...'** (*Surah* 4, *An-Nisa*, verse 12).

The mother will receive one sixth of the estate, because the deceased had more than one brother. Again this is in accordance with the *Qur'anic* verse, **'... and to each of his parents, a sixth share of the inheritance if he (the deceased) has a son; and if he has no son and the parents are (the only) heirs, the mother has a third; and if he has brothers, then his mother has a sixth – after (the distribution) of any legacy he may have bequeathed.'** (*Surah* 4, *An-Nisa*, verse 11).

The father will receive the rest of the estate, i.e. seven twelfths, because he is the nearest male relative, in accordance with the tradition related in *Al-Bukhari* and *Muslim*: 'Give the shares of the inheritance which are prescribed in the *Qur'an* to those who are entitled to receive them. Then whatever remains should be given to the closest male relative of the deceased.'

As for the rest of the brothers and sisters, married or not married, they have no share in the estate, because the father precludes them as the nearest male relative.

Q : *Does Islam share the Western concept of ghosts – that a dead soul which refuses to rest 'haunts' the people who live in its former house?*

A : The folk-idea of the existence of ghosts which haunt houses and disturb people is not shared by Islam. I do know of an old Arab myth which says that the soul of someone who has been killed will continue to roam above his tomb until his death has been avenged – but this has nothing whatsoever to do with Islam. Muslim opinion as to the exact final abode of a soul after it has departed the body tends to vary. According to one opinion, a person's fate after death depends on his or her individual state of faith, *Iman*. Some souls will be in the High Heaven, like the Prophets, who were observed by the Prophet Muhammad, upon whom be blessings and peace, during his *Miraj*, the Night Journey, to Jerusalem and then through the seven heavens to the Presence of Allah. Some souls will be kept outside Paradise, others will be kept on earth.

Muslim scholars who have researched the subject say that nothing can be said for definite without support from either *Qur'anic* verses or a well-authenticated saying of the Prophet, blessings and peace be on him. It is not an area where we can employ reasoning or rationality, they say, as it relies heavily on a Muslim's ability to believe in and perceive the Unseen. However, none of the opinions expressed, either oral or written, talk about the concept of a ghost which haunts householders and those who live in its former home.

Q : *We are told that the souls of dead people are questioned in the grave and will remain there until the Day of Judgement. What happens to the souls of people who are cremated or those who are destroyed in major disasters?*

A : It is true that the souls of the dead are questioned in the grave, and the grave of every individual should be in the place where he passed his life, although it is not necessary to be too particular about the burial site. We have to remember that understanding the nature of the whole arena of the afterlife relies upon authentic traditions for explanation. We do not have any objective tests whereby we can go and 'test' what happens.

The Prophet, blessings and peace be upon him, narrated the incident of a man who lived before the time of Islam and who left a will for his children. In it he asked to be cremated after his death, and for his ashes to be thrown into the air, the earth and the sea – in the hope that God would not be able to resurrect him. On the Day of Reckoning, after God had ordered the earth, the air and the sea to give back what they had received, He asked the man why he had done this. The man replied that he done so out of the fear that he would be brought before his Lord and asked to account for his deeds. God forgave him.

However, as Muslims we must understand that cremation is absolutely prohibited. The Prophet, blessings and peace be on him, said that breaking the bone of a dead person is like breaking the bone of a living being. The body has to be respected in death as it is expected to be respected during life.

In the End

Q : *If someone who professes Islam denounces his belief in life after death, is he still a Muslim?*

A : No, he is not still a Muslim – because a Muslim has to believe in the articles of faith mentioned in the *Hadith* which recounts the visit by the Archangel Jibril when he came to ask the Prophet, in front of his Companions, blessings and peace be on him and them, to 'tell' him the fundamentals of Islam and the articles of faith – which include belief in the life to come. So to believe in the Hereafter is an act of faith required of all Muslims.

The life to come is mentioned in the *Qur'an* in *Surah* 2, *Al-Baqarah*, verse 4. Referring to the Prophet, blessings and peace be upon him, and to those for whom the *Qur'an* is a guidance, Allah says: ***'And those who believe in what has been revealed to you, and what has been revealed before you, and who are certain of the Hereafter.'*** There are no less than 177 *Qur'anic* verses which refer directly to the life to come. So anyone who denies its existence is denying part of the faith and ceases to be a Muslim.

Q : *On the last day of Judgement, is it the Prophet Muhammad or Jesus who will be present?*

A : Both the Prophet Muhammad and the Prophet Jesus will be present on the Last Day, blessings and peace be on them – as well as all the other Prophets, and everyone who has ever lived!

You speak about the Day of Judgement as if it is many days. It is one day – and your question perhaps should be: 'Who will come *before* the Last Day as a sign that this day is approaching?' The answer for this question has been given in many *Ahadith* of the Messenger of Allah, blessings and peace be on him, when he was informing his Companions about the great signs of the coming of the Day of Judgement.

Let us remember that we, the *Ahl'ul-Sunnah wa'l-Jama'ah*, the community united behind the true way of the Prophet Muhammad, blessings and peace be on him, believe that 'Isa (Jesus), peace be on him, was raised to heaven alive. He still has to die, just like any other human being. So it is authentically reported in many traditions that before the Day of Judgement, 'Isa will come down to earth, break the crosses and declare that those who continued to follow that religion after the coming of Al-Islam were not following the true religion. He will kill the pigs and fight the false messiah, the *Dajjal*, remain on earth for forty 'days', marry and have children, and then die – and after all this the Last Day will take place.

Some people in the past, and at present, who have claimed to be Muslims, have doubted the whole idea of the future coming of the Messiah, Jesus, peace be on him. They have claimed that 'Isa is dead, and that since we do not believe in reincarnation, there can be no second coming of 'Isa, peace be on him. There are many books which have been written refuting this notion. Prominent among them is the book of the great Indian scholar, *Imam* Muhammad Anwar Shah, *At-Tasrih bima Taw'at-Arafi Uzal'al-Masih*, which explicates what has been reported by a group of traditionalists on the coming of *al-Masih*, the Messiah. Another book was written recently by Shaikh Abd'al-Muhsin al-'Abbad, vice-rector of Al-Madina University, refuting a short treatise denying the second coming of 'Isa, peace be on him. Again, I have to emphasise that the Sunni community of Muslims believe that 'Isa is up in heaven, alive and well. He will come down before the Day of Judgement, as one of its great signs, and will follow the *Shari'ah* of the Prophet Muhammad, blessings and peace be on them.

Q : *Will the good non-Muslims go to Jannah, Paradise? I would like to know whether there is a place in Jannah for kind-hearted, sincere and genu-*

inely honest non-Muslims – particularly those who are involved in selfless acts of humanitarianism towards Muslims. Sometimes I find it quite difficult to reconcile their not being Muslim when all around me, I see my Muslim brothers and sisters constantly at each other's throats, exhibiting totally un-Islamic behaviour.

A: If we look into the *Qur'an, Surah* 3, *Ali 'Imran*, verse 85, it is very clear that God says: ***'And as for anyone who desires a religion other than Islam (submission to Allah), it will not be accepted from him – and in the Hereafter he will be among the losers.'***

As far as the *Ahadith* are concerned, it is authentically reported in *Sahih Muslim*, Vol. 1, p. 91, translated by Abd'al-Hamid Siddiqui, in a *Hadith* narrated by Abu Hurayrah, that the Prophet, blessings and peace be on him, said: 'By Him in Whose hands is the life of Muhammad, whoever among the community of the Jews or the Christians hears about me, but does not affirm his belief in that with which I have been sent, and dies in this state of disbelief, shall only be one of the denizens of Hellfire.'

The commentary on this passage states that the Holy Prophet, may Allah bless him and grant him peace, has been sent as the final dispenser of the will of Allah, and that the *Holy Qur'an* is the last scripture from our Lord – which embodies the teachings of all the earlier Prophets and all the principles and values of life which humanity will stand in need of until the Day of Resurrection. *Surah* 5, *Al-Ma'idah*, verse 3, of the *Qur'an* confirms this by saying: ***'This day I have perfected your religion for you, and I have completed My blessing upon you, and I have chosen Al-Islam for you as your religion.'***

So there is an obstacle in the path to *Jannah* for those who are good-natured, well-mannered, warm-hearted people who do a lot of good to others – but who at the same time do not believe in Allah, and in His last Messenger and in the Final Day. As justice is one of God's attributes, He will compensate them for their kindness, but only in this life. He will bestow them with good health, peaceful existence, and many blessings on this earth – but that does not amount to safety in the life to come.

As for what Muslims do as bad things in this life, they will be punished for that – unless they repent and correct their misdeeds – but because they have crossed the barrier dividing faith from disbelief, the fact that they chose faith will finally be the saving grace on their part.

So encourage and invite the good non-Muslims whom you know to find out about and embrace Islam. It will be the best thing they have ever done. Believe it or not, the truth of the matter is:

'There is no god but Allah
and Muhammad is the Messenger of Allah'

may the blessings and peace of Allah be on him and on all his Family and on all his Companions, and on all who follow him and them with sincerity in what they are able until the Last Day.

Amin